Two week loan

Please return on or before the last
date stamped below.
Charges are made for late return.

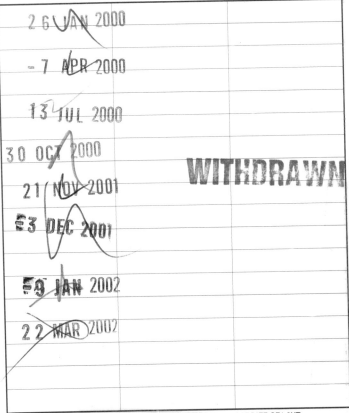

Control and
Ideology in
Organizations

Control and Ideology in Organizations

edited by
Graeme Salaman
and
Kenneth Thompson

The Open University Press
Milton Keynes

The Open University Press
A division of
Open University Educational Enterprises Limited
12 Cofferidge Close
Stony Stratford
Milton Keynes MK11 1BY, England

First published 1980

Printed in Great Britain by
The Anchor Press Ltd, Tiptree.
Typeset by
R James Hall Typesetting &
Book Production Services

British Library Cataloguing in Publication Data

Control and ideology in organizations.
   1. Organization 2. Industrial sociology
   I. Salaman, Graeme II. Thompson, Kenneth,
   b. 1937
   301.18'32   HM131

ISBN 0-335-00258-7

Contents

Acknowledgements

Grateful acknowledgement is made to the following for permission to reproduce material in this book:

Front cover: George Grosz, Untitled (Kunstsammlung Nordrhein-Westfalen Düsseldorf).

Page 18 Table 1 from Galenson and Lipset (eds) *Labour and Trade Unionism*, Blauner, R. (1960): reproduced by permission of John Wiley & Sons, Inc.

Page 29 Figure 1 from the Matsushita Electronics Corporation Visitors' Guide: reproduced by permission of National Panasonic (U.K.) Limited.

Page 31 Figure 2 from Pym, D. (ed) *Industrial Society: Social Sciences in Management* (1968) © Penguin Books: reprinted by permission of Penguin Books Ltd.

Page 34 Figure 3 from Tannenbaum, A.S. *Control in Organizations* (1968) © McGraw-Hill Book Company: used with permission of the McGraw-Hill Book Company.

Page 51 Table 1 from Hinings, C.R., Hickson, D.J., Pennings, J.M., and Schneck, R.E. 'Structural Conditions of Intraorganizational Power', *Administrative Science Quarterly*, March 1974, pp 22–44: reproduced by permission of the authors.

Page 67 Figure 1 from Perrow, C. 'A Framework for the Comparative Analysis of Organizations', *American Sociological Review*, vol 32, April 1967: reproduced by permission of The American Sociological Association.

Page 205 Figure 1 from Thompson, J.D. *Organizations in Action* (1967) © McGraw-Hill Book Company: used with permission of the McGraw-Hill Book Company.

Editors' Introduction

This textbook is directly based on the Open University course — *People and Organizations*. The chapters in the book are modified, edited and updated versions of the units or written lectures that make up the major element of the Open University course. This book's origins in a third year teaching course give it, we think, a number of strengths. For one thing the course, and subsequently this book, was planned with great care and deliberation. The team of contributors, with help from publishers, educational technologists, consultants and teachers, spent a great deal of time and effort in attempting to design a coherent and intelligible introduction to the analysis of modern, large-scale organizations. These are complicated phenomena, and understanding them is a complex business, often involving reference to theoretical and conceptual issues and distinctions. Nevertheless, we were convinced that a useful introduction to these issues, which was straightforward but not simplistic, was possible. This book represents the outcome of that conviction.

The origins of this book in an Open University course have another crucial significance. The book is first and foremost a teaching text. Obviously, we hope that it will be read and enjoyed by our academic colleagues. Indeed, since a number of the foremost names in the field are contributors to this volume, we confidently expect some attention from other teachers and researchers in this area. But our first audience is students, not teachers. These materials were originally designed to constitute the major element in a package of distance-teaching materials. And here lies, we think, another possible advantage of the present volume : that it is designed to catch the attention and interest of relatively uninformed students with little prior experience of the social sciences, and to build on that attention an increasing awareness of the complexity of the issues surrounding organizations and how these have been variously illuminated by social science research and theorizing. Thus we should also raise interest in the social sciences as a whole, not assume it, by judiciously introducing social science concepts and theories such as role, bureaucracy, rationality, and so on. Many years of experience of presenting the course to Open University students seem to confirm the effectiveness of these teaching materials.

We should add that originally these materials were accompanied by a 'custom-built' anthology – *People and Organizations*, edited by us and published by Longman. For those wishing to use the present volume as teaching material, we would recommend the associated anthology as a resource book.

The main theme of this book is organizational control. From a number of points of view, the origins, mechanisms, implications and consequences of processes of organizational control seem to be the most important and interesting features of organizations. Certainly for the early theorists – Weber and Marx, for example – organizations were most interesting as mechanisms of control, as represented in the design of work or bureaucracy. Similarly, for most members of organizations – or students of organizations (who often draw on experience of organizational membership) – exposure to various processes of organizational control is a major source of interest and theorizing. Hence the fascination with 'red tape', with selection interviews, with 'good' or 'bad' bosses, with successful or unsuccessful careers, with conflicts between administrators and professionals, with the deprivation of much repetitive manual work, with various employee organizations (formal or informal) which oppose the dictates or manipulations of 'them' – the management.

The chapters are arranged in sections, as follows.

The opening chapter considers organizations in terms of their wider social and political relevances and attempts to relate the analysis of organizations to theoretical themes and debates initially introduced by the classical, early sociologists. It takes as its focal point the concept *bureaucracy*.

The second section continues this general strategy with reference to the internal features of organizations. If organizations are important it is important to understand how they operate. However, sociology cannot and does not simply present descriptions of 'how things work', because such descriptions and accounts depend upon the choice of topic, the theoretical approach, and methodology, and so on. Consequently, the discussions in this book will not only address the question: how do organizations work?, they will also, and at the same time, be considering: what are the assumptions lying behind this sort

of account of how organizations work? What does it take
tion or analysis of an organization to be sensible?

This book takes as its theme the issue of organizati
Control means that members of the organization have
(and, possibly, attitudes and orientations) determined, or influenced,
by membership of the organization. This process involves power. It
would be impossible to consider organizational control without considering the nature of power within organizations, how it is distributed,
how it originates. Such issues constitute the topics of Chapter 2. Two
points of particular importance are made by this chapter. First, that
despite the crucial importance of organizational power in any attempt
to study organizations, the concept suffers from a wealth of overlap-
ping and conflicting definitions and applications. Therefore, conceptual
and theoretical debate is essential to any serious interest in organizations, or anything else. This point is made frequently in the following
chapters. Secondly, David Hickson and Arthur McCullough point out
the connection between power and uncertainty, a point that is developed by Hickson *et al.* in Salaman and Thompson (1973). Senior
members of organizations will attempt to reduce uncertainty about the
behaviour of subordinates by limiting and controlling their activities.
For this they need power. At the same time members of the organization
will attempt to create or negotiate some area of discretion, of creativity,
and consequently also, of uncertainty. And capacity to cope with
organizational·uncertainty is a source of power.

The fact that organizations involve attempts to reduce uncertainty,
and to create order and stability (indeed this stability is usually what
is meant by an organization) is the central topic of Chapter 3. This
chapter considers the concept and manifestations of organizational
structure. This concept is used to refer to the most dramatic and
obvious feature of organizations: the way they involve a relatively
stable patterning of activities over time. And the chapter considers
the origins of this structure and its relationship to various determining
factors. There is also a discussion of a number of classifications of
organization in terms of the suggested relationships between features
of organizations, and other factors. Although noting the importance of
the concept structure with respect to organizations, the discussion also
stresses the variable, but existent, possibility of choice that lies behind
the attempts to impose structure on organizations, and the behaviours
which give rise to the emergent regularity that is considered as organizational structure. Finally, attention is devoted to the variety of forms
of control employed by organizations, since there is reason to believe,
and many studies support the idea, that organizations make use of more

than one method of controlling personnel.

The systems approach to organizations, outlined in Chapter 4 is particularly interesting — and problematic — because it derives from a model of functional interdependence — systems theory — which comes from outside sociological theorizing and which, its enthusiasts claim, is applicable to many sorts of phenomena, and many academic disciplines. Here, possibly, lie its main advantages and deficiencies. In particular it will be suggested in later chapters that, with respect to the sociological study of organizations, systems theory suffers from a commitment to an excessively abstract level of generalization, and, usually, from a relative lack of interest in developments within sociological theory and research which are critical of the application of systems theory to social phenomena.

Section three contains four chapters that are all concerned, in various ways, with exploring the methods by which the behaviour of members of organizations is constrained and limited. They focus on the individual, his priorities and aspirations, rather than on the somewhat abstract factors that are involved in the use of such concepts as 'formalization', 'structure', 'centralization', and so on, that are intrinsic to the structural approach. In terms of traditional sociological theoretical distinctions these approaches may be said to be primarily interactionist in character.

This book, however, is not simply about organizations; it is about the *sociology* of organizations, and as such it involves consideration of problems of sociological theory, since any analysis of organizations depends upon theoretically derived concepts. Therefore, this section considers some of the concepts that have been used in investigations of organizational control (such as rules, roles, motivation, etc.), and their significance for organizational members. Sometimes then, roles, or rules, will be considered in terms of the variety of ways in which these concepts have been used by *sociologists*, and in terms of the theories from which they derive, or emerge; at other times these concepts will be considered in terms of how valuable they are in adding to our understanding of organizational events and processes.

There are, however, two exceptions to this — the two chapters contributed by Hedy Brown, who is a social psychologist. These two chapters consider topics and employ concepts and theories that derive from social psychology. They are included in this book not only because these topics — motivation, the nature and impact of group processes on members of work groups — are indispensable features of any course on organizations, but also because they are topics of concern to those who have a professional interest in studying organizations with a view to improving efficiency or increasing production. Once again the discussion operates on two levels: on the one hand, the discussions consider some of the factors that may have some controlling influence over organizational members' behaviour; on the other hand, it is noted that attempts to increase organizational efficiency (as defined by senior members of the organization) or organizational control frequently involve a manipulation of these factors, and these manipulative efforts are often guided and inspired by the sort of academic theorizing discussed in these chapters. In other words the sort of academic theorizing and analysis of possible sources and types of workers' motivation, or the impact of peer group attitudes and pressures, discussed by Hedy Brown, have been used in and have inspired attempts to increase the efficiency and scope of organizational control. This sort of reflexivity between academic research and the organizations that constitute the context and subject matter of that research is discussed later in the book by Martin Albrow.

Chapter 5 by David Weeks is directly concerned with presenting the interactionist approach to organizations, and, more specifically, with assessing the nature and contribution of the social action approach. One of the special features of this chapter is the way it relates this theoretical discussion to a variety of different empirical studies, some of them outside the traditional boundaries of Organization Theory. In so doing, this chapter follows one of the main tendencies of the book: to view with indifference the traditional demarcations between the various sociological sub-specialities that are concerned with work.

Chapter 6 continues this interest in the interactionist approach, and considers in detail two concepts which have been widely used in studies of organizations: role and rule. This chapter reviews some of the ways in which these concepts have been employed in studies of organizations, and the different events and phenomena they have been used to describe and understand.

Section four is about knowledge and information in organizations in relation to choice and selection regarding alternative courses of action. Organizations are ongoing accomplishments, the products and constructions of people who become involved with them in various capacities. Strictly speaking it is not the *'organization'* that *'acts'* in these respects but powerful groups or individuals in the organization. In a sense, almost all social action in organizations involves choices and decisions. Frequently, however, organizations seek to maintain their stability and reduce uncertainty by restricting the opportunities and possibilities for variation or deviation. They do this by such devices as setting the premises of decision-making, securing the pre-eminence of certain rationalities over others, supplying ideologies to legitimate goals, authority and the unequal distribution of benefits, and by select-ing suitably motivated and pre-socialized personnel.

Chapter 9 provides a critical examination of various approaches to the study of decision-making and assesses the importance of a number of structural factors in influencing the decision-making process. It also considers the ways in which decisions and decision-making procedures are legitimated, and so relates the whole topic to our theme of organ-izational control.

On the whole, accounts of organizations as decision-making systems take for granted the given-ness of many of those aspects of organiza-tion that this book shows to be problematical. Chapters 10 and 11 return to the examination of the problematical nature of these features of organizations. We will be looking at issues concerning the social construction of the reality about which decisions are made. In Chapter 10 the social construction of reality in organizations is analysed with regard to the different types of rationalities and logics-in-use favoured by various groups. This chapter also traces the process by which some rationalities become legitimating or justificatory ideologies as, for example, in the case of certain managerial ideologies. Chapter 11 continues this focus on organizational techniques for creating, trans-mitting and enforcing definitions of reality. It also considers the organ-izational construction of reality with particular reference to processes of recruitment, selection, training and appraisal of personnel.

The final section of the book looks back over some of the main issues that have been discussed and tries to relate these to general questions about the different perspectives within the study of organiza-tions, the relation of this field to the discipline of sociology, and the kinds of values and commitments that are entailed in adopting one perspective rather than another.

Section one
The problem of organizations

CHAPTER 1

Kenneth Thompson

The organizational society

Introduction

In subsequent chapters we will be looking in detail at some specific aspect of organizations and examining associated theories and research. In this first chapter, however, our primary intention is to emphasize the wider social relevance of organization studies.

All too often in the field of organization studies (and in many other areas of academic study) the important issues which give the subject its original impetus are lost sight of as the 'total phenomenon' is broken down into sub-disciplines, dimensions, variables, etc. Academic, or 'scientific', analysis usually takes the form of this progressive dissection. The advantage of this process is that we may promote analysis of structure by minute attention to the nature and relations of the parts. The disadvantage is that the whole and its effects disappear from view. This may not be too serious from a purely academic standpoint. And it may be a positive advantage from the point of view of those who wish to focus attention on lower level, specific problems with regard to organizations. For example, there has been a great deal of research focusing on specific factors within organizations which facilitate or impede efficiency at various levels. Concepts and theories are then generated which are relevant to those issues. But it is a serious loss as far as some of the wider issues and problems are concerned.

The problem of bureaucracy is a good example of this and that is why Chapter 1 takes it as a major theme. Industrial societies are increasingly dominated in all spheres by large, complex organizations, staffed by full-time, expert officials, acting in accordance with detailed rules. The power of such organizations and their officials is great, and the processes of control exercised by, and within, them are constantly being refined. Just what aspect of bureaucratic control is seen as problematic depends on the particular values and concerns of the observer. This chapter concentrates on aspects connected with the deceptive control exercised by seemingly 'impersonal' processes, and the alienating effects on individuals. It does not pursue other aspects, such as the influential criticism by Talcott Parsons and Alvin Gouldner of earlier conceptualizations of bureaucracy on the grounds that they did not distinguish between authority based on expertise and that based on position in a hierarchy. (Cf. Albrow 1970.) On the whole, our emphasis is on the great extent to which bureaucratic hierarchies successfully co-opt expertise into their control systems.

1 The concept of bureaucracy

There has been a widespread political concern about bureaucracy for more than two hundred years. It was thought by the English to be a French 'disease', and the view was shared by some Frenchmen: Balzac's novel of 1836, *Les Employés*, has been described as being at least half a treatise on bureaucracy, and in it he set the vituperative tone for many subsequent discussions of the subject:'. . . Bureaucracy, the giant power wielded by pigmies . . .' (Albrow 1970 p. 18).

The 'disease' spread, however, and we find a motion condemning 'the continued growth of bureaucracy' being put forward in the House of Commons in 1968.

Max Weber, the German sociologist, was responsible for providing the most influential and systematic social scientific analysis of the phenomenon of bureaucracy. He judged it to be the most important development of modern industrial society — indispensable to both capitalism and socialism:

> The development of the modern form of the organization of corporate groups in all fields is nothing less than identical with the development and continued spread of bureaucratic administration. This is true of church and state, of armies, political parties, economic enterprises, organizations to promote all kinds of causes, private associations, clubs, and many others . . . Its development, largely under capitalistic auspices, has created an urgent need for stable, strict, intensive, and calculable administration. It is this need which gives bureaucracy a crucial role in our society as the central element in any kind of large-scale administration. (Weber 1964 pp 337–8)

Bureaucracy has certainly been a problem for democrats in capitalist societies (the problem of controlling multinational corporations is an example, as are issues of civil service power, privacy of the individual, and 'red tape'), but it has been no less of a problem for socialist societies. Marx tended to neglect the subject (although see Perez-Diaz 1975 for a discussion of Marx's ideas on bureaucracy in relation to state and society), and even the great realist Lenin began to sound unrealistic when it came to explaining how the new socialist bureaucracy would bring about the withering away of bureaucracy:

> *We ourselves*, the workers, will organize large-scale production on the basis of what capitalism has already created, relying on our own experience as workers, establishing strict, iron discipline supported by the state power of the armed workers; we will reduce the role of the state officials to that of simply carrying out our instructions as responsible, revocable, modestly paid 'foremen and book-keepers' (of course, with the aid of technicians of all sorts, types and degrees). This is our proletarian task, this is what we can and must *start* with in accomplishing the proletarian revolution. Such a beginning, on the basis of large-scale production, will of itself lead to the gradual 'withering away' of all bureaucracy, to the gradual creation of an order, an order without quotation marks, an order bearing no similarity to wage slavery, an order in which the functions of control and accounting — becoming more and more simple — will be performed by each in turn, will then become a habit and will finally die out as the *special* functions of a special section of the population. (Lenin 1970 pp 57—8)

1.1 Control

'Bureaucracy' is a good concept to begin with in starting a book on organizations because it has proved so durable and flexible in expressing so many of the concerns that people have had about their own relations with organizations. The quotations at the beginning of this chapter express some of these concerns as they have been felt by people with varied interests and outlooks. Most of these concerns can be summed up under the heading of *control*. They are concerns having to do with the ways in which modern complex organizations exercise control in society — both internally with respect to their members, and externally with respect to their environment. Most of the early writers on bureaucracy had this as their major interest (e.g. Max Weber and Robert Michels especially) and they would not have thought it fruitful to divorce questions of internal organizational control from issues of external control. Their belief that the two sets of issues are intimately related was probably well founded, and the study of organizations is impoverished when it rigidly separates them. We will reject the kind of view that suggests the modern study of organizations is necessarily different in this respect, as for instance in the unfortunate distinctions drawn in the second half of the following statement:

> In modern society it is impossible to escape from the influence of organizations of one type or another. It was an awareness of this influence that encouraged the early sociologists to develop their interest in organizations. As seen already, however, this interest differs from the interest of present-day sociologists. The difference between the two is not simply the difference between the levels of analysis — whether macro or micro — but also between an interest in the external political sphere of society and the internal political structure of the organizations. (Dunkerley 1972 p 2)

In fact, it can be argued that the central questions for sociologists in this field are still those posed by Weber. His achievement was precisely in showing how systems of internal organizational control were intimately related to wider systems of control of social action. In particular, it should be made clear that, although the earlier, nineteenth-century interest in bureaucracy was a reflection of a debate about the place of public officials in developing governmental machines, it was still a debate about who (*which people*) control whom. Weber was a pivotal figure for the subsequent development of this debate in a direction which makes it relevant to current issues. For he represents a shift from this older perspective, with which he began, to a concern with the control of men by organizational rules — control by impersonal rather than personal factors. In other words, whilst it may be true that nineteenth-century writers on bureaucracy focused on the problem of the civil service in a democracy, the modern sociology of organizations' concern, stemming from Weber, is with the relation between organizational systems of action and the individual actor.

2 Different uses of the concept

Although social scientists are often accused of inventing unnecessary new terminology to conceal a poverty of ideas, the failing is somewhat different in the case of the term bureaucracy. Here there seems to be a 'poverty of terminological inventiveness' or, more specifically, a process of 'terminological conservation and conceptual change' (Albrow 1970 pp 120–3). The same term is used to refer to a variety of things, depending on the particular interest of the layman or social scientist concerned. We will confine ourselves to discussing two of the most influential usages: bureaucracy as rational organization, and bureaucracy as modern society.

2.1 Bureaucracy as rational organization

Most of the social scientists who adopt this conceptual strategy claim to be following the usage of Max Weber, but, they would add, only after first correcting Weber's conceptual ambiguity. For example, Peter Blau states:

> Weber conceived of bureaucracy as a social mechanism that maximizes efficiency and also as a form of social organization with specific characteristics. Both these criteria cannot be part of the definition, since the relationship between the attributes of a social institution and its consequences is a question for empirical verification and not a matter of definition (Blau 1963 p 251).

Blau and others choose to interpret Weber's description of bureaucracy as 'rational organization' as being a definition of bureaucracy in the sense of an 'organization that maximizes efficiency in administration'. (Blau 1956 p. 60) They then find this to be inconsistent with what they take to be his list of *a priori* essential characteristics of bureaucratic organization. Blau states that Weber saw the following list of characteristics as making up his 'ideal', pure or most rational type of bureaucracy:

1. specialization of tasks;
2. a hierarchy of authority;
3. a system of rules;
4. impersonality;
5. employment based on technical qualifications, and constituting a career;
6. efficiency. (Blau 1956 pp 28–31)

Blau then goes on to show that efficiency may not always be best served by some of the other characteristics in the list. For example, he notes that in his own study of a federal law-enforcement agency, efficiency was often best served by *unofficial* practices and *informal personal* relations among the staff, in contravention of the rules and disregarding formal impersonal structures. One of his major conclusions was that: 'Maximum rationality in the organization, therefore, depends on the ability of operating officials to assume the initiative in establishing informal relations and instituting unofficial practices that eliminate operational difficulties as they occur.' (Blau 1963 p. 255)

But Blau is misleading in suggesting that Weber equated rationality with efficiency. In referring to the formal rationality of bureaucracy, Weber had in mind formal procedures involving correct calculation — either in numerical terms, as with finance and statistics, or in logical terms, as with law. Such calculations are formal procedures which allow us to determine what level of efficiency has been reached, but they do not in themselves guarantee efficiency. To put it another way: Weber was all too aware that *formal* rationality did not guarantee *material* or substantive rationality (the most efficient attainment of goals or values). He sometimes spoke of the 'paradox of consequences' whereby highly rational procedures frustrated or defeated the purposes and values which had inspired them. For example, bureaucracy might be democracy's most rational form of administration, but sometimes it was also its worst enemy.

In fact, far from Weber's definition of the concept of bureaucracy being set in the context of a discussion of organizational efficiency, it is set in the context of a larger discussion of *authority* as a form of control (or 'imperative co-ordination'). He distinguished between power and authority along the lines that, whereas power referred to any relationship where one member could enforce his will despite resistance, authority existed when obedience to commands rested on a belief in their legitimacy — a belief that orders were justified and that it was right to obey. It was this idea of legitimacy which provided him with his criterion for classifying organizations. Along with different forms of belief in the legitimacy of authority went different authority structures and corresponding forms of organization. Three kinds of authority were distinguished: *charismatic* authority, based on the sacred or outstanding characteristic of the individual; *traditional* authority, based on respect for custom; *rational legal* authority, based on a code of legal rules and regulations.[1] The purest type of exercise of rational legal authority was that which employed a bureaucratic administrative staff.

Weber's full list of ten bureaucratic characteristics should not be taken in isolation from his longer list of preceding propositions on *legitimacy* and *authority*. He first of all set out five related beliefs on which the legitimacy of legal authority depended; this was followed by eight propositions about the structuring of legal authority systems; and finally, the ten characteristics of bureaucratic administration based on

---

[1] Of course most organizations contain a mixture of all these elements, but Weber was concerned with distinguishing the most logically pure types of combinations of authority and administration. These were not simply abstract types, however, but were typical of actual historical periods and circumstances.

these rational legal principles. The legitimacy of legal authority depends on the following beliefs:

i   That a legal code can be established which can claim obedience from members of the organization.
ii That the law is a system of abstract rules which are applied to particular cases; and that administration looks after the interests of the organization within the limits of that law.
iii That the man exercising authority also obeys this impersonal order.
iv That only *qua* member does the member obey the law.
v   That obedience is due not to the person who holds the authority but to the impersonal order which has granted him this position. (Albrow 1970 pp 43–5)

On the basis of these conceptions of legitimacy Weber formulated his propositions about the structuring of legal authority systems:

a   Official tasks are organized on a continuous, regulated basis.
b   These tasks are divided into functionally distinct spheres, each furnished with the requisite authority and sanctions.
c   Offices are arranged hierarchically, the rights of control and complaint being specified.
d   The rules according to which work is conducted may be either technical or legal. In both cases trained men are necessary.
e   The resources of the organization are quite distinct from those of the members as private individuals.
f   The office holder cannot appropriate his office.
g   Administration is based on written documents and this tends to make the office (*Bureau*) the hub of modern organization.
h   Legal authority systems can take many forms, but are seen at their purest in a bureaucratic administrative staff. (Albrow 1970 pp 43–5)

Bureaucracy in its most rational form presupposed the preceding propositions on legitimacy and authority, and had the following characteristics:

1   The staff members are personally free, observing only the impersonal duties of their offices.
2   There is a clear hierarchy of offices.
3   The functions of offices are clearly specified.

4 Officials are appointed on the basis of a contract.
5 They are selected on the basis of a professional qualification, ideally substantiated by a diploma gained through examination.
6 They have a monetary salary, and usually pension rights. The salary is graded according to position in the hierarchy. The official can always leave the post, and under certain circumstances it may be terminated.
7 The official's post is his sole or major concern.
8 There is a career structure, and promotion is possible either by seniority or merit, and according to the judgement of superiors.
9 The official may appropriate neither the post nor the resources which go with it.
10 He is subject to a unified control and disciplinary system. (Albrow 1970 pp 43–5. This is an abbreviation from Weber 1964 pp 329–34.)

Weber's definition of rational organization is, therefore, significantly different from those of many who thought they were following him in conceptualizing bureaucracy as rational organization. The difference is particularly evident when Weber's whole theoretical stance is compared with that of the management theorists. The latter tend to define organizations in a reified fashion as single entities with goals. And rational organization is then simply a matter of adopting whatever means are most efficient for attaining the goals. For Weber an organization (*Verband*) signified an ordering of social relationships, the maintenance of which certain individuals took as their special task. Thus the presence of a leader and usually an administrative staff was the defining characteristic of an organization. Furthermore,

> Weber regarded the fact that human behaviour was regularly oriented to a set of rules (*Ordnung*) as basic to sociological analysis. The existence of a distinctive set of rules governing behaviour was intrinsic to the concept of an organization. Without them it would not be possible to say what was and what was not organizational behaviour . . . Commands and rules ranked as equally important factors in the structuring of social relationships. In an administrative order they were linked in that the rules regulated the scope and possession of authority. (Albrow 1970 pp 38–9)

The spread of the bureaucratic form of organization to all spheres was part of a general process of rationalization in modern society. The reason why it would inevitably spread was because its characteristics of precision, continuity, discipline, strictness and reliability made it technically the most satisfactory form of organization for those who sought to exercise organizational control.

Bureaucracy, therefore, meant control by experts – men with the skill and knowledge to be able to apply the technical rules and norms that govern the functioning of modern organizations. The importance of technical rules and of experts to interpret and apply them is summarized in two of Weber's key statements: 'Bureaucratic administration signifies authority on the basis of knowledge. This is its specifically rational character.' (Weber 1964 p 339) And, 'Bureaucratic authority is specifically rational in the sense of being bound to discursively analysable rules.' (Weber 1964 p 361) The formal rationality of bureaucracy refers to the expert application of rules. And, as we have seen, Weber did not confuse such technical formal rationality with efficiency. It is worth noting Weber's statements on this subject, delivered at a conference in Vienna in 1909. No one denied, he argued, the 'technical superiority of the bureaucratic machine'. But when it came to comparing the national power position of different countries the German bureaucracy achieved far less than the corrupt machines of France and America.

> Which kind of organization has at the moment the greatest 'efficiency' (to use an English expression) – private capitalistic expansion, linked to purely business officialdom, which is more easily open to corruption, or state direction under the highly moral enlightened authoritarianism of the German officialdom? (Quoted in Albrow 1970 p 64)

In other words, Weber was not trying to state *a priori* sufficient conditions for the attainment of any organizational goal. He was describing the form of administration that went along with rational legal authority – in contrast to the kinds of administration that accompanied two other quite different types of authority, the traditional and the charismatic. As this type of authority and administration spread it pushed out all other types. The reason for its triumph is *not* adequately summarized in the single word 'efficiency'. Weber's explanation for its success includes a wider list of operational virtues: precision, speed, unambiguity, knowledge of the files, continuity, discretion, unity, strict subordination, reduction of friction and of material and personal costs. Certain other developments in industrial society also favour the spread of bureaucracy, such as the speed up in communication and transport, the adoption of modern accounting methods, the demand for equal treatment by citizens in a democracy and the growth of mass production and mass administration. Weber was thus offering a general theory of modern culture, centred on the process of progressive rationalization in all spheres. This leads us to the other common usage of the term bureaucracy:

2.2 Bureaucracy as modern society

Some theorists who have adopted this usage think in terms of forms of organization simply reflecting the economic or political character of the larger society. This is the view of Marx. But it is possible to see the process operating in the opposite direction as well so that bureaucratization is the subjection of society to the influence of the attitudes, values and techniques of bureaucrats. Why should this be the case?

The answer to this question of why bureaucracy as the administrative form of rational legal authority should spread so easily is that it moves into the vacuum left by the disappearance of administration based on traditional or charismatic types of authority. The control of members of modern organizations is rendered problematic because their commitment or allegiance is so partial. This contrasts with a traditional order in which participation in one social activity was closely intertwined with participation in all other activities, and where all these activities were regulated on the basis of norms and values sanctioned by ancient custom (although often backed by force as well). When this basis of order disappears the only alternatives are: (a) coercion based on naked power, (b) allegiance to a charismatic figure as in some religious or political sects, or else, (c) acceptance of rational legal authority specific to each activity. Because such authority is activity-specific, and because members' commitments to that organizational activity are partial, there is a problem of control. Bureaucracy refers to the structure of control in organizations based on rational legal authority. As Perrow puts it:

> For our purposes then, the bureaucratic model refers to an organization which attempts to control extra-organizational influences (stemming from the characteristics of personnel and changes in the environment) through the creation of specialized (staff) positions and through such rules and devices as regulations and categorization. (Perrow 1970 p 59)

3 Professionals and bureaucracy

There are some social scientists who have so defined bureaucracy as to be able to contrast it with a form of organization that relies on professional expertise. In so doing they suggest that the distinguishing characteristic of bureaucracy is a proliferation of detailed rules with close surveillance to ensure members' observance of those rules. This is then contrasted with organization based on professionals who do not require detailed rules or close surveillance. Weber himself did not make any such distinction, although he would probably have regarded both professional organization and bureaucracy as forms of administration based on the legal rational principles, but differing in the degree of specificity of the rules. Perhaps the real difference between the two types is pointed out in the comment by Perrow:

> The less the expertise, the more direct the surveillance, and the more obtrusive the controls. The more the expertise, the more unobtrusive the controls. The best situation of all, though they do not come cheap, is to hire professionals, for someone else has socialized them and even unobtrusive controls are hardly needed. The professional, the prima donna of organizational theory, is really the ultimate eunuch — capable of doing everything well in that harem except that which he should not do, and in this case that is to mess around with the goals of the organization, or the assumptions that determine to what ends he will use his professional skills. (Perrow 1972 p 10)

The effect of this statement if accepted, is to minimize the difference between bureaucrats and professionals, at least as far as the issue of organizational control is concerned. For it implies that the actions of professionals in organizations are just as programmed as those of bureaucrats — the only difference being that they are more '*pre-programmed*'. Some people would dispute this on the grounds that professionals in many organizations seem to have more initiatory power and capacity to re-direct organizational goals. Obviously this must be a matter of degree: it will depend to a large extent on the type of profession involved, and the type of organization in which the professional is operating. Wilensky, in his ironically titled article 'The Professionalization of Everyone?', discusses some of the factors that affect the professionalization of an occupation and the subsequent preservation of such professional characteristics as autonomy and a 'service' ideal in different organizations. He notes that an increasing percentage of professionals work in complex organizations (scientists, engineers, teachers, architects, even lawyers and doctors) and that these organizations have non-professional control structures — bosses, not colleagues, rule. On the whole, the salaried professional has neither exclusive nor final responsibility for his work; he has to accept the final authority of non-professionals. But whether the professional in a bureaucracy manages to maintain some of the autonomy typical of the classical independent professional will depend on several factors:

The crux of the issue of autonomy for salaried professionals is whether the organization itself is infused with professionalism (as measured, say, by a large percentage of professionally trained employees and managers) and whether the services of the professionals involved are scarce (as measured by a large number of attractive job offers from the outside). (Wilensky 1970 p 491)

As for maintaining their professional ideals, such as disinterested service to clients, Wilensky maintains that it is not always the case that professionals in bureaucracies are less independent.

It is true that one of the main centers of resistance to Nazi terror in Germany between 1933 and 1939 was a bureaucratic profession — personified by Pastor Niemöller of the Protestant Confessional Church and some of the leading Catholic clergy. But it is also true that many salaried professors in Nazi Germany prostituted their scholarship to ends which they knew were false. Teachers generally were among the earliest and most enthusiastic recruits for the Nazi Party. At the same time, however, fee-taking lawyers were subverting the rule of law and fee-taking physicians were conducting bizarre medical experiments in the concentration camps. (Wilensky 1970 pp 491–2)

However, Wilensky does conclude that bureaucracy enfeebles the service ideal more than it threatens professional autonomy. In effect he seems to be saying that professionals pressured by the demands of a bureaucracy are more likely to sacrifice their clients' interests than their own (and their profession's) interests. But he goes on to suggest that this will vary depending on the particular role orientation of the professional, and whether that orientation is primarily towards the profession, the organization, or a social movement (political or religious) (Wilensky 1970 pp 494–8).

4 Bureaucracy and social control

Has the bureaucratization of society brought about a new and more effective control of individuals? And is that insidious control even more dangerous than previous tyrannies because it appears to be a 'neutral' force which is non-partisan and value-free?

According to Blau and Schoenherr,

The new forms of power that are developing in modern society are closely connected with the great efficiency of indirect mechanisms of organizational control. Slave drivers have gone out of fashion not because they were so cruel but because they were so inefficient. Men can be controlled much more efficiently by tying their economic needs and interests to their performance on behalf of employers. Calling this wage slavery is a half-truth, which correctly indicates that workers dependent on their wages can be exploited as slaves can be, and which conveniently ignores the basic differences between economic exploitation and slavery. The efforts of men can be controlled still far more efficiently than through wages alone by mobilizing their professional commitments to the work they can do best and like to do most and by putting these highly motivated energies and skills at the disposal of organizations. (Blau and Schoenherr 1973 p 18)

The professionalization of organizations, in which decisions are made by technical experts, enhances both the internal efficiency and the external power of organizations. But the pursuit of efficiency is accompanied by an increase in insidious control. It is all the more dangerous because it is often not identified as power, and the individual may not experience it in terms of feeling oppressed. The individual operates less according to specific directives given by superiors, and more in accordance with an internal obligation to perform tasks in ways determined by an inherent rationality.

The pressure to make the most rational decision in terms of the interest of the organization requires that the recommendations experts make on the basis of their technical competence govern as much as possible such decisions of organizations as whether to shut down a plant and lay off its workers; in which city to build a new plant; whether to back the British pound against inflation or not; or in which company's stock to invest funds. Decisions like these have far-reaching implications for the lives of people, and sometimes they have deleterious consequences for society. But if experts have reached their recommendations on the basis of technical judgements, they cannot be censured for having arrived at these conclusions, because there is no animus in them, technical criteria govern them, and other experts would have reached the same conclusions. Whereas not all administrative decisions are based purely on technical grounds and exclude all political considerations, it is in the interest of organizations to make most decisions largely on these grounds. Inasmuch as experts judge issues in terms of universal criteria of rationality and efficiency, they cannot be blamed for the conclusions they reach, even though these conclusions may lead to actions of powerful organizations that are contrary to the interest of most people. (Blau and Schoenherr 1973 p 21)

This was the real issue that concerned Max Weber as far as bureaucracy was concerned. It lies behind some of the most stimulating discussions in the study of organizations that will be referred to in later chapters (especially those concerned with the various aspects of control within organizations — recruitment, selection, appraisal, decision-making, information flow, uncertainty reduction viz-à-viz external environment, etc.). It is also related to one of the main themes in contemporary sociology — the issue of social control versus individual freedom, as expressed in the contention of the German sociologist Jürgen Habermas that the element of choice for individuals in situations is being eroded by the spread of instrumental action systems (Habermas 1970). Habermas defines instrumental action as purposeful rational behaviour that proceeds according to technical rules based on empirical knowledge. He views instrumental action systems as the result of the development of science and technology (Weber would add to these the concomitant development of bureaucratic administration) as major forces of production. The problem with such action systems is that it is not feasible to deviate from technical rules. In contrast with the breaking of social norms, which can be labelled *deviant* behaviour, and is punished by sanctions external to the norms, the breaking of technical rules is simply *incompetent* behaviour which is sanctioned by the immediate failure of the intended strategy. The claim to rationality thus becomes a *legitimism in itself* (an ideology) — hence the link between the study of bureaucracy and the political issue of the threat to democracy of technocracy.

The importance of Weber's contribution to the founding of the study of complex organizations was that it set out to explore the ways in which the incorporation of a particular kind of rationality into a particular form of administrative structure gave rise to a similar pattern of organization in quite diverse fields of activity. This book seeks to follow Weber in discussing both these sets of factors in organizations, for it is the combination of such factors that structures social action. A controversial statement by Blau and Schoenherr sets out in extreme form the point about the interrelationship between social problems, which provide the context within which we discuss organizations, and the theory and methodology which guides our analysis.

> . . . in our sociological analysis as well as our political thinking, it is time that we 'push men finally out', to place proper emphasis on the study of social structure in sociology, and to recognize the power of organizations as the main threat to liberty in modern society. The enemy is not an exploitative capitalist or an imperialist general or a narrow-minded bureaucrat. It is no man. It is the efficient structure

of modern organizations which enables the giant ones and their combinations to dominate our lives, our fortunes, and our honour. (Blau and Schoenherr 1971 p 357)

5 Alienation

Blau and Schoenherr are close to Max Weber's position in their assertion about new forms of power that it is not individual or group interests such as those of the exploitative capitalist which are the main threat to liberty in modern society. Like Weber they reserve their deepest pessimism for the prospect of the domination of men by their own organizations. No doubt they have good cause for their pessimism and in this book we will examine many examples of the ways in which organizations seem to develop an entrenched logic of their own which is different from, and more than, a direct reflection of the interests of any single group or individual. In this respect the emphasis of non-Marxists regarding power in society has tended to be on the issue of rational bureaucracy rather than economic class struggle.[2] However, it might seem that the organization theorists in this tradition do draw closer to the Marxists when it comes to discussing the likely consequences for the individual of these developments. They focus on alienation. But they differ from Marx in that they view alienation as the product of a particular form of organization — bureaucracy.

> Marx's emphasis upon the wage worker as being 'separated' from the means of production becomes, in Weber's perspective, merely one special case of a universal trend. The modern soldier is equally 'separated' from the means of violence; the scientist from the means of enquiry, and the civil servant from the means of administration. Weber thus tries to relativize Marx's work by placing it into a more generalized context and showing that Marx's conclusions rest upon observations drawn from a dramatized 'special case', which is better seen as one case in a broad series of similar cases. The series as a whole exemplifies the comprehensive underlying trend of bureaucratization. Socialist class struggles are merely a vehicle implementing this trend. (Gerth and Mills 1948 p 50)

Some critics, such as Gouldner (1955), have condemned this 'metaphysical pathos' about bureaucracy and have sought to focus attention on the possibilities for reversing the process of bureaucratization and

---

[2] Although this need not exclude the concomitant conclusion of the Marxists that bureaucracy is often an effective means of oppression in the class struggle.

alienation, on the grounds that 'if the world of theory is grey and fore-doomed, the world of everyday life is green with possibilities which need to be cultivated'. (Gouldner 1954 p 29) Thus Gouldner in his study of the enforcement of rules in a gypsum plant found that morale and efficiency were higher when rules were not backed by close supervision and the threat of sanctions (Gouldner 1954). Other researchers claim to have found a persistent trend in modern organizations towards a decentralized and more flexible structure of authority (Likert 1961; Lawrence 1958; Guest 1962; Burns and Stalker 1961). Even military bureaucracies, which Weber and others regarded as the epitome of authoritarian bureaucratic organization, have recently been described as undergoing a shift towards less strict and rigid methods of control (Janowitz 1959).

5.1 Occupational differences

The nature of the rules in an organization and the degree of conformity and supervision that is expected and attached to them is obviously an important factor in either exacerbating or mitigating alienation. As Gouldner observed, 'In the last analysis, proliferation of . . . rules signify that management has, in effect if not intention, surrendered in the battle for the worker's motivation' (Gouldner 1954 p 175). We would expect to find some variation between organizations and even between occupational groups with respect to alienating conditions of work and alienated attitudes to work. Research cited by Blauner (1960) found the following differences between occupational groups regarding satisfaction with their work:

Table 1 Occupations and work satisfaction

Occupational group	Mean Index*	Number in sample
i Professional and managerial	560	23
ii Semi-professional, business, and supervisory	548	32
iii Skilled, manual and white collar	510	84
iv Semi-skilled manual workers	483	74
v Unskilled manual workers	401	55

*(In this index, the figure 100 would indicate extreme dissatisfaction, 400 indifference, and 700 extreme satisfaction.)

Source: Blauner (1960) p 342.

These findings reflect not only differences in alienation, or in the objective conditions of work for people in various jobs, but also occupational differences in the norms with respect to work attitudes (Caplow 1954). The professional is expected to be dedicated to his profession and to have an intensive intrinsic interest in his area of specialized competence: the white-collar employee is expected to be 'company-oriented' and like his work. But for the manual worker, 'his loyalty is never taken for granted and more than any other occupational type, cultural norms permit him the privilege of "griping" ' (Blauner 1960 p 343). J. A. C. Brown makes the same point: 'The working classes, as we have seen, are supposed to dislike work and therefore need "discipline" (the time clock, for example), to keep them in order.' (Brown 1954 p 99)

A number of factors contribute to occupational differences in alienation. In the case of manual workers in occupations in which the physical environment or the technological work process is particularly challenging, control over it seems to alleviate experienced alienation (Friedman and Havighurst 1954). Similarly, research by Brewer showed some support for two propositions that highly complex organizational tasks and dangerous, isolated tasks also lead to the debureaucratization of authority relations (Brewer 1970). Blauner suggests that satisfaction derived by professional and white-collar workers from control over their *social environment* parallels the control over the *technical environment* sought by manual workers, i.e. they seek to control clients and customers in the same way that manual workers desire to control the technical means of production. Blau illustrates this with regard to officials' efforts to exercise control over clients in a state employment agency and in a federal law enforcement agency. Similarly, Gouldner found that the gypsum miners had a lower level of work alienation than surface workers (even though they had less status in the community than surface workers) because the miners themselves were responsible for deciding the pace at which the machines worked, where the machines should operate, and what happened to them when they broke down.

5.2 Informal organization

Another important factor that can reduce alienation is the degree to which an organization allows workers to organize informally. Coal mining is a good example of an occupation where technological conditions favour the development of integrated work groups. Technological changes in mining which have had a disruptive effect on informal organization – such as the change over from hand-got to long-wall procedures – had an alienating effect on the miners (Trist and Bamforth 1951). One of the functions of groups that is relevant to alienation is the adoption by individuals of the group's norms to define their own actions. Where such norms are internalized, the individual does not feel that his normatively channelled behaviour is a response to coercive dictates over which he has no control. Leonard Pearlin, in a study of nursing personnel, defined alienation as subjectively experienced powerlessness to control one's own activities, and found that behaviour supported by group norms can create a sense of personal commitment and voluntarism (Pearlin 1962). Organizations and occupations vary in the extent to which they facilitate such processes. Some occupations would seem to rank higher than others in this respect in almost all circumstances; thus, professionals seem to be able to impose their own autonomous group norms on their work situation more easily than manual workers. But the degree of autonomy is also relative to the particular organizational context in which it exists. The basic process of steel making requires more small group operations than car-assembly-line plants (cf. Walker 1950). Even the individual factory, at a particular time, may vary enormously in this respect from otherwise similar factories. It may even vary internally from time to time, as Donald Roy shows in his description of a small work group in 'Banana Time: Job Satisfaction and Informal Interaction' (Roy 1973).

5.3 Managers

The same considerations apply to management groups in organizations. In industries experiencing rapid change and a constant need for innovation, the structure of organization may become more 'organic'. That is, instead of a 'mechanistic' structure characterized by a highly specialized division of labour and a rigid hierarchy, jobs can lose some of their formal definition of methods, responsibilities and powers and the definitive or enduring demarcation of functions may become more difficult to prescribe. (Burns and Stalker 1961)[3] The managers have to

---

[3] Professor John Child who has carried out research similar to that of Burns and Stalker has expressed doubts about the prevalence of this trend:
   Burns and Stalker only found one example of an organic structure, and that was confined to the R and D division of Ferranti's. Some parts of companies in changing, science-based industries may adopt organic type systems, but my own research carried out over a much wider comparative base than Burns and Stalker's shows that companies in electronics and pharmaceuticals are highly bureaucratic. Project teams, matrix systems, etc. seem generally to be set on top of this structure rather than instead of it. (Personal communication.)

engage in much more 'lateral' communication and informal ties are likely to increase as a result and so reduce alienation. Also, when each manager's tasks have to be discharged more in the light of knowledge of the total situation, in a turbulent environment, then his feelings of powerlessness or purposelessness may not be so marked as in the former mechanistic system. But some firms have a deeply entrenched resistance to such developments, and are just as likely to respond to external turbulence and change by redefining roles in more precise and rigorous terms and reinforcing the formal structures, thus creating more alienation. Even where informal peer groups do develop among managers, they may create alienation by accentuating careerist competition and inducing the manager to see his colleagues as commodities, to be used to further his own career. In such groups, behind the superficial friend-liness and co-operation there is distance, indifference and distrust.

5.4 Professional commitments and career interests

The new forms of power, or unobtrusive controls, discussed by Blau and Schoenherr (1973) include the harnessing of professional commit-ments and career interests to the service of the organization. Career interests are a valuable resource at the disposal of organizations. Robert Merton has noted that in order for a bureaucracy to operate successfully, it must attain a higher degree of reliability of behaviour, an unusual degree of conformity with prescribed patterns of action. To ensure this, it plans the bureaucrat's life for him in terms of a graded career, and he is tacitly compelled to adapt his thoughts, feelings and action to the prospect of that career. Career success by organizational standards is measured by the alienated yardsticks of money, power and prestige, rather than spontaneous involvement in the work for its own intrinsic and fulfilling value.

There are at least two strategies open to the professional in a bureau-cracy when faced with these organizational pressures. He can utilize conformity as a tool, for example, by following rules and regulations to the letter and so protect himself against interference. Michel Crozier's study of French officials found that subordinates tacitly agreed to play the management game, but they tried to turn it to their own advantage and to prevent management from interfering with their independence. (Crozier 1964) Or, alternatively, the professional within a bureaucratic organization can seek to maintain wider professional norms of behaviour that foster autonomy and expectations of involvement in shaping the goals of the organization. In the case of the first strategy, as described by Crozier, there tends to be a high degree of dissatisfaction with the conditions of employment and little worker solidarity. In the second strategy, different types of professionals are found to have somewhat different expectations and to experience alienation for subtly different reasons, although they can all be included under such general rubrics as desire for participation in goal setting and decision-making, and freedom to pursue autonomous professional goals. (Miller 1970, and Aiken and Hage 1970)

Conclusion

Although it is useful for the purpose of academic research to break down such broad concepts as 'alienation' and 'bureaucracy' into different dimensions and to test propositions about empirical correlations between them, in the manner suggested by Aiken and Hage, there are dangers. One danger is that such research may become purely academic because the issues begin to appear as matters of detail and requiring only minor adjustments. This may well suit the interest of some of those who sponsor research. They naturally welcome information which may help them to manipulate less essential aspects of the system so as to increase worker motivation or operating efficiency. The broader issues are then lost sight of and matters concerning different goals and values never come to the fore.

This brings us back to the point made earlier in discussing the inter-relationship between social problems, which provide the context within which we discuss organizations and the theories and method-ologies which guide our analysis. The single example of the use of the concept *bureaucracy* in the field of organization studies provides us with rich material for analysing these interrelationships. The quotations at the beginning of this chapter alerted us to the different problems and interests that have been associated with bureaucracy. The tendency of many organization theorists and researchers to associate the concept with problems of efficiency, as faced by managers, has given rise to a particular set of theories and empirical studies. A completely different set of theories and findings can emerge when a researcher on bureau-cracy and alienation starts out with a different perspective and different associated problems in mind. This is illustrated in the introduction to a report of the participant observation study of the New York Telephone Company, by Elinor Langer:

> I brought to the job certain radical interests. I knew I would see 'bureaucratization', 'alienation', and 'exploitation'. I knew that it was 'false consciousness' of their true role in the imperialist economy

that led the 'workers' to embrace their oppressors. I believed those things and I believe them still. I know why, by my logic, the workers should rise up. But my understanding was making reality an increasing puzzle: Why didn't people move? What things, invisible to me, were holding them back? What I hoped to learn, in short, was something about the texture of the industrial system: what life within it meant to its participants. (Langer 1970 p 1)

Her account of the functioning of that organization includes reference to many of the factors discussed by researchers with a quite different perspective, and they will constitute the main topics of this book: structure, system, control, interaction, roles, rules, knowledge and information. But what she found was affected by what she was looking for (problems), how she looked (theory and methodology), and what she hoped her findings would be used for (values).

This volume will present a variety of perspectives on organizations and it will be clear that the author of this chapter, like the authors of other chapters, has his own preferences. The reader is likewise free to make a choice. What our discussions can provide is help in making that choice as well informed as possible. And perhaps also instil the feeling that these are socially and intellectually relevant issues.

Section two
Structure and system: basic concepts and theories

CHAPTER 2

David J. Hickson and Arthur F. McCullough

Power in organizations

This chapter looks first at who has power in and over organizations, and then at why, in eight sections as follows:

1 The concept of power: a brief look at terminology
2 Hierarchical power: how power is distributed 'up and down' organizations
3 The power of subunits: how power is distributed across organizations
4 Interorganizational power: how organizations have power over each other
5 Why power?: some explanation
6 Resources as power bases: the kinds of resources used for power in organizations
7 Power and decision-making: how power shapes decision processes and premises
8 Views of power.

1 The concept of power

1.1 Definition

Any understanding of organizations must take account of the differential distribution of power between positions in them, and between the occupants of those positions. At its most obvious, doctors have more power than nurses, and some doctors have more power than others: managers have more power than clerks, and some managers have more power than others; some factories are said to be 'sales dominated' and some 'production dominated'. Power is the essence of organization, from Weber's analysis of its basic legitimation in charismatic, tradition-alistic, or bureaucratic terms, to the mutual control of one person by another inherent in social interaction day by day on the job.

The study of power is plagued by terminological confusion. Here we will use the word power as the generic term to encompass all the subtleties of authority, coercion, influence, force, domination and control. For our purposes in examining power in work organizations we can regard *power as the capacity to use resources, for example wealth, status or expert knowledge, to affect others.*

It is useful to recognise three aspects of power which Kaplan (1964 pp 14 and 15) has defined clearly. These are:

1 *weight* (or amount of effort on others); i.e. how far 'A can at his choice affect the probability that B will act in a certain way in certain circumstances';
2 *domain*: i.e. 'the range of persons or groups influenced';
3 *scope*: i.e. 'the range of . . . responses whose probabilities are affected'.

For example, the power of a workers' leader in a factory may have such *weight* that at a word from him his fellow workers down tools without question, or so little weight that it takes him weeks of argument to get a response. His *domain* may be every worker in the plant, all of whom strike, or only his immediate workmates. Although the *scope* of his power includes behaviour on the job it may stop short of determining the political party allegiances of those who otherwise accept his power over their work.

In *sections 2, 3* and *4* we will now examine how power is distributed within organizations, and then in the subsequent sections analyse the resources on which power is based and look at some of the explanations of these distributions of power that have been put forward.

2 Hierarchical power

2.1 Official hierarchy

The two structural fundamentals of organization, hierarchy and division of labour, are each bound up with power in organizations. We will look at power first from the perspective of hierarchy, and then from the perspective of the division of labour as that is represented by subunits (or departments or sections).

The two concepts overlap, since hierarchy is partly a division of labour because the supervisory and administrative tasks of bosses differ from the tasks of those who are their subordinates; but, primarily, hierarchy is a division of power. The higher the level in the hierarchy, the greater the recognized or legitimate right – the authority – to control the use of resources and the behaviour of others. For instance, managers may allocate money, and so be able to buy machinery, or may alter wages and thereby attempt to affect the behaviour of personnel below them: workers usually can do neither.

Figure 1 shows a conventional organization chart of a factory – conventional, that is, except for the written characters on it which very few readers of this text will be able to comprehend. The chart comes

Figure 1 Japanese organization chart

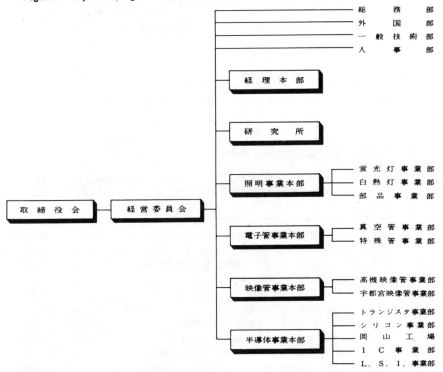

Source: The Matsushita Electronics Corporation Visitors' Guide

from a Japanese factory. Yet it is immediately recognizable for what it is, irrespective of the language of its written content: the formal hierarchy of authority is plain to see.

Reading from left to right, it proceeds level by level from a single top position whose authority is greater than that of any other single position (which is not to say that its authority is absolute, i.e. greater than that of any combination of others in the organization).

The chart shows the overwhelmingly prevalent type of hierarchy, but there are other variations, mainly multiple apexes. For example, a group of doctors may come together to work in a small health centre but avoid naming any one of themselves as having the final say: hospitals often have three sub-hierarchies, of doctors, of nurses, and of administrative and ancillary personnel, without either the senior medical consultant, the senior nursing officer or the hospital secretary or executive being top for all matters; in a trade union, the part-time president and the full-time secretary may jostle for position; a few rare companies claim to be run by a committee with a non-executive chairman. But these are the exceptions.

Hierarchy makes an organization work. It ensures that the variety of jobs in an organization are co-ordinated and that what is done in one is not too far out of step with what is done in another. It holds together the diversity of individuals in the jobs.

2.2 Hierarchical power distribution

Pugh and Hickson, in their article, 'The comparative study of organizations' (reprinted in Salaman and Thompson 1973 pp 50-66), present a chart (see Figure 2) of the characteristics of six heterogeneous British organizations: a municipal (local government) department, assorted private companies, state-owned manufacturing, and a retailing chain. The key indicates that the fourth bar of each organization's histogram represents its comparative degree of centralization of formal decision-making authority. It can be seen that the centralization of the two governmental or publicly owned organizations is comparatively high. Why should this be? Pugh and Hickson suggest that demands for decisions to be made openly, in public scrutiny, are a pressure for decisions to be referred upwards to representative committees and councils (so that the public who demand democratic control will also fume at the 'bureaucratic' delay thereby created?!). In local governments, for example, decisions and action have to wait for Committees and Councils to meet. But these authors also suggest that a similar

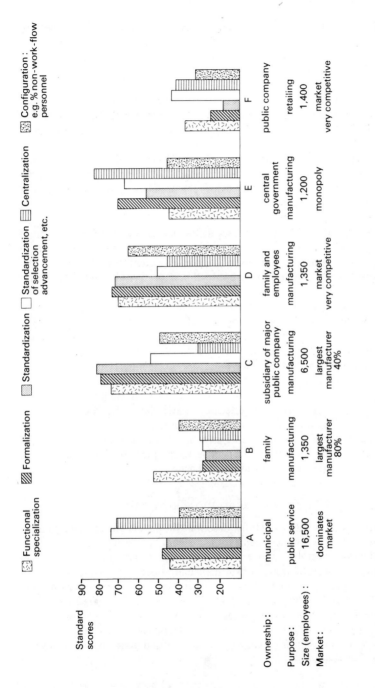

Figure 2 The comparative study of organizations

pressure for accountability in the use of resources forces the small units of large *private* combines to refer decisions upwards.

In contrast, organizations C and D in the same figure show comparatively high functional specialization, formalization, and standardization, which in combination amount to highly bureaucratic administration — or, as Pugh and Hickson call it, 'structuring of activities' of employees. That is, control is maintained not so much by centralizing decisions towards the top but by setting prescribed tasks, rules, and procedures to regulate behaviour. It is a less visible form of power, which sets the limits of what others may do, shapes the premises by which they decide, and then delegates authority within these constraints. A kind of freedom of manoeuvre within bounds.

So subordinates can either await the bosses' decision (centralization) or use their own discretion within the rules they have learned (decentralization). In either case power is present governing what they do, though research results imply that most people prefer the latter where they feel free of irksome interference. In Britain, people mostly prefer doing what they have learned and sticking by the rules, even if this sometimes seems a bit futile, rather than be ordered about personally by someone else which can 'make your blood boil'. In this way they have some autonomy, even if they have little power.

But what kind of data are Pugh and Hickson reporting? (Full details can be found in Pugh and Hickson, 1976.) They studied official authority levels, i.e. the levels in the hierarchy at which top management said decisions were taken and acted upon (Whisler *et al*, 1967, report an alternative method of doing this). Yet more goes into power than this: it includes the total process of influence of one person by another, and one group by another. A perspective which picks up something of this is taken by Tannenbaum and his colleagues.

2.3 How hierarchy looks to those involved

Tannenbaum's method (fully described in papers collected in Tannenbaum 1968) is to ask organization members to respond on a questionnaire to questions about 'influence'. There are many possibilities including asking about the influence of different hierarchical levels (e.g. managers or supervisors or workers) in the organization in general, or over each other, or, as it ideally should be, compared to how it actually appears to be, and so on.

For example, in thirty-two geographically separate sites of an American delivery company, which carried goods by road, respondents were asked:

In general, how much say or influence do you feel each of the following groups has on what goes on in your station?, as follows:

	Little or no influence	*Some influence*	*Quite a bit of influence*	*A great deal of influence*	*A very great deal of influence*
Your station manager	——	——	——	——	——
The other supervisors in your station	——	——	——	——	——
The men in your station	——	——	——	——	——

The same question was repeated on what the influence of each 'should' be. Figure 3 (overleaf) shows the result (full details are on pp 73-79 in Tannenbaum 1968). It plots the average scores representing the views of supervisors and of non-supervisors (men), and joins the points with a graph line. Each respondent can score from 1.0, little influence, to 5.0, a very great deal, on his view of each of the three hierarchical levels.

In this case both supervisors and men see influence as following an orderly step by step hierarchical sequence, but the men think they themselves ideally *should* have more influence than they feel they do have. That is, the hierarchy of power should not be so 'steep', and the slope of the control graph, as it is called, should not be so negative in direction. This is shown by their ideal of influence for themselves being over 3.0 whereas they score the reality as near 2.0. In general, they feel all three grades have less influence than they should have, so the graph line joining the men's (non-supervisory) ideal points is well above the actual.

As in this example, personnel in industrial or business organizations always perceive these as more hierarchical in power terms than organizations with some 'voluntary' (non-paid) membership appear to be to their members (Tannenbaum and Cooke, 1979). In these latter organizations, such as trade unions, or the local branches of the American League of Women Voters, which were once studied, the slope of the control graph is not so steeply negative or, indeed, may be positive. So in some American unions the members were seen as having as much or more influence than the officials who headed the hierarchy. Research on organizations which employ substantial proportions of highly trained professional personnel, such as universities and research institutes, shows that these, too, have a less hierarchical power distribution

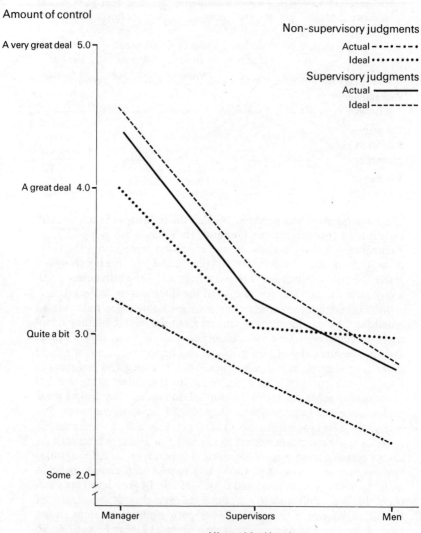

Figure 3 Average control curves for 32 stations of a delivery company:
Actual and ideal control—non-supervisors and supervisors (from
Tannenbaum, 1968 p 78)

than is common in industry and commerce. So professional training is a third alternative way of controlling people in organizations, alternative to direct authority or to rules and regulations.

Whatever the pressures, whatever the spread of decisions (in Pugh and Hickson's terms) or the slope of the graph (in Tannenbaum's terms), the balance of power rarely if ever tilts wholly one way. Few organizations have overwhelming power 'weight' over every aspect of the behaviour of every one of their members (total 'scope' and 'domain'). That is, few approach what Goffman (1968) has called the 'total institution', controlling its members day and night, waking and sleeping, throughout the twenty-four hours. At times the armed forces, or religious organizations such as monasteries or nunneries, or boarding schools, or merchant ships, come close to it. Limited control 'off the job' is quite common, e.g. senior civil servants in Britain are not allowed to be active in politics. But mostly there is a great deal of scope for behaviour outside such control, even 'on the job'. For example, the importing of working-class culture into the factory, with a whole range of behaviour officially unrecognized or forbidden by management, is vividly and often amusingly described by Katz (1968) and Roy (1960). Roy himself worked on a routine industrial job in the United States, and at first he was taken aback by the apparent absurdities of banana time, peach time, opening the window time, coke time, and so on. Every day, for example, one worker would bring in a banana for a snack, and every day the others would sneak it away, eat it, and taunt him. How futile – until Roy realized that these goings on made a useful break with light relief from the monotonous work and helped keep everyone socially companionable. They flourished irrespective of managerial authority which frowned on 'horseplay' or any kind of distraction viewed by managers as frivolous and time-wasting.

Also, there is frequently delegation and participation of the kinds described by Strauss (1963) and advocated by writers such as Likert (1961), though how far this should be called 'power-equalization', as Strauss terms it, is a moot point. Welcome though it may be to the subordinates concerned to have more say in what they themselves do or in changes which may affect them, the power hierarchy continues and eventually the decision is probably taken above them. On the one hand, egalitarian optimists see better organizations when lower level employees can participate more in decisions by being consulted on what their views are and by having their representatives to press their case on committees and boards. On the other, cynical pessimists claim that unless the basic hierarchy of power is changed in some yet undiscovered way this participation serves only to underline it. Through participation those in charge know more readily how to act to get what they want with less trouble, and those without real power still do not understand all that is being done. Indeed, those in power may even become more powerful (Mulder 1971; Rus 1980).

3 The power of subunits

3.1 Interdepartmental systems

So far we have a picture of power in organizations divided step by step down a hierarchy. This is power 'up and down' organizations. There is also power 'across' organizations. Although organizations are bound together by a controlling hierarchy, they are at the same time shifting coalitions of interested parties. They are more or less open systems reconciling the aims or goals of employees or managers or owners or customers or suppliers, etc., etc. The larger an organization becomes, the more the problems in which these parties are interested tend to be divided into sub-problems and assigned to subunits. As a small business grows, for instance, its owner can no longer manage the money on his own. He employs an accountant, then wages clerks to pay the employees, then a cost accountant, and so on. This is part of the development of bureaucracy and is another way of describing the division of labour. Thus organizations can be seen as being composed of subsystems designed to deal with basic system problems. This gives a view of organizations as being inter-subunit or interdepartmental systems, some subunits with more power and some with less, each pursuing its own ends within the whole. In industry, for example, a sales department may see its marketing campaign as necessitating a larger budget for sales staff salaries and expenses, whilst production stresses the need for more money to be invested in stocks of raw materials in case demand increases for the product.

Strauss (1962) found that 'purchasing agents' (i.e. the buyers or purchasing managers in firms he studied) were in a weak position, but struggling for more power. (He observed, interviewed, and gave questionnaires to purchasing agents in a number of firms.) As he saw it, an agent has two primary tasks, placing orders for supplies, and expediting their delivery. But agents feel they should do much more than this. They should keep management informed on new materials, on prices, etc., and should take part in the planning stage of new products, not merely place orders after all the decisions have been taken. So the agents studied used a variety of tactics to try and influence decisions, including exploit-

ing friends in other departments, and manipulating rules to give themselves greater power to affect what happened. Agents could do little
where standard supplies were routinely bought, but their chances of
power were greater where companies made goods to customer order so
that there was a continual variety of supplies needed for varying products.

Any change, of course, may favour some subunit(s) rather than
others. New machinery, for example, which runs with very little maintenance required, may help a production department, but put the
maintenance engineers in a precarious position because their job
becomes less important. When Normann (1971) followed the development of new products in twelve Swedish companies in food processing,
packaging, pharmaceuticals, construction, electronics, and engineering,
he found that the departmental power structure served as a filter for
new ideas. Departments attempted to mould changes to their own
viewpoint. This is corroborated by Carter (1971 p 418) who traced
major decisions in an American computer company, and reports that
when a decision was to be made, 'By bargaining within departments
the staff would preprocess investments to ensure that projects sub-
mitted for the president's consideration fitted the wishes of the
members of the department' (Carter 1971 p 418).

3.2 Generalization?

It is clear that the pattern of power among subunits differs from one
organization to the next, but research has not yet established whether
there is sufficient stability and uniformity to enable generalizations
as to which are the most powerful in which organizations in what
circumstances.

In the United States, Zald (1962) has inferred that as the aims of
penal institutions shift from punishment to treatment, so power slips
away from the 'custodial' staff. Clark (1956) has analysed educational
institutions. But most of the meagre research has been in industrial
organizations.

For instance, Hinings *et al* (1974) investigated power in five breweries
and two cardboard container factories in Canada and the United States.
They found that production was consistently more powerful than
marketing, engineering, or accounting. In each organization these were
the only four subunits, making a complete interdepartmental system.
A range of power data were obtained from detailed interviewing about
departmental activities, from questionnaires, and from chief executives'
definitions of departmental authority. All data presented a consistent
picture over multiple analyses.

An example from questionnaire data alone is given in Table 1. In this small branch brewery of 300 employees, the heads of all four departments or subunits were asked to rate their own and each of the other departments on five point scales, from 'very great influence' to 'little influence', on each of the seventeen issues listed on the table. These issues were reported by the department heads to be recurrent interdepartmental topics. In this way Hinings and his colleagues applied Tannenbaum's method, discussed in *section 2.3* above, not to hierarchy as is usually done but to power across departments. Highest influence scores are underlined in the table, picking out production not only as unchallenged within its own task area but as frequently having considerable power in the other departments' areas of work. Marketing, on the other hand, whilst dominating its own area of sales, shares that power with production and has a lesser place outside the sales area.

These results, on an unusually full range of power data but on a small sample, do not fit Perrow's (1970) picture of the dominant power of *sales* departments in the American market economy. In the small units Hinings *et al* studied, the belief (in brewing) that brewing beer has a special skill, the complexities (in container production) of making a variety of special packagings, and in both brewing and container manufacture the central position of production in the organization's workflow and its involvement in everything that happens, all helped make the *production* department the most powerful.

The maintenance or engineering section can also exert a great deal of power. In twenty-three small tobacco plants in France investigated by Crozier (1964), the maintenance personnel were able to monopolize the knowhow necessary to repair machine breakdowns. Since all else ran smoothly, mostly under central administrative control from Paris head office, machine breakdowns were the only critical problem. Since the maintenance personnel could deal with the problem, they were powerful.

In studies such as these the power differences can be held to arise in some way from a department being 'critical' to an organization (to use Perrow's word). Thus Landsberger (1961) argued from the histories of three engineering firms that when money is scarce, accounting is more powerful; when raw materials are short, purchasing is more powerful; and, conversely, when demand is insatiable, sales are less powerful. This question of why power arises is examined in *section 5* below.

4 Interorganizational power

4.1 External interests

Power is not only a matter of hierarchical authority or of the influence of internal subunits. It also governs relationships between organizations, which are more and more important to contemporary societies. Here organization theory overlaps with economics and political science. Starting from an economics perspective, Williamson (1975) points out that transactions in a society can be undertaken in two ways. There are market transactions in which it is possible to place a price on what is being done and so there is buying and selling. And there are bureaucratic transactions within organizations. With these it is not so easy to arrive at a monetary value so they are brought within organizations and in some degree routinized, as when a buyer firm takes over one of its suppliers which then becomes one of its internal subunits making components which are passed to other subunits or departments without a monetary reckoning between them.

Similarly, Wamsley and Zald (1973) see in the political economy of public (i.e. state) organizations an external system of interest groups including competing public organizations, legislative committees, and control agencies, as well as the internal system of subunits.

Thus all organizations, most obviously those in industrialized societies, function in an interlocking network of relationships with others. This is so whether they are public or private, manufacturing or service or administrative. A private factory will have contracts with suppliers and customers, contacts with numerous governmental units from the factory health and safety inspectorate to the Department of Trade, the Inland Revenue, and the local planning authority, links with banks and trades unions, and many more. A local government county or district will have much the same except that the proportion of other state organizations will be even larger.

4.2 Power and choice

How great is the power of one over another? It can range from domination to negligible power. Butler *et al* (1978) vividly describe two organizations, calling the one 'paralytic' and the other 'politicking'. The paralytic case is a nationalized public service organization which has a single unalterable source of supply, a range of customers fixed by government, prices fixed largely by the charges it has to pay its supplier and beyond that by a Prices Commission, and large competing organizations preventing it changing the services offered. This organization is paralysed by the power of other organizations on which it is totally dependent. The politicking case, a university, has comparatively much less constraint from external powers and much more politicking among internal subunits.

Organizations – or, strictly speaking, those who manage them and take strategic decisions – usually have more choice than was apparent in the paralytic case above. There is some degree of strategic choice as to what products to make, what services to offer, where to sell these or make them available, and what other organizations to deal with (Child 1973). A firm concerned over the regularity of its supplies can choose one or more supplier organizations with which to sign long-term contracts. A firm concerned over its costs may be able to arrange direct or indirect state subsidies. In short, organizations can ensure a secure future by arranging a network of supporting relationships and, as it were, choosing and negotiating their environments.

This changes their internal power, both hierarchically, up and down, and across. For example, a firm may secure a long-term contract for supplies but this can have the effect of making it dependent on, say, one supplier. In turn one of its own customer organizations, following the same policy of ensuring supplies, may take it over. It is now dependent on a single supplier of materials, and on its new owner as a single source of capital as well as for taking all its output – an extreme case, but common enough. Research has demonstrated (Pugh and Hickson 1976) that greater external dependence on a few other organizations is strongly correlated with greater internal centralization. External dependence affects the hierarchical distribution of power. This is because when there are a few crucial external relationships, any decisions which might impinge on them become so important that they are taken at the top (centralized), and some may be centralized beyond the unit of organization itself in the headquarters of an owning group.

Second, external links change the uncertainties from which power may be derived. For example, a marketing department which is powerful because it gets orders despite an unpredictably fluctuating market is likely to lose power if it succeeds in signing a contract with a big customer. The market uncertainty which was the source of its power has now gone. A firm with guaranteed distribution channels has little need of marketing expertise.

To this question of the sources of power we now turn.

5 Why power?

5.1 A theory

From Marx (1930) to Weber (1948) to Blau (1964) and onwards, a great deal has been written on why there is power and why some have more than others. The whole of this question cannot be covered here.

However, the references in *section 3.2* above to the work of Landsberger (1961) and Perrow (1970) have the beginnings of an explanation as to why there are differences in power between subunits, why one has more and another less, and why this is a shifting distribution of power. For this distribution of power across organizations, based on the division of labour, i.e. on who does what, is likely to be more dynamic than the hierarchical structure of power. It changes faster. Hickson *et al* (1971) drew together the threads of explanation into what they called a 'strategic contingencies theory of power' (Figure 4 overleaf). Though they cautiously applied it only to departmental power, where it was supported in a limited empirical test (Hinings *et al* 1974), it may well apply more widely.

The theory hinges on ideas about uncertainty introduced by March and Simon (1958) and brought out by Crozier (1964). Power derives from what, for the organization, is critical, and is for it a major problem. But not just any problem. Most power potentially derives from those problems about which there is greatest *uncertainty*. A problem to which there is a ready answer is not a source of differential power. But a subunit which can cope with uncertainty will gain in power. *Coping with uncertainty* yields power.

Even so, this is only in certain circumstances. If anyone and everyone could do what is needed then all would have some power but one party would not have more than the others. That can only happen when that one can do the job and no one else can, i.e. that subunit has a degree of monopoly, and is *non-substitutable*. So a marketing department which, despite an uncertain fluctuating market, is able to bring into its organization a steady flow of orders will gain power provided also that marketing consultants (for example) cannot be hired to cope just as well. Such a department is in the best possible position if it is also *central* to the organization as a system (a point made by Woodward 1965), in the sense that if it failed the output of the whole organization would immediately be affected *(immediacy)*; and also that the flows of work connect it pervasively to all or most other departments so that it is a focus of what happens rather than being on the fringe of activity *(pervasiveness)*.

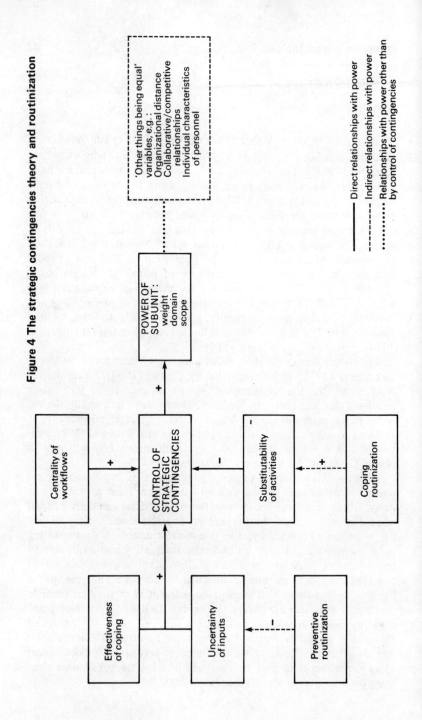

Figure 4 The strategic contingencies theory and routinization

'Other things being equal'
variables, e.g.:
Organizational distance
Collaborative/competitive
relationships
Individual characteristics
of personnel

POWER OF
SUBUNIT:
weight
domain
scope

Centrality of workflows

CONTROL OF
STRATEGIC
CONTINGENCIES

Substitutability
of activities

Coping
routinization

Effectiveness
of coping

Uncertainty
of inputs

Preventive
routinization

——— Direct relationships with power
– – – Indirect relationships with power
········· Relationships with power other than
            by control of contingencies

In sum, the theory argues that a subunit will be most powerful if it copes effectively with high uncertainty, is non-substitutable, and is central both in terms of immediacy and of pervasiveness. These variables combine to explain differing amounts of power because they give subunits differing degrees of control over contingencies that affect the work of other subunits. It is a theory stated specifically in organizational terms but in line with the general propositions of Dahl and Emerson. Dahl, a foremost student of power in the wider community setting, writes: '. . . power terms in modern social science refer to subsets of relations among social units such that behaviours of one or more units (the responsive units) depend in some circumstances on the behaviour of other units (the controlling units)' (1968 p 407). Emerson has formulated this idea of dependence explicitly: 'The dependence of actor A upon actor B is (1) directly proportional to A's motivational investment in goals mediated by B, and (2) inversely proportional to the availability of those goals to A outside of the A – B relation' (1962 p 32). That is, B depends on A to the extent that he can only get what he wants from A or via A.

The theory explains the moving patterns of power in organizations. First, events beyond the organization may change what for it are the uncertainties; markets change, technical advances change the information and processes that are needed, governments alter regulations, and so on. More than that, the organization's own goals and strategic choices, referred to earlier, may change what are for it the primary uncertainties. Second, alternative ways arise of doing what a department does and make it substitutable, e.g. a computer may make a statistical department largely superfluous. Third, managerial changes in structure in the interests of efficiency alter flows of work and so some become more central and others more peripheral.

Hence the constant flux in power. Further, it is possible for subunit members to deliberately seek uncertainty, non-substitutability and centrality, and Hickson *et al* (1974) go so far as speculatively to suggest some routes of power in these terms. In particular, Crozier's (1964) analysis of how engineers held on to power emphasizes that routinization of work must be avoided if power is the aim, for if a subunit's work can be done routinely by anyone who can understand the rules or instructions for doing it, then that subunit can be substituted for. Indeed, it may even be that the uncertainty with which it was coping can be removed, as the uncertainties of machine breakdown with which only the engineers could deal would have been removed by routine preventive maintenance.

The appropriateness of this theory to explain power between organizations has not been directly empirically tested, but there seems no obvious obstacle to transferring it to external power also. To continue an earlier example, a marketing department which loses its source of power by signing a contract which removes uncertainty has thereby moved the problem on to the customer organization. It now in its turn has to ensure the steady orders contracted for by coping with any uncertainties that face it, and if it succeeds it continues to have power to influence the organization from which it is buying. As Jacobs (1974 p 53) says: 'Organizations are controlled by those who comprise or control the organization's most problematic dependence', and Benson (1975) notes the close resemblance of his analysis of inter-organizational relationships to analyses of intraorganizational subunit relationships.

Conversely, the idea of non-substitutability is the transfer to internal analyses of the economics notion of monopoly. Hickson *et al*'s (1971) theory stresses subunit monopoly of the know-how or expertise which copes with an uncertainty, and the same idea helps to explain hier-archical power (and its limits). Mechanic (1962) has stated plainly what it means. In all organizations, superiors are inclined to see themselves as having more power over subordinates than subordinates see them as having (see the control graph in Figure 3). Subordinates are aware of the counterpower they possess which limits the power of the boss. They come to know their own jobs better than their superiors know these jobs, and so, Mechanic argues, superiors then have to depend on their subordinates' expertise and the latter gain power as a result. This necessarily assumes that superiors cannot get the job done in any other way because the subordinates are non-substitutable. On the other hand, Michels (1949) shows the same tendency working in the opposite direction. Because the officers of voluntary-membership organizations acquire experience and skill in leadership and administration which other members do not get, they become a powerful self-perpetuating oligarchy; and this tendency is present in all organizations, something which applies to managers as much as to union officials (Michels 1970).

5.2 Legitimacy

If, as has been suggested, the effective and exclusive use of expertise can lead to power, it can only be used legitimately within limits. The expertise of a specialist department, for instance, is intended legit-imately to be used only for the benefit of the whole organization, even if at the same time it furthers that department's own interests. Conflicts do arise where the implicit limits are overstepped and sectional interests are pursued regardless.

In just the same way the hierarchical power of bosses is only to be used within legitimate limits (e.g. violence may not be used on subordinates in most circumstances), and within those limits it is termed authority, accepted and respected for charismatic, traditionalistic, or bureaucratic reasons (Weber 1948) or because of trained professional commitment. Similarly, and even more fundamentally, the very existence of organizations as systems of power rests on a legitimacy accorded by society. In Britain, companies are permitted by Parliament under the Companies Acts, local governments are set up in their present form by specific acts, so is the Independent Television Authority, and so on for all kinds of organizations. They are legally legitimate creations thought up by society and with what they may legitimately do defined by law and by informal norms or standards of conduct.

Organizations yield society benefits which range from wealth to health. The legitimation which they are accorded approves their use for these purposes of resources such as capital, which they may have a right to own, and certainly to use, or information which they may retain as trade secrets or patents, and so on.

But the acquisition and use of 'power-full' resources by organizations does not go unquestioned. In most, if not all, 'organizational societies' there are groups, large or small, blatant or concealed, which deny the legitimacy of the use of resources by certain organizations. In Europe or North America there are histories of demonstrations against the scientific development of weapons, or against mining in scenic countryside. There are recurrent fears that the powers of multinational corporations may exceed the power of any one state to control their activities. Their vast yet dispersed economic assets can enable them to make investment and price decisions which affect economic trends and employment in countries which have no influence on those decisions. There are also less conspicuous organizations legitimated only by some sections of a society, for example clandestine presses or resistance fighters/terrorists.

So there is no such thing as legitimate power in an absolute sense. There is continual conflict in societies and in organizations over what resources can be legitimately used in which way for what. That is, legitimacy of the weight, scope, and domain of power is a matter of degree and a matter of who sees it that way and who does not. Compliance with power is not only a matter of being dependent and having little choice, but is also affected by whether that power is felt to be rightfully exercised. Moreover, the legitimacy of the power of organizations and the power in organizations is inevitably partly defined by organizations, in the process of negotiating their own rightfulness and acceptance. They lobby, they have representatives on committees and commissions, public and private, they advertise, they wine and dine, they improve working conditions; and from such activity flows their own legitimacy.

6 Resources as power bases

6.1 Classifications

Organizations, then, are (more or less) legitimately established institutions for the use of resources that confer power. Our initial definition regarded power as the capacity to use *resources* to affect others, and this is what is done inside and outside organizations both beneficially and to exploit.

The notion of resources, which when used for power are usually referred to as power *bases*, frequently confuses the subject. It is largely responsible for the numerous power-like words, some of which were mentioned at the beginning of the chapter. For example, if different authors at different times write about coercive force, or persuasive influence, or normative control, they are all writing about the same concept, power, but labelling it according to the resource bases that are used. Coercive force probably means that physical resources are used such as weapons or prison walls; persuasive influence probably means that special knowledge or expertise, or the implication of it, are used to back verbal pressure; normative control probably means that an ideological attraction is the supporting resource.

Etzioni's (1970) account of different types of power resources classifies power as coercive (physical resources) or remunerative (material resources) or normative (symbolic resources). Some organizations emphasize one kind of resource, some another, though any one organization may use all three kinds of resource.

Organizations relying mainly on physical force to affect behaviour are exemplified by prisons, concentration camps and custodial mental hospitals. Material resources are the primary means for business, commercial, administrative and industrial organizations which reward their members with income and fringe benefits. Symbolic resources are rituals or objects which act as symbols of love, esteem, or prestige as in religious and sometimes in political organizations, universities or colleges, and voluntary associations. Etzioni suggests that this last could also be called persuasive or suggestive power.

Thus bureaucracies, for example, are not all identical in the resources on which their power is based. They differ sharply in which resources they rely on the most for legitimate control. A bureaucracy may rely more on coercive power (a prison) or on remunerative power (a factory or bank) or normative power (a hospital).

Attractive though Etzioni's analysis is, it has been very little tested empirically. Hall *et al* (1967) made one attempt to do so, an attempt whose adequacy is challenged by Weldon (1972). Nothing can be said about the *degree* to which organizations differ in this way. And is this extremely simple classification exhaustive or not?

A similar analysis put forward by French and Raven (1959) has been used more often for research purposes, but rarely to explore differences between organizations as such (for example, inconclusive results are reported by Bachman *et al* 1968).

French and Raven view power from the standpoint of the member of an organization who is subject to it. They suggest that superior levels — supervisors and managers of all kinds — use any or all of the following bases of power:

coercive: the individual conforms because be believes he will otherwise suffer negative consequences, punishment;
reward: the individual believes he will benefit if he conforms;
referent: the individual is attracted to and identified with another, and so conforms to his desires;
expert: the individual believes that another has superior knowledge or expertise to which he defers;
legitimate: the individual accepts the right of another to power over him.

So a supervisor can have an employee's pay withheld for late attendance, or allocate him the most troublesome work, i.e. use coercive power. Or a supervisor can recommend a pay increase, i.e. reward power. If the supervisor is personally admired by his subordinate then he can confidently ask for a special extra effort, i.e. referent power. Should the supervisor be known for his skill at the job then a subordinate will accept a supervisor's authority to tell him how to do it as in the proper order of things, i.e. legitimate power.

These five bases resemble Etzioni's categories, though his are meant to show broad differences between organizations whereas French and Raven imply that within any one organization individuals may differ in their reasons for complying. French and Raven's coercive power includes Etzioni's physical coercion, but extends also to the negative aspect of his remunerative power: reward power and remunerative power appear to match: referent power matches Etzioni's normative or identitive power, and expert power may also come within the normative category.

6.2 Legitimacy of resources

Legitimacy is treated differently, however. In Etzioni's scheme, coercive, remunerative, or normative power may each be used legitimately or non-legitimately or in some degree legitimately. In this light, the listing of legitimacy among bases of power by French and Raven is confusing, even mistaken. Legitimacy is not an exclusive category of power base, but a variable quality of each of the other bases. For example, coercion can be legitimate (the control of deserters in any army) or non-legitimate (physical brutality to factory workers); expertise can be legitimate (the chief accountant's decision on a budgeting problem) or non-legitimate (the physics professor's attempt to tell sociology lecturers how to teach). And Weber's (1948) authority of office (based on the *reward* systems of the organization) and authority of expertise (the *expert* base) are both legitimate.

Here again we see the constant conflicts in all societies over the rightful – legitimate – use of power. In Britain, for example, the potentially coercive resources of business organizations are questioned as trained security guards multiply around factories and to guard money. Equally, the pressures put by trade union members on their fellows to come out or stay out on strike are regarded suspiciously. Thus the use of coercive power is the most carefully watched and defined, though, as was said earlier, there are always differing views on legitimacy. Strikers dealing rather forcefully with blacklegs may not see coercion in the same light as do the journalists who write about the brutal misuse of union power.

As with coercive power so too the legitimacy of reward power is limited: nothing 'smells worse' than the over-use of rewards (e.g. money). Likewise, the exploitation of someone else's devoted loyalty (i.e. wrong use of referent power) may be frowned on; and so might be the use of moral commitment to minimize wage costs, such as low pay in hospitals (i.e. wrong use of normative power).

In contemporary organizations it is likely that expertise power is becoming more important as specialist knowledge grows. It is a power based on a division of labour which generates the expertise, and it is from this that the strategic contingencies theory of power (Hickson *et al*, 1971) discussed in *section 5* above derives. This theory assumes that as well as the reward power used hierarchically in organizations there is an expertise power base which subunits and others can take advantage of irrespective of hierarchical position. Its potential for power is greater when it is used to cope with uncertainty.

6.3 Responses to the power of resources

Which brings us to the other aspect of our definition of power: *effect* upon others. How are the members or employees of organizations affected by the use of these several kinds of resources to motivate and control them? How do they respond?

Over this there is a fundamental obscurity in analysis of power, arising from the empirical difficulty, even impossibility, of distinguishing responses to someone's power (or to an organization's or subunit's power) from responses to everything else that happens.

However, Etzioni's typology again offers a sweeping perspective, untested though it is. He hypothesizes (see the summary in Dunkerley 1972 p 60) that the use of coercion brings an alienative response, the use of remuneration in the widest sense of that word brings a calculative response, and the use of normative bases brings a moral response. On the face of it, this is appealing. People who are coerced don't like it, people who are paid do count the cost, and people who are offered ideological aims do morally commit themselves. Of course, most cases are mixed: hospital staffs have gone on strike for more pay when the normative power of appeals to their moral commitment has waned, and armies have been led by highly paid mercenary foreigners though they themselves have been expected to give more in patriotism than they got in cash.

Alienation, of course, is frequently used as a wider concept which would include both Etzioni's alienative and calculative categories of compliance. It is seen as an effect of power, or rather of powerlessness. Those whose sole resource is their labour and expertise, and who do not have the power that goes with the control of the capital and technology resources of organizations, are regarded as alienated from or non-involved in the organizations and societies to which they nominally belong.

7 Power and decision-making

7.1 Decision processes

Often there is a tendency to speak as if decisions are made at a single moment of time, as if they all emanated from the mythical men of decision created by the wilder Westerns and the less novel novelists.

Yet even if a decision does seem to be made quickly on the spur of the moment, it is necessarily the culmination of experience which includes being influenced by the power of others. And even in a crisis when one man or a few may have to make up their minds with no chance to contact anyone else, they will implicitly or explicitly weigh up the likely views of any especially powerful others.

Attempts to trace what leads up to a decision reveal confused sequences which suggest that the very term 'a decision' is misleading (Mintzberg *et al* 1976). More accurately, there are processes of decision, or many sub-decisions. The record by Cyert *et al* (1956) of an American company's decision to install electronic data processing equipment spans no less than three years (and even then, where is its beginning and its end?), and shows that a variety of managerial and other personnel from accounting and sales departments were involved: a range of executives on a management committee, the company president, various computer company representatives and consultants, and influential outsiders met at conferences. Pettigrew's (1973) study of a similar decision in a British company shows the power of a manager who was the nexus of a similarly wide range of internal and external contacts over about five years. His position meant that the information reaching the company board which made the decision was in effect screened so that it reflected primarily the view he favoured. Again, Mintzberg *et al*'s (1976) twenty-five cases spanned from one year to beyond four years of complex activity. In short, there is a maze of talking and more talking considering and further considering, informing and re-informing, in most decision processes, except perhaps the more programmed and trivial. So major strategic decision processes are political power processes. It is here that more attention is paid to one individual than to another, that the members of powerful subunits can get their cases accepted.

As Lindblom (1959) points out in a provoking analysis, the optimum decision made in a detached way by exact calculation from all relevant information, somehow uncontaminated by other affairs of the world, probably does not and never did exist outside books of maths exercises. Much more likely, a process of decision-making moves spasmodically within a restricted set of possibilities, priorities switching from one time to another and different aspects being weighed in the balance from one point to the next (Simon 1947; Cyert and March 1963: as summarized by Pugh *et al* 1971). It arrives gradually at a compromise that will do for the time being, within the bounds of power and practicability. That is, it 'muddles through' incrementally to a satisfactory solution.

Table 1 lists as many as seventeen decision issues which even in rather

Table 1 Perceived power (weight) of four subunits in organization S (brewery)

On each of 17 issues, means of the questionnaire ratings of every subunit by heads of all 4 subunits (scores at or above the mean for the table underlined)

17 ISSUES, as allocated to task areas (or functions)

SUBUNITS	Sales area: interpretation of liquor regulations	Sales area: price	Sales area: product packaging	Sales area: introduction of new products	Sales area: marketing strategies	Engineering area: operating performance of equipment	Engineering area: obtaining equipment	Production area: overall production plan	Production area: product efficiency	Production area: product quality	Production area: obtaining raw materials	Finance area: reviews of the non-capital budget	Finance area: overall non-capital budget	Finance area: overall capital budget	Personnel area: personnel and labor relations	Personnel area: personnel training and development	Personnel area: salary revision	OVERALL MEANS
Accounting	2.75	4.5	1.5	1.5	1.5	2.75	1.75	2.0	1.0	2.25	2.75	3.5	3.75	4.0	3.25	3.5	3.25	2.7
Engineering	1.5	1.00	3.25	1.75	1.25	4.25	5.0	2.25	1.75	4.75	2.5	2.5	2.75	3.5	1.5	2.75	1.75	2.7
Marketing	4.5	3.0	3.5	5.0	5.0	1.75	2.0	2.0	2.75	2.0	2.25	2.5	2.75	2.75	2.25	3.0	2.25	2.9
Production	2.5	2.0	4.0	3.75	3.25	4.5	4.5	5.0	5.0	5.0	4.0	2.5	2.75	3.5	3.0	3.25	2.25	3.6

(Hinings et al 1974)

small stable organizations (brewing plants) were recurrent and involved different departments. The most widely powerful subunit is Production (beer brewing). However, whilst Production might well have the lion's share of any decision over 'obtaining raw materials' (from hops to bottle tops), as it scored much the highest influence on this issue, if it tried to alter 'product packaging' it might enter a drawn-out process of reconciling the interests of the Marketing and Engineering (Maintenance) departments which are more influential on that particular issue. We have mentioned earlier the studies by Normann (1971) and Carter (1971) who found powerful departments bargaining one with another, and putting up to higher management only those innovations which fitted in with what they wanted. So some alternatives are thought of as realistic and some are ruled out, some consequences are seen and others are ignored, partly at least because of group pressures. Indeed, those with interests at stake may have power to shape the premises from which decisions ensue, and the limits of what is considered: they may shape the structure within which the decision is arrived at.

A decision, then, is arrived at within a power structure in which various interests prefer certain outcomes before even the decision process could be said to have begun. Cohen *et al* (1972) sees an organization as a collection of decision-makers looking for opportunities, solutions looking for problems to which they might be the answer and feelings looking for issues on which they can be aired. It is a situation they have colourfully dubbed a 'garbage can'. To quote them:

> To understand processes within organizations, one can view a choice opportunity as a garbage can into which various kinds of problems and solutions are dumped by participants as they are generated. The mix of garbage in a single can depends on the mix of garbage available, on the labels attached to the alternative cans, on what garbage is currently being produced, and on the speed with which garbage is collected and removed from the scene (Cohen *et al* 1972 p 2).

A startling description, but often an appropriate one.

7.2 Invisible power

Yet even though power may be omnipresent, it is not necessarily self-evident. This is a major obstacle to empirical researchers who find power easy enough to talk about with managers and administrators, for example, and obtain extensive data as the published sources quoted above indicate, yet sometimes feel they are not quite reaching the heart of the matter. For instance, on the face of it power may seem obvious enough in union-management negotiations. On each issue raised, from the rate of pay per hour to number of hours worked, the power balance might be detected. But what then of those issues *not* raised? Power will also have played a part in determining that the union will not raise issues which directly question the right to supervise, nor management raise issues which directly question the right to strike. In short, there are everywhere in organizations unspoken issues from the trivial to the revolutionary, the 'unspokenness' of which is itself evidence of power. Not only are decisions the outcome of power processes, so are 'non-decisions' as they are often called (Bachrach and Baratz 1962; Lukes 1974).

More than that, Silverman (1970 chapter 6) emphasizes that the meaning in language itself is evidence of power. Suppose that a university staff group proposes to a committee that a new course on 'Organizations' be offered. In the university many people think of 'sociology' as a 'soft' subject and of sociologists as 'unreliable', whereas management is 'hard-headed' and 'sound' (!). If so, the first issue is not the proposed course itself, but the word(s) by which it will be known and the associated language in which it will be discussed, and hence the concepts by which it will be construed. If the course should be called 'Organizational Sociology' its fate may be different than if it is called 'Organizational Analysis' in which case the negative associations of the word 'sociology' disappear; or if (irrespective of its title) it is discussed in terms of being an exercise in theoretical sociology rather than as being a contribution to practical management. The several interest groups concerned may even spend more effort on the 'language issue' than on the substantive syllabus. In such ways the whole 'language' of an organization becomes an indication of its power structure, from its 'cost-consciousness' (or its 'cheese-paring') to its 'personal initiative' (or its 'rat race'); with its 'bosses', 'pay packets' and 'absenteeism'. This is a major factor in the complexity and protractedness of many decision processes.

8 Views of power

There are many ways of shelling an egg, and there could be as many ways of looking at power in organizations. The chapter you have just read is, therefore, inevitably inadequate; and your aim must be to formulate your own judgements. One cheerful thought is that, though you will never get everyone to agree you are right, neither will they agree you are wrong!

For example, from one point of view, power is distributed 'up and down' organizations, but mainly 'up'. This is reflected in *section 2* on hierarchical power. So Parkin summarizes Dahrendorf's view that 'every single large scale organization has a dominant and subordinate class; administration and students in university, clergy and laity in the church, warders and inmates in prison, managers and workers in factories, and so forth' (1971 pp 45–6). The dominant group forms an élite of powerholders and their associates. Its dominant power is because it has the capacity to use those resources which have the most weight over the domain and scope at issue. It may own the capital under capitalism, or have the party memberships which confer reward and referent power under communism. It may have the special skills denoted by Michels' 'iron law of oligarchy'.

However, this élitist perspective does not necessarily mean that total power is with the élite. Mechanic's case for the power of subordinates has been discussed above in relation to Michels'. Subordinates too have know-how. Further, they can band together to exercise their power in the form of massed labour resources. Collective action by underdogs, whether workers in unions, or middle managers facing a crisis together, or firms resisting government pressure, adds the power of one to the power of all and brings 'strength in numbers', not least because it makes each one less substitutable.

From another point of view, power is distributed 'here and there' around organizations. This is partly reflected in *section 3* on subunit power, and in Blau and Scott's (1963) classification of the groups who benefit from organizations. Owners, customers, suppliers, government legislators and public officials, trade unionists, competitors, associated organizations or agencies, consultants – are there more? – all play a part in the life of an organization, as do its internal subunits, its managers, and its subordinate clerks, workers, or whatever. All of these also have power in the life of an organization, because of the part they play. There is a plurality of power-holders, when seen from this pluralist perspective.

So are organizations tools for control in the hands of those who set them up, and those élites who hold most power? Are they coalitions between powerful sections or interests? Are they collaborative entities in which power is dispersed for the common aim? What do you think?

The very word 'power' has a chilling ring to it, a hollow threatening sound. The word itself is an example of the subtle power of language to influence thinking in a particular way. For power is neither good nor bad. Like many things in life, that depends on what it is used for. Organizations as power systems may create wealth and give their members good incomes and their customers and clients good value, or they may dominate and exploit. They may produce desirable material goods, but also pollution. They may cure patients, but also market tobacco which contributes to ill health. They may educate, but also manipulate ideas. Are they a power for good — what do you think?

CHAPTER 3

Graeme Salaman

Classification of organizations and organization structure: the main elements and interrelationships

Introduction

The concept organizational structure is used to refer to the observed, patterned continuity in the behaviour and activities of organizational members over time. This regularity is, on the one hand, what is meant by organizational structure, but is also held to be the *result* of the ways in which events, activities, responsibilities, authorities and so on are officially *structured* and controlled within and by the organization.

The concept of structure has a long sociological pedigree. It has been used to refer to the apparent existence of regularities (in societies, organizations and so on) in the behaviours and values of members which can be analysed without reference to the predispositions and decisions of those individuals. Thus Durkheim says there is '. . . a category of facts with very distinctive characteristics: it consists of ways of acting, thinking and feeling, external to the individual, and endowed with a power of coercion by reason of which they control him' (Durkheim 1938 p 3). With reference to organizations the concept structure is used to refer to the uniform, standardized properties that may be discerned; for example the fact that some people (called salesmen) spend a lot of time attempting to sell (but not to manufacture or design) a variety of products that are produced by the company that employs them, while other employees spend their time performing a series of repetitive operations which, in combination, result in the manufacture of the finished product. Clearly there are a number of ways in which the structure of an organization can be considered: differences in task are just one; level of authority and type of function or product are others.

It will be clear that Weber too was interested in the structure of organizations. His interest was in organizational rules and procedures, the ways in which tasks, responsibilities and duties are distributed and organized, also how it was that members were controlled by these constraints; why people were prepared to behave in such ways as to produce organizational structure.

Sociologists tend to employ two main perspectives in viewing the problem of the origins of structure. Simply, structure can be seen as an emergent feature of ongoing negotiations and interactions, or as a result of imposition and constraint.

It is worthwhile mentioning this distinction between processes that are held to produce the regularity and predictability that is meant by organizational structure and the regularity and orderliness itself, because research into and discussion of organizations has sometimes tended to confuse official definitions of what the organization is like with analysis of actual behaviours and events. That is, official attempts to create organizational structure (or descriptions and definitions of that structure) have been taken for descriptions of organizational structure even though it is clear that they constitute only one of a number of possible determinants of actual behaviour, although of course a highly salient and important determinant. This distinction between official descriptions of the organizational structure and actual behaviours displayed by organizational members (and, presumably, observed by the sociologist) has serious methodological implications, since members of organizations themselves tend to perceive their jobs and activities in terms of their conception of what they *ought* to be doing. Burns' study of managers' estimates of their work activities showed that a manager's estimate was considerably affected by '. . . the assumptions (he had) about the context of organized activity in which his own work was being done' (Burns 1967 p 117). This makes the description and analysis of organizational structure problematic since a number of different structures will be apparent to those within the organization, who view it in terms of different priorities.

For many who study organizations the analysis and description of organizational structure constitutes the most interesting and important job.

Blau and Schoenherr, for example, see this as a necessary beginning to any attempt to control and regulate the potential power of organizations, and the threat to democracy they represent: 'Unless we take seriously the simple fact that organizations are not people, we as citizens shall not be able to meet this threat to democracy, and we as sociologists shall not be able to meet the main challenge our discipline poses.' (Blau and Schoenherr 1971 p 357) It is, however, only fair to add that others have argued that a concern for the structure of organizations restricts attention to the internal aspects at the expense of a sufficient interest in the social impact and consequences of large scale organizations.

1 Typologies of organizational structure

Is it possible to speak, generally, about organizations, as though they held characteristics in common? If membership of an organization means exposure to rules, procedures, job specifications and so on, are there different *types* of such control, or organizational structure, and if so how do they differ? And what causes these differences? In what ways are hospitals, prisons, commercial companies, churches and army camps similar?

Such questions have considerable relevance and importance for those in senior positions within organizations who are concerned with the efficiency of the organization. For organizational structure will be seen by such members in terms of its appropriateness, its capacity to achieve what such people take for the goals of the organization. Thus Pugh and Hickson remark:

> All organizations have to make provision for continuing activities directed towards *the achievement of given aims*. Regularities in activities such as task allocation, supervision, and co-ordination are developed. Such regularities constitute the organization's structure, and the fact that these activities can be arranged in various ways means that organizations can have differing structures. (Pugh and Hickson 1973 p 51. My emphasis.)

It has been suggested that Weber's work on bureaucracy hints at a basic distinction between two bureaucratic types. Gouldner, for example, suggests that:

> ... bureaucracy is not a single homogeneous entity but that there are two types of bureaucracy, the representative bureaucracy and the punishment-centred bureaucracy. The representative bureaucracy is, in part, characterized by authority based upon knowledge and expertise. It also entails collaborative or bilateral initiation of the organizational rules by the parties involved ... The punishment-centred bureaucracy is characterized by authority based on incumbency in office, and by the unilateral initiation of organization rules which are enforced through punishments. (Gouldner 1959 p 403)

It is by no means established that this distinction, which has been frequently used in analyses of the circumstances of professionals employed in large organizations, is valid. For one thing administration too demands expertise and knowledge; for another, as will be seen, it is very likely that the claimed incompatibility of professional (expert) and bureaucratic (incumbency in office) authority has been overstated.

This distinction is one of a number of different classifications of organizations that have been presented and utilized in the literature on organizations. The essence of these schemes is the suggestion that certain organizational characteristics tend to cluster together, to correlate; and organizational classification is thus closely related to the practical (managerial) task of finding and designing an organizational structure which is most *appropriate* for particular environments, technologies, personnel etc.

In considering the three classificatory schemes outlined below two questions should be borne in mind, namely: what are the key differences between the organizational types? And what are the mechanisms or determinants that are held to produce these differences in organizational structure? These questions will be considered later.

2 Talcott Parsons

Parsons has applied his general theoretical framework to the analysis of organizations. And the results, predictably, are ambitious and idiosyncratic. As is well known Parsons' conception of the societal social system emphasizes the importance of four basic systemic problems, which societies (as systems) must resolve. These are:

1 *adaptation:* the accommodation of the system to the reality demands of the environment coupled with the active transformation of the external situation;
2 *goal achievement:* the defining of objectives and the mobilization of resources to attain them;
3 *integration:* establishing and organizing a set of relations among the member units of the system that serve to co-ordinate and unify them into a single entity;
4 *latency:* the maintenance over time of the system's motivational and cultural patterns. (Blau and Scott 1963 p 38)

For Parsons any system is made up of other systems. He sees organizations as societal sub-systems which are mechanisms for achieving societal requirements, but which are also composed of sub-systems which attempt to resolve the organization's four basic system problems. Analysis of organizations, for Parsons, is unequivocally part of '. . . the study of social structure' generally (Parsons 1970 p 75). And organizations are defined in terms of their '. . . primacy of orientation to the attainment of a specific goal' (Parsons 1970 p 75). This orientation has both internal and external organizational consequences. Internally the fact that organizations are goal-attaining systems has consequences for its 'special features', and '. . . gives priority to those processes most directly involved with the success or failure of goal-oriented endeavours' (Parsons 1970 p 76). Externally Parsons' conceptualization of organizations in terms of their orientation towards the meeting of societal requirements and needs leads to a concern for the ways in which organizational *products* (consumer goods, students, decisions) are used by other sub-systems within the society — sometimes other organizations, for example.

Organizations not only must address the same four problems as societies (and for this they will require specialized organizational departments or mechanisms), they can also themselves be categorized in terms of these four functional imperatives. Thus Parsons distinguishes four types of organization which he discriminates by reference to '. . . the type of goal or function about which they are organized' (Parsons 1970 p 80). In this way Parsons arrives at a classification of the following four organizational types: economic organizations, political organizations, integrative organizations and pattern maintenance organizations.

A provocative feature of Parsons' approach to organizations follows from his determination to consider them in terms of their functions for the larger, societal system. Parsons envisages organizations as ways of getting things done. This leads to a possibly misleading conception of power (which, presumably, is needed to get things done, as he would see it) as '. . . the generalized capacity to mobilize resources in the interest of attainment of a system goal' (Parsons 1970 p 79). Such a definition seems to beg important questions that arise from the possibility that organizations may in fact pursue goals that could be seen as contrary to those of the society as a whole, and that within organizations different groups might hold very different conceptions of their interests, and the nature of the relationship between them. Multinational corporations, for example, are by no means concerned with national, societal goals; instead they can be seen as pursuing their own organizational interests (as these are seen and evaluated by policy-making personnel) as against the goals of their native society (whatever they might be).

Parsons' theoretical scheme is heavily oriented towards the legitimating importance of values. For example, he sees organizations as operating under a societal mandate, as it were, a grant or allocation of power which is given in order to achieve what are generally held to be legitimate organizational objectives, from the society's point of view. This appears to be an extraordinarily optimistic view, in face of the realities of organizations. The obvious possibility that organizations may seek to generate or utilize political or economic power to seek the ends of senior and powerful organizational members seems to be defined away; as does the possibility that organizations ostensibly entrusted with the attainment of a societal goal may deliberately withhold information from government personnel in order to pursue their own ends, or simply act in secret so as to create a *fait accompli*.

Finally, without entering into the debate about what society's goals are, it is important to mention that the existence of some degree of legitimation for an organization (or a political party, or whatever) is not the end of the story. Anyone with an interest in understanding the dynamics and conflicts inherent in society (or an organization) will also wish to consider where these legitimations come from. In the area of organizational analysis this question is particularly important since organizations include as members, personnel (representing the senior members of the organization, or its owners) who will make strong, systematic and plausible efforts to justify the activity of the organization in terms of available and acceptable justifications or rhetorics. Thus hospitals will claim to be concerned with the nation's health, and not the interests of doctors or the medical industry; and industry will be concerned with 'giving the customer what he wants', rather than achieving profit. Thus, a value, goal, or symbol is invoked to justify actions which would seem to conflict with it.

Apart from the difficulties mentioned above, Parsons' scheme is also vulnerable to the criticism that while it elegantly connects the study of organizations to a grandiose societal theory it fails to distinguish between organizations even in its own terms since it is extremely difficult (and possibly misleading) to allocate organizations to Parsons' categories, or to know what is an economic organization, or a political organization. To use such classificatory categories directs attention away from the ways in which organizations that would assert, say, their economic aspects have political ones as well. The fact that organizations have implications and objectives over and above those they assert in their public relations pronouncements, their capacity to define and legitimize the nature of their activity and objectives, and interconnections between elite personnel and their interests in dominant positions in organizations that Parsons would consider to be different types, are simply not considered.

But why bother with this consideration of Parsons' proposed organizational classification? There are three reasons. For one thing the somewhat extreme nature of the Parsonian classificatory scheme draws attention to the fact that organizations, or any other social phenomena, do not exist as unquestionable facts to be measured and described by the sociologist. Social phenomena are only apparent through the theories and concepts that are brought to bear on them. This point is made most emphatically with reference to the Parsonian scheme because, it is suggested, of its irrelevance to other, rather obvious, possibilities and considerations that are held to be apparent. But the existence and evaluation of these possibilities stems from the utilization of another, implicit, scheme.

Secondly, the Parsonian scheme is interesting because it is vulnerable for theoretical reasons. A few of the theoretical difficulties have been suggested above. A more thorough treatment is contained in Silverman (1970). The theoretical debate that revolves around Parsons' approach to organizations thus serves to emphasize that theoretical discussion is absolutely central to any consideration of social phenomena, no matter how pressing their practical significance. (See also Mouzelis 1967.)

Finally, the scheme considered above introduces an issue that will be allocated more attention later: the relationship between what are claimed to be the organization's goals and the structure of the organization. Another approach to organizational analysis and classification has been suggested by Etzioni. This scheme is outlined below.

3 Etzioni

Unlike Parsons, who sees organizational power as an unproblematic capacity allocated to organizations by 'society' with a view to attaining society's requirements or at least socially legitimate goals, Etzioni focuses on intra-organizational aspects of organizational power and control. For Etzioni, as for Weber, the interesting feature of organizations is: '. . . why do people in organizations conform to the orders given to them and follow the standards of behaviour laid down for them?' (Pugh et al 1971 p 30) Etzioni, like Parsons and others, argues strongly for the advantages of the comparative method. Such an approach requires a classificatory scheme. The scheme he offers involves, as he sees it, both motivational and structural elements. It is also firmly related to sociological thinking and discourse in other fields.

The key classificatory variable in the Etzioni scheme is *compliance*, which refers to the obedience of an organizational member (with respect to some command or rule) and the reasons for this obedience. Compliance is the result of two sorts of factors: the power means and the members' orientation towards (or involvement in) the organization's power system. Since Etzioni considers there are three sorts of power means (called coercive, remunerative and normative) and three sorts of involvement (alienative, calculative and moral) he necessarily argues for the theoretical possibility of nine compliance structures, although he maintains that in practice three types are found more frequently than the others. The reasons for this are interesting and will be considered later.

Etzioni maintains that classifying organizations by their compliance structures — that is, by whether they are utilitarian, normative or coercive organizations — is more useful than employing previous classifications. As he says:

> The use of such common sense categories as labor unions and corporations to isolate the units of comparison creates considerable difficulty. This method of classification tends to attach the same label to organizations which differ considerably, and to assign different names to organizations which are analytically similar in many significant ways, particularly in their compliance structure. (Etzioni 1970 p 112)

Using this variable, traditional organizational categories or types are subdivided. For example, Etzioni distinguishes between peacetime and combat units within 'military organizations'. Such a distinction is justified by the argument that peacetime and combat units display different compliance structures and so differ in various other significant respects. These associated variations are held to derive from the compliance variable. For example, Etzioni claims that organizational goals are related to compliance. 'Organizations that have similar compliance structures tend to have similar goals, and organizations that have similar goals tend to have similar compliance structures' (Etzioni 1961 p 71). Similarly, Etzioni argues that the way in which power is distributed within the organization is related to the compliance structure, for example coercive organizations involve a sharp distinction between inmates and officials, or rulers and ruled, but normative organizations emphasize the amalgamation or assimilation of *all* participants in the control process. Compliance is also related to the degree of cultural integration that exists within organizations. In support of Etzioni's claim for the predictive utility of his classificatory scheme he argues that coercive, utilitarian and normative organizations differ considerably in the degree to which reliance is placed upon normative agreement and commitment in order to achieve efficient operation. With respect to utilitarian organizations he argues that '. . . utilitarian organizations require consensus in those spheres which are directly related to instrumental activities — namely, cognitive perspective, participation, and performance obligations.' (Etzioni 1961 p 150)

Etzioni's classificatory scheme is interesting for our purposes not only because of the way in which it deliberately sets out to replace and reject what he classes as 'common sense' categories, such as military organizations, or unions, business organizations and so on, but also because it is directly concerned with organizational control, which is the central theme of this book. It will be seen that Etzioni's scheme is also interesting for the way in which it raises two questions which will be discussed later, namely, how far is it empirically true that certain organizational characteristics tend to cluster around this (or any other) key classificatory variable, and if such empirical clusterings are discernable, then why do they come about? It has already been noted that for Etzioni the mechanism that produces what he claims to be the three most common organizational types (in terms of their compliance structure) is organizational efficiency.

It has been argued that 'The essence of the typological effort really lies in the determination of the critical variables for differentiating the phenomena under investigation' (Hall 1972b p 41), a sentiment with which both Parsons and Etzioni would agree. They would disagree, however, as to *which* variables are critical in this context. One way to choose between the existing typologies is to discover, empirically, how organizations actually differ with respect to their structure. A study by Hall, Haas and Johnson (1967) found that although the theoretically derived classifications were helpful up to a point (that is as Hall reports, '. . . prisons were classified as "coercive" . . . and so on') (Hall 1972b p 48), the applicability and relevance of these classifications was decidedly limited, not only with respect to the possibility of allocating an organization to one category or another, but also in terms of the determinate importance of the selected variable. With reference to what Hall takes to be significant features of organizational structure he concludes of the Etzioni classification that it has '. . . only a limited application insofar as total organizational analysis is concerned' (Hall 1972b p 51).

The criticism that the theoretically derived classifications are empirically inaccurate and misleading, at least on occasion, and fail to pinpoint the organizational characteristic that empirically can be seen to correlate with (or determine) the form of the organizational structure (or those characteristics that are held to be generally important) leads us to consider the sorts of classification discussed below. This involves a significantly different approach from Parsons' and Etzioni's classifications and is worth serious consideration.

4 Technology as a basis for classification: Woodward and Perrow

Woodward's classification of different types of organization grew out of an empirical effort to investigate the applicability of the sorts of management principles that litter the management textbooks. The survey conducted under the auspices of this interest '. . . revealed considerable variations in the pattern of organization which could not be related to size of firm, type of industry, or business success' (Woodward 1969 p 196).

Woodward continues, 'When the firms were grouped according to similarity of objectives and techniques of production, and classified in order of the technical complexity of their production systems, each production system was found to be associated with a characteristic pattern of organization' (Woodward 1969 p 196). Three types of technology are isolated: small batch and unit production, large batch and mass production, and process production. These types are seen to differ with respect to technical complexity, which is defined as: '. . . the extent to which the production process is controllable and its results predictable' (Woodward 1969 p 203). A number of organizational characteristics are seen to be related to the technical complexity of the work processes, for example, the number of levels of authority, the span of control of the first line supervisor, and the ratio of managers and supervisory staff to total personnel.

Furthermore, Woodward claims that the relative importance of management specialist activities and the nature of the co-ordination and integration also varied with the technical system. For example, the nature of the technical process determined where the manufacturing cycle began – in unit production getting an order was the first step, whereas in mass production the goods were researched, developed and produced, and then sold. More specifically Woodward argues, on the basis of her findings, that a number of structural features are positively related to the degree of complexity of the production system. She remarks:

> Among the organizational characteristics showing a direct relationship with technical advance were: the length of the line of command;

the span of control of the chief executive; the percentage of total turnover allocated to the payment of wages and salaries, and the ratios of managers to total personnel, of clerical and administrative staff to manual workers, of direct to indirect labour, and of graduate to nongraduate supervision in production departments. (Woodward 1970 p 279)

Woodward's argument that technology determines organizational structure has been tested by Hickson *et al* (1972). Using a more precise notion of technology the authors found a complex and variable relationship between their findings and Woodward's; they write '. . . although a sweeping "technological imperative" hypothesis is not supported, a residual seven variables have been identified in the tests on manufacturing industry that do have associations with technology' (Hickson *et al* 1972 p 148). The crucial point about these features is that they are most directly concerned with the technology (e.g. variables like the proportion of personnel in maintenance, or inspection, which are obviously directly affected by the nature of the technology in a way that the proportion of personnel in accounting is not). The authors hypothesize that '. . . structural variables will be associated with operations technology only where they are centred on the workflow' (Hickson *et al* 1972 p 150). One corollary of this is that Woodward's findings would be most applicable to small firms.

Woodward, like Parsons and Etzioni, considers that the goals of the organization are, indirectly, important as determinants of organizational structure since '. . . differences in objectives controlled and limited the techniques of production that could be employed' (Woodward 1969 p 202). Woodward also argues that if objectives give rise to differences in technology and thus, ultimately, to differences in organizational structure and process, then there '. . . can be no one best way of organizing a business' (Woodward 1969 p 202). The optimum (from the point of view of efficiency) organizational structure must be seen not in terms of conformity with management principles, but in relation to the goals and technology of the enterprise.

Woodward's findings have been most influential, and she is by no means alone in arguing that technology is an important determinant of organizational structure. Such a line has also been adopted by Perrow. Perrow sees organizations as phenomena within which things are done to raw materials of some sort. The things that are done — and the ways that they are done — constitutes the technology of the organization. The way in which individual members of the organization interact with other members in the course of doing things to the raw material (which may of course be other people) constitutes the organization's structure.

Perrow distinguishes two relevant aspects of the technology of an organization that he claims are important determinants of organizational structure:

> ... the number of exceptional cases encountered in the work, that is, the degree to which stimuli are perceived as familiar or unfamiliar ... The second is the nature of the search process that is undertaken by the individual when exceptions occur. We distinguish two types of search process. The first type involves a search which can be conducted on a logical, analytical basis ... The second type of search process occurs when the problem is so vague and poorly conceptualized as to make it virtually unanalysable ...In this case one draws upon the residue of unanalysable experience or intuition. (Perrow 1972a pp 40–50)

Using these two dimensions (each one varying between high or low, and present or absent) Perrow finds four types of technology, see Figure 1.

Perrow attaches a great deal of importance to the nature of the raw material that the organization processes. He conceives of the raw material as varying with respect to two variables: its understandability and its stability and variability. But he emphasizes that these distinctions do not refer to some actual state of the raw material, but to the

Figure 1 Technological variable (industrial example)

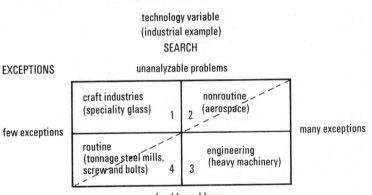

Source: Perrow 1972a p 51

way in which it is considered and defined within the organization. He notes that organizations attempt to so define their raw material as to '. . . minimize exceptional situations' (Perrow 1972a p 51). And so to open the way for rule-bound procedures and routineness.

Perrow's argument that '. . . technology is a better basis for comparing organizations than the several schemes which now exist' (Perrow 1972a p 48) is supported by Hage and Aiken who report on the basis of their study, which attempted to explore the relationship between routine work, organizational structure and organizational goals, that Perrow's hypotheses concerning routine technology and centralized decision making were empirically substantiated (Hage and Aiken 1972 p 70).

Perrow's suggestions — and their application by Hage and Aiken — are relevant to the subject matter of this chapter and previous discussions not only because Perrow is concerned with modifying and refining the hypothesized significance of technology as an independent variable in analyses of organizational structure, but also because in doing so he makes some pertinent points about Woodward's conception of technology. Obviously Perrow's specific conception of technology in terms of the degree of routineness of work could be seen as broadly similar to Woodward's interest in the extent to which the '. . . production process is controllable and its results predictable' (Woodward 1969 p 203). But there are also differences between the two definitions of technology. For one thing Woodward's definition is restricted to industrial applications; her three types would make little sense in organizations that process, or deal with, people. Another difficulty has been noted by Perrow who although asserting the importance of technology also notes the variety of phenomena that have been variously included in definitions of this term. Of Woodward he writes:

> Her independent variable is not, strictly speaking, technology, but is a mixture of production, size of production run, layout of work and type of customer order. These distinctions overlap and it is difficult to decide how a particular kind of organization might be classified in her scheme or how she made her final classification. (Perrow 1972a p 66)

Perrow's analysis is also important because it clearly demonstrates not only the close links between technology and goals — for technology is used *in order* to achieve certain prescribed changes in the raw material, but also because he demonstrates the crucial connections between technology and processes of organizational control. The connections are various and complex. Some technologies have control built into them — they are pre-programmed. This is only possible, of course, when the raw material is regarded as stable. Other technologies rely on the discretion of the operative or technician. In this case these employees must be monitored and regulated so that they do not deviate from overall organizational priorities and principles. These inter-connections are discussed more fully in Davies *et al* (1973). The important point to make, however, is that by considering the relationship between technology and organizational structure Perrow also demonstrates the direct connections between the organization of work and the organization of control. For some writers it is this relationship which constitutes one of the main criteria behind the choice of technology — i.e. work technologies may be chosen precisely because of their 'built in' and therefore, possibly, somehow de-humanized and de-politicized, constraints.

One of the points that emerges with overwhelming certainty from any review of attempts to develop organizational classification, is that, as Pugh and Hickson remark, despite the central importance of the notion of organizational structure to those who theorize about — or classify — organizations, the concept of structure '. . . remains primitive in empirical application. So far neither manager nor researcher has any means other than personal intuition of knowing how far the structure of Company A is the same as, or different from, that of Company B, or State Agency C' (Pugh and Hickson 1973 p 51). The attempt made by these authors to develop some sort of acceptable, reliable, statistical measurement of discrete and unitary organizational characteristics has proved enormously influential. It represents a definite change in strategy from those typologies which derive purely from some *a priori* theoretical or conceptual interest. This work will be considered in more detail later.

5 Organizational structure, organizational goals

Although, as Child argues, a number of different factors have been considered as determinants of such empirical variation in organizational structures as has been discovered or claimed, this section will restrict attention to the role of organizational goals in this debate. The next section will consider some alternative ways of regarding the determinants of organizational structure.

It has been seen that for Parons '. . . primacy of orientation to the attainment of a specific goal is used as the defining characteristic of an organization' (Parsons 1970 p 75). This, it is claimed, has consequences for the structure and external relations of the organization. The relationship with the environment is regarded in terms of the 'maximization' of some output which supplies criteria by which the internal structure of the organization may be assessed. This has consequences for organization which Parsons sees as suffering 'deprivation' if the desired output is not achieved.

Etzioni directly addresses the importance (and nature) of organizational goals. In his scheme the theoretical possibility of nine organizational types is, it is claimed, seldom realized because three types constitute what are called *congruent* relationships between power means and orientation, and six do not. This argument has two elements. We are told that to some extent organizational power means tend to generate certain sorts of reactions (and here lies the tautology), but that organizational members also bring involvements with them into the organization. When their prior orientations are similar to the involvement they develop as a result of exposure to the organization's power the situation is described as congruent.

But it is also stated that such congruence is more *efficient*, and that organizations are '. . . under pressure to be effective' (Etzioni 1970 p 109). Therefore, '. . . organizations tend to shift their compliance structure from incongruent to congruent types' (Etzioni 1970 p 108). Since compliance structure is seen as a key variable in determining other features of the organization, and since congruence is achieved as a result of the pressure efficiently to achieve the organization's goals, it is clear that goals and goal attainment play a central part in the Etzioni model.

As mentioned earlier Woodward's scheme for differentiating organizations according to what are claimed to be the observed, empirical bases of organizational, structural variation also hinges around the objectives that are being pursued. Organizational goals are held to determine the nature and organization of the manufacturing process; and this affects the structure of the organization.

One of the major difficulties with the approach is illustrated by the following quotation from a report by the Health Policy Advisory Center into the American health system, and its current crisis:

> . . . the American health system is not in business for people's health . . . even within the institutions that make up America's health system – hospitals, doctors, medical schools, drug companies, health insurance companies – health care does not take top priority. Health is no more a priority of the American health industry than safe, cheap, efficient pollution-free transportation is a priority of the American automobile industry. (Ehrenreich 1971 p.vi)

In other words, from the point of view of organizational analysis the problem with the goal achievement approach to organizations is that it is by no means clear just what the goals of the organization are. Certainly the stated goals should be considered sceptically. Depending on the stance taken towards organizational goals, i.e. whether the official statements and rhetoric are accepted or viewed with cynicism, the actual behaviours and choices of senior members of the organization can be viewed with or without indignation, as extraordinarily and inexplicably deviant, or as quite natural and logical, given these 'real' goals. This initial point is made by Perrow when he argues that organizations are indeed tools, but that they are tools for many different purposes only *for those who control them.* It is thus irrelevant to criticize organizations as being inefficient because they display, for example, particular rather than universal criteria in, say, the choice and treatment of organizational personnel, because such behaviour can only be assessed as efficient or not in terms of the *actual* goals of those members who display them. '. . . organizations are tools designed to perform work for their masters, and particularism or universalism is relative to the goals of the masters' (Perrow 1972a pp 16–17).

It has been argued that when Weber talked of organizational rationality he was referring to, or assessing, the efficiency or adequacy of some means-ends link. That is, that he was concerned with the efficiency with which organizational procedures and processes achieved the goals they were designed to achieve. Such an interpretation of Weber has been criticized (see Chapter 1) but it is still common for those who write about organizations to attend to the relationship between what *they* take to be, or infer as, the organizational goals and organizational procedures, although this may mean rejecting one view of the organizational objectives in favour of a more realistic, or cynical one. For example, Perrow has distinguished between official goals and operative goals, the latter being seen as '. . . those that are embedded in major operating policies and the daily decisions of the personnel' (Perrow 1961 p 854). In the same vein the Ehrenreichs argue that the American health crisis is only problematic as long as it is assumed that the health system exists to improve or look after the health of Americans, in which case its 'inefficiency' is surprising. But these authors argue that the 'health' system is oriented towards profit-making, and that in these terms, '. . . the health industry is an extraordinarily well-organized and efficient machine' (Ehrenreich 1971 p 23).

The famous study by Michels refers to the necessity to consider how organizations pursue goals other than those they were originally set up to achieve. Michels considers how the fact of organization creates, through its inevitably *oligarchic* structure, groups and interests that are in conflict with the democratic basis and concerns that were the original inspiration and objective of the organization (Michels 1970). Michels' work also raises the likelihood that organizational goals may vary over time; that the procedures set up to achieve a state of affairs may either produce power and ability for organizational groups to pursue alternative ends, or that the means in themselves become objectives. Gross suggests the importance of distinguishing '. . . private (personal, individual) goals from organizational goals . . . what a particular person desires *for the organization as a whole* (Gross 1969 p 278). This leads to the difficulty described by Silverman: how can organizational goals be pinpointed and described? To refer back to the Ehrenreichs' analysis of the 'real' goals of the American health industry, how do these authors know what these 'real' goals are? Whose actions or words can reliably be taken as genuine indicators or expressions of organizational goals? Are they the stated goals of the organization's public relations rhetoric (what Perrow would call the official goals), the goals of certain key personnel as they describe them to themselves, each other, or the researcher; the goals as they are inferred by some omniscient observer, or the requirements and constraints that members operate under in their decision-making? (Silverman 1970 pp 8—11). Furthermore, the article by Thompson and McEwen (1973) suggests that it is important to consider organizational goals not as givens, fixed for ever, but as an aspect of an organization's functioning. They write: 'It is possible, however, to view the setting of goals (i.e. major organizational purposes) not as a static element, but as a necessary and recurring problem facing any organization.' (Thompson and McEwen 1973 p 155) But whatever the difficulties and problems that surround any attempt to discover what an organization's goals are, the established view is that such goals are reflected in the structure of the organization, which is seen as being designed to achieve (under pressures of efficiency or 'situational demands') the 'official' or formal goals. However the difficulty with this argument is that a lot of what goes on in organizations has little to do with such official regulation and control and the organizational structure itself does not reflect a concern for such goals.

The sociological literature on organizations frequently contains reference to a distinction between formal and informal aspects of organizational structure. As Mouzelis and others have noted, this distinction can mean a number of different things (Mouzelis 1967). One common usage involves a reference to aspects of the organization's structure or process which are not defined by the organization chart or the organizational rules, procedures and prescriptions as these are described by senior organizational personnel. Such a distinction does have the benefit of drawing attention to the symbolic rather than descriptive status of such official statements of organizational structure or purpose, but it also carries dangers. Albrow notes that aspects of the organization's structure are the result of outside factors; that 'unoffical' behaviours and relationships can serve to assist the attainment of desired objectives; that the behaviour of members of organizations is not simply the result of organizational rules and constraints, and that 'the notion of the specific goal as the origin and cause of the organization is an unhistoric myth' (Albrow 1973 p 402). Albrow too notes that organizational goals tend to be general, multiple and confused, and asks, how then can it be argued that organizational structure (which implies some degree of orderliness and regularity) is determined by these organizational goals? His solution to the difficulty is to offer an alternative definition of organizations which does not conceive of them in terms of some social contract-like consensus between the members of a co-operative group, who agree to work together in certain specific ways in order to achieve their goal. On the contrary, Albrow's view of organizations contains reference to structure or regularity between the *emergent consequence* of competition and conflict between membership groups and their various goals. Such a view of organizations, and of organizational goals, is also presented by Crozier, on the basis of his analysis of two French bureaucracies. Although by no means denying the importance of official, formal rules and statements of goals he notes that, inevitably, organizations contain conflicts and divisions; by no means all organizational members are committed to the overall organizational goals, and the behaviour of organizational members cannot realistically be viewed as attempts to attain such goals. Instead Crozier sees bureaucratization itself as an *attempt* by senior organizational members to reduce behavioural uncertainty and eliminate unofficial power and resistance. But uncertainty survives, as do the multitude of conflicting goals and priorities, and the job of a manager, Crozier concludes, is not to pursue the clearly stated organizational goal, but to '. . . settle conflicting claims in a maze of rules, arbitrate between opposing forms of rationality, and face the difficult moral issues of the ambiguity of means and ends' (Crozier 1964 p 298).

Albrow's definition raises another interesting issue in connection with this discussion of organizational goals. He sees organizations as '. . . social units where individuals are conscious of their membership and legitimize their co-operative activities primarily by reference to the attainment of impersonal goals rather than to moral standards' (Albrow 1973 p 409). This raises the suggestion that organizations are phenomena which make available to their members ways and procedures for justifying (or legitimizing) their actions. Goals are now seen not merely as determinants of actions, but as ways of 'rationalizing' them – ways of making them sensible to those others who, as members, can be relied upon to inhabit the same symbolic and cultural community and thus to accept a particular sort of explanation, complaint or suggestion as sensible and rational. Clearly this immediately introduces the possibility that different conceptions of the 'proper' organizational interest, and so different organizational rationalities, may exist.

The suggestion that members' statements about goals should be seen not only as determinants of behaviour or social structure, but as ways of explaining sensibly to competent and qualified others, those behaviours which are seen as displaying ordered properties, comprises the main thrust of C. W. Mills' famous essay on 'Situated actions and vocabularies of motive'. Mills' comments in this essay are relevant to the considerations of this section in as much as Mills argues for a view of motives (or goals) as '. . . typical vocabularies having ascertainable functions in delimited societal situations . . .' (Mills 1940 p904). He continues, '. . . motives are the terms with which interpretation of conduct *by social actors* proceeds. This imputation and avowal of motives by actors are social phenomena to be explained' (Mills 1940 p 904). Later Mills comments that particular 'historical epochs and specified situations' (which of course include organizations) make available situational vocabularies of sensible, unquestioned motives and answers. The goals of an organization can be seen in the same way, as organizationally available acceptable verbalizations. One interesting if rather ominous implication of such a view might be that sociologists who study organizations have shown an excessive preparedness to accept what passes – within the organization, or among organizations in general – for sensible justifications and accounts; in other words in their own (sociological) accounts and descriptions they have relied upon organizational members' descriptions and explanations.

Finally, Selznick's study of the Tennessee Valley Authority in America is also pertinent to this discussion. Selznick notes how this particular organization attempted to disseminate statements of its intentions and goals – he writes of the leaders of the TVA that they '. . . have been especially active . . . in propagating a systematic formulation of its own meaning and significance' (Selznick 1966 p 21). But Selznick goes on to show how these goals, although indisputably important as overall symbols, were not in fact always realized in action. The notion of grass-roots administration was a key element in the organizational rhetoric. But Selznick notes that the '. . . needs of maintaining the organization tend to drive it toward alliances and mechanisms of participation . . .' which are at odds with the spirit of the rather vaguely phrased commitments to '. . . the exercise of democracy' (Selznick 1966 p 60).

A number of points emerge: first that official goals tend to be so vague and general as to be inadequate as guides to action although important symbolically. Secondly, that the actual behaviour of members of organizations is determined more by the conflict between opposing factional interests within the organization or between it and the environment, than by any overarching organizational goal. Finally, that in these conflicts between competing groups — and their goals — senior organizational members with control over organizational resources and the ability to manipulate the official control and reward mechanisms, and to design work systems and promotion structures, etc., will seek to structure and monitor the activities of subordinate members, who, in turn, will very often seek to resist such control. If organizations are arenas of conflict, senior organizational members usually are able to achieve some measure of dominance over their potentially recalcitrant employees. But such dominance will require a battery of techniques and strategies, and will involve the manipulation of all sorts of sanctions and resources and mechanisms.

This chapter started with some discussion and justification of the structural perspective on organizations. Attempts to classify or measure organizational structure have encountered a variety of difficulties. The goal-attaining model has been shown to be particularly suspect. But if variations in organizational structure do exist and can be measured or observed, then what determines these differences? This will constitute the subject matter of the next section.

6 The determinants of organizational structure: the role of choice

Blau and Schoenherr — two notable representatives of the structuralist approach to organizations — explain their approach in terms of the 'regularities' that organizations exhibit which may be 'analysed in their own right, independent of any knowledge about the individual behaviour of their members (Blau and Schoenherr 1971 p viii). It has been seen that analyses of these regularities frequently tend to be based either upon pre-existing theoretical commitments or upon the analyses and descriptions of senior members of the organization, and their 'knowledge' or view of the organization and its symbolic, cultural equipment.

However, it is one thing to point out the difficulties that are often encountered in using a concept, or an approach, and another to reject the concept altogether. Few would deny that organizations do exhibit regularities of one sort or another; although some would maintain that such regularity and orderliness as is displayed and made apparent is not the result of organizational members' obeying official rules and regulations, but of a series of ongoing negotiations and compromises between conflicting and competing groups whose power in these negotiations derives from internal and external factors. Position within the organization and control over various organizational activities (among which would be the capacity or prerogative to design and enforce organizational procedures) constitutes an important source of organizational power. In these interest conflicts the goals of the organization and other symbols will be mobilized for legitimating purposes.

Such a conception of organizational structure does not deny that organizations reveal or create regularities, it merely emphasizes that these are the consequences of the combinations and interactions of various individual or groups priorities, aspirations and constraints. Man *need not* be left out of discussion of structure.

The discussions of a selection of organizational classifications, however, revealed another way in which man had been left out. This omission concerns the mechanisms whereby the claimed relationship between the selected key variable (goals, compliance structure, technology) obtained. Frequently, as noted, this imputed mechanism involved some reference to the goals of the organization and their achievement. This sort of suggestion has been critically considered, but the question of the nature of the processes that produce the correlations between elements within organizational structure, or between other variables and the organization's structure, remains.

Here, as elsewhere, there has been a tendency to leave men out, to consider the relationship between, say, technology or environment and the structure of the organization in a mechanical way as the outcome of some 'necessary' or functionally imperative process. As Child points out, however, this argument is inadequate because '. . . it fails to give due attention to the agency of choice by whoever have the power to direct the organization' (Child 1973 p 91). The regularities that lie behind discussions of organizational structure consist of the behaviour of men; men do not normally consider a 'functional imperative', system need or 'situational demand' when choosing and planning their own behaviours. Consequently any *explanation* (rather than merely description of an observed correlation) must at some stage contain reference to men's choices.

How then does the claimed relationship between, for example, compliance structure and organizational structure or technology and structure come about? Presumably unless it occurs through some process whereby organizations that do not display the correlation go out of existence, or unless the classification is entirely axiomatic, the relationship between the key variable and organizational structure must rest upon decisions taken by those persons responsible for and able to control and design the structure of the organization in terms of what could be taken to be their 'rationality', that is *their* grasp or conception of the relationship between the organizational goals as they see them and the optimum organizational structure or design. Recent work has argued this case strongly, that organizational structure is not the consequence of some inexorable organizational logic, but a result of the values, aspirations and notions of what a proper organization looks like that are held by those members of the organization with the power to control and initiate structure. Thus organizational structure which consists of restriction on and control over members' decision-making, is itself the outcome of power struggles between politically salient groups within the organization (with the help, prescriptions and principles of organizational ideologues and theoreticians such as the 'classical management thinkers').

Child's article considers a number of orthodox models of the determinants or correlates of organizational structure and argues convincingly that all involve a considerable element of choice. For example, with respect to technology he suggests that, 'The prevailing technology is now seen as a *product* of decisions on workplans, resources and equipment which were made in the light of certain evaluations of the organization's positions in its environment' (Child 1972 p 6 my emphasis).

Child argues then, on the basis of his review of the three most significant and appealing models of structural determination that decisions and choices made by '. . . those who have the power of structural initiation – the dominant coalition' (1973 p 105) are important causes of variation in organizational structure. Such decisions and choices must of course be made within a framework of organizational activity, structure and environment which is constraining, but these factors themselves involve choices, as well as leaving considerable room for manoeuvre.

The concept structure, when it is applied to organizations, refers to the extent to which and the ways in which organizations' members are constrained and controlled by the organization and distribution of activities and responsibilities and the organizational procedures and regulations. Not surprisingly, therefore, types and procedures of organizational control have always been a central concern of those sociologists who theorize about or study organizations, and organizational structure.

Earlier sections distinguished between theoretically derived typologies and empirically grounded taxonomies (although this distinction should be seen as involving a quantitative rather than qualitative difference). Both sorts of classification have been concerned with theorizing about or investigating processes and types of organizational control. The next section will consider some of this work on what are claimed to be variations in organizational structure with special reference to processes of organizational control.

7 Differences in organizational structures: types of organizational control

Max Weber's delineation of the bureaucratic ideal type has served as the inspiration of a great deal of work into organizational control mechanisms and types. The characteristics Weber regarded as bureaucratic – the existence and application of rules, hierarchic offices, emphasis on technical competence and so on – constitute a particular sort of organizational control, but *possibly not the only one.*

Two points of interest each deriving from Weber's writings lie behind a great deal of work discussed below. A number of writers have concerned themselves with establishing the empirical interrelationships between the characteristics that Weber considered to be distinctively bureaucratic. Such work argues that bureaucracy – in terms of Weber's dimensions – can be seen not as '. . . a condition that is either present or absent . . .' but as '. . . a form of organization which exists along a number of continua or dimensions' (Hall 1963 p 33).

The empirical interrelationships between Weberian bureaucratic dimensions have also been investigated by Udy. He argues that Weber himself implicitly distinguished between two types of bureaucracy and that these suggested clusterings of interrelated variables are empirically apparent. More specifically Udy suggests that Weber distinguished between bureaucratic elements ('. . . hierarchic authority structure, an administrative staff, and differential rewards according to office'), and rational elements ('Limited objectives, a performance emphasis, segmental participation and compensatory rewards'.) (Udy 1959 p 793) Udy claims that 'Bureaucracy and rationality tend to be mutually inconsistent in the same formal organization' (Udy 1969 p 794).

The suggestion that bureaucratic administration and control can be distinguished empirically from other sorts of (rational) organization and control is supported by Stinchcombe (1970). The two forms of organization isolated by Stinchcombe differ in the ways in which members are controlled — in one case by training and socialization into the '. . . empirical lore that makes up craft principles', in the other by '. . . centralized planning of work' (Stinchcombe 1970 pp 262 and 263).

Stinchcombe's work not only suggests that the Weberian bureaucratic dimensions tend to interrelate in a greater variety of ways than has been considered by those who regarded bureaucracy as an empirical realization of the Weberian ideal type, but also introduces a much discussed distinction between types of organizational control. This distinction, which has been variously defined stems from Parsons' comment that Weber's view of bureaucracy involved two sources of authority, one based on technical expertise, and the other on bureaucratic position, on sheer incumbency of office. As noted earlier, this distinction has been taken up and elaborated by Gouldner, most notably in his classic *Patterns of Industrial Bureaucracy*. Gouldner distinguishes between two types of bureaucracy, one where authority is based on technical expertise and knowledge, and where there is a considerable degree of low level involvement in decisions and commitment to what are seen to be sensible and mutually agreed rules and procedures, and the other where procedures, rules and decisions are highly centralized and enforced through discipline.

This distinction between organizational control of a bureaucratic sort, exercised through centralized, rule-bound procedures and decisions, and organizational control through delegated decision-making based upon occupational professional standards, techniques and knowledge (with all the concomitant implications for the 'shape' of the organization) found early exposition in the work of Burns and Stalker (1961) and obviously relates to the two types of organizational authority described by Gouldner and mentioned earlier. These authors argued that the bureaucratic type (which they call mechanistic) consists of specialized differentiation of work duties and tasks, very specific delineation of areas of activity, responsibility and authority and a hierarchic control structure. The organic type of organizational control is characterized by constantly changing definitions of members' jobs and a greater emphasis of technical knowledge and expertise — as it is distributed throughout the organization.

Interestingly Burns and Stalker, like Stinchcombe, maintain that these different types of organization are appropriate to, or efficient in, different conditions and circumstances. The key environmental variable in both cases is stability. Stinchcombe argues, for example, that '. . . professionalization of manual labour is more efficient in construction because bureaucratic administration is dependent on stability of work flow and income, and the construction industry is economically unstable' (Stinchcombe 1970 p 262). Burns and Stalker argue that the mechanistic organizational form is most suitable for stable environmental conditions, while the organic variant is 'appropriate to changing conditions, which give rise constantly to fresh problems and unforeseen requirements for action which cannot be broken down or distributed automatically arising from the functional roles defined within a hierarchic structure' (Burns and Stalker 1961 p 120).

Hall considers that although the gross polarization of bureaucratic and professional forms of control is overstated, '. . . a generally inverse relationship exists between the levels of bureaucratization and professionalization. Autonomy, as an important professional attribute, is most strongly inversely related to bureaucratization' (Hall 1973 p 132). Hall goes on to add that this conflict can however be overemphasized, and that the structure (that is the degree of bureaucratization) of an organization is affected by the demands and expectations — and bargaining power, presumably — of the professionals who enter the organization. In considering organizational structure as a result of compromise and conflict between various organizational groups, Hall is employing a conception of organizational structure that is more fully discussed in Strauss' article (1973).

The important distinction to emphasize is between a real devolution of power (which may occur with professionals who can obtain some degree of discretionary autonomy because of their powerful bargaining position) and the sort of apparent delegation of decision-making responsibility where it is found that any delegation is hedged around with rules and procedures. This is the sort of situation described by Blau and Schoenherr.

The established way of conceptualizing and operationalizing the suggested variation in organizational control processes is to consider the relationship between what is called formalization (which refers to the existence and use of rules within the organization) and centralization (which refers to where decisions are taken within the organization).

It has already been pointed out that the various features of a Weberian, ideal type bureaucracy do not always co-exist, and this is also true of the suggested co-existence of formalization and centralization. These bureaucratic dimensions vary independently, indeed to some extent they are inversely related. This suggests that each characteristic represents a distinct type of organizational control, and that organizational members may be controlled *in one of two ways*: they can be constrained through their subjection to a large body of defined rules, regulations and procedures (high formalization) or they can be constrained by the fact that all the significant decisions are made at the top of the organization (highly centralized). It has often been found that when there is a high degree of formalization – clearly defined and rigidly obeyed rules and procedures – then power is delegated within organizations. Blau for example, maintains that 'Formalized procedures and centralized authority may not be two expressions of the same underlying emphasis on strict discipline, but they may rather be two alternative mechanisms for limiting the arbitrary exercise of discretion' (Blau 1970b p 152). When organizational personnel can be relied upon to conform with certain general organizational priorities and procedures they may be allowed to 'exercise their own discretion' and make the appropriate decisions themselves. It may of course be asked with Argyris whether such 'decentralized' decision-making can genuinely be considered as evidence of decentralization – since what seems to be occurring is that '. . . managerial decisions in organizations are either significant, in which case they are not delegated, or delegated, in which case they are not significant' (Blau 1970b p 172).

There is considerable support for the argument that organizations control their members either directly, through centralized decision-making, or through ensuring their obedience with or conformity to such procedures and systems that an appearance of decentralization can be achieved without any real risk of 'irresponsible' behaviour. As mentioned, Blau and Schoenherr's work argues this position strongly. It is also one of the findings of Pugh and Hickson's study (1973). These authors noticed that their empirical investigations suggested the existence of certain clusterings of interrelated organizational characteristics. Two such types that they discern which are relevant to this discussion are differentiated in terms of the sort of structuring they involve. The *workflow structured* organizations, which are relatively decentralized, '. . . have gone a long way in *structuring* activities; that is, the intended behaviour of employees has been structured by the specification of their specialized roles, of the procedures they are to follow in carrying out these roles, and of the documentation involved in what they have to do' (Pugh and Hickson 1973 p 62).

But another organizational type these authors delineate involves a positive relationship between centralized authority and the existence of procedures and regulations. This relationship exists only with reference to the recruitment and selection of organizational personnel. Organizations which exerted strong central control over these activities are called *employment structured*. They tend to leave actual daily work activities relatively ill-defined, possibly because control here is exercised through the '. . . central control of recruitment, central interviewing by formally constituted selection boards', and so on (Pugh and Hickson 1973 p 62). As noted, Blau and Schoenherr argue most forcibly for the significance of what they consider to be a discernible shift in emphasis from control through centralized decision-making to control through selection, recruitment and allocation of personnel and through the allocation of personnel resources. This new form of what they term 'insidious control' enables senior members of the organization to delegate decision-making (which they are forced to do through the pressure of large volumes of complex activities and responsibilities) to middle managers, confident in their ultimate capacity to control and influence the resultant decisions by establishing the parameters of the decision-making, ensuring that the personnel involved are 'properly' trained, motivated and informed, and so on.

Clearly, investigation of the degree of centralization within organizations is going to be a problematic exercise since merely to discover where decisions within the organization are typically taken is inadequate since the most significant form of power within organizations or elsewhere is the ability *to establish the premises upon which organizational decisions are taken.* There are numerous ways in which the decisions and choices of members of organizations can be influenced and constrained. Two obvious examples are assembly line work and automation. But more subtle examples are apparent: for example statistical performance records, or standardized selection procedures.

Various sorts of decisions are taken within organizations. The most apparent may be the least important. In his analysis of the relationship between workers' expectations of their employment situations and the nature of such situations (and how this affects workers' notions of legitimacy) Fox suggests a distinction between substantive and procedural norms. Procedural norms are those which lie behind and govern '. . . the decision-making methods by which norms are formulated' (Fox 1973 p 322). Substantive norms '. . . emanating from these decision-making procedures, cover every aspect of organizations' activities' (Fox 1973 p 322). Fox notes what this means: '. . . decisions constantly have to be taken, explicitly or implicitly, about which norms are to be used in dealing with a particular situation, problem, or instance' (Fox 1973 p 322). This has an obvious application to the discussion of types of organizational control over decision-making. Organizational members may appear to be free to make decisions according to their judgements and evaluations, but such freedom may be more apparent than real, because they may be so hedged around with insidious controls which limit the available resources and options, so limited by the organizational definition of the nature of the problem, so well trained, motivated, selected, appraised, evaluated and generally processed, that when it comes to making a decision they fully conform with higher levels' priorities and expectations. They are reliable, even though they are relatively free from centralized control. In other words the decisions they make are about procedural rather than substantive matters.

The question remains however: if organizations with large numbers of professional and expert staff tend to display somewhat different structures, and if professionals and experts (of whom there are ever-increasing numbers in organizations) are oriented towards and committed to their professional body of knowledge and colleague control — rather than organizational control, then does this mean that professional/expert members of organizations are less controlled by the organization, that they are to some extent free to pursue their own (professional) objectives rather than the organization's? It is difficult to answer this question because, as has been argued, the structure of an organization can be seen as a result of the interactions, compromises and conflicts of competing groups within the organization — and their expectations, ideologies and definitions. In this process professionals, as Hall shows, have some possibility of influencing organizational structure and activities. But at the same time there is little, if any, evidence that organizations which employ professionals behave in a markedly different way from other organizations. Indeed it would seem that professionals — despite their agonized protestations of alienation and frustration — conform, on the whole, to their organizationally determined tasks, objectives and procedures. This leads to the possibility that professional knowledge, training and commitment are by no means necessarily antipathetic to organizational activities and objectives, except with respect to the actual organization of the work situation, and that professionals are in a rather similar situation to those other members of organizations, described by Blau and Schoeherr and others, who are free to act autonomously as long as their decisions are appropriate and conform to organization notions of rationality. However, the question of the interrelationship between bureaucracy and professions probably depends on the type of professional, and especially the strength of the professional ideology, commitment to it, and to the professional association, and the importance or centrality of the professional's contribution. Doctors and academics probably have greater influence than research experts in a 'line' function in a commercial company.

Similarly, professionals in organizations can be seen as simply applying their expert knowledge and skills to the resolution of problems set by the organization. As Perrow has remarked, it is still the organization that defines the problem and sets the standards. And certainly it is the organization that has final control through the manipulation of resources. It is best to leave the last word on this discussion of suggested varieties of organizational control structures to Perrow: 'If we should fear large, bureaucratic organizations . . . we will not be saved from their selfish ravages by believing that they are disappearing, to be replaced by highly decentralized, problem-solving, profession-loaded organizations concerned with a responsible approach to society's multiplying social problems' (Perrow 1972b p 175).

CHAPTER 4

David Elliott

The organization as a system

. . . from the commencement of my managements, I have viewed the population with a mechanism and every part of the establishment as a system composed of many parts, and which it was my duty and interest to combine, so that every hand as well as every spring, lever, and wheel should effectively co-operate to produce the greatest pecuniary gain to the proprietors. (Robert Own 1813, quoted in Cleland and King 1972 p 80)

Summary

General systems theory purports to cover all types of system and leans heavily on cybernetic, biological or organic analogies. In this chapter I look first at the concept of goals, since this is central to systems and cybernetic concepts, and show that in the case of social systems, the goals are more complex and fragmented than in physical systems. I then try to show that a simple equilibrium model does not suffice and that organizations display a *managed* equilibrium rather than an automatic stability.

Systems analysis using the concepts of inputs and outputs provides an introduction to methods for identifying the factors that must be managed in order for the system to be controlled.

Two system models, which help to identify important interactions and interfaces, are introduced, leading to the construction of a general systems model.

Finally, the cybernetic approach is reviewed, concentrating first on its organic origins. I then introduce the modern cybernetic approach which attempts to accommodate the non-deterministic action approach, by emphasizing the generation of interpretations and meaning structures.

The main object of this chapter is to raise the question – can we study organizations as systems? What are the limitations of this approach? What assumption does the systems perspective make about the nature of organizations?

For example, it is possible to consider organizations as in some way similar to biological organisms: this approach can be criticized for stressing the equilibrium aspect, which is not necessarily strong in organizations, and ignoring conflict. Can we view organizations as merely complex arrangements of interacting entities which have fixed operational responses, with behaviour determined by the inputs to the network? This can be criticized as too mechanistic or as being dangerously close to reductionism. Similarly, the concept of an organization as a sentient being with a simple goal of its own can be criticized as ignoring the variety of its human components – and as being dangerously similar to reification. The abstract entity, the system, has no goals – but the individual actors, whose relationships in the system or groups make up the system, have goals, and maybe these unite into a single consensually held goal. Or maybe the sub-systems which make up the system have a multitude of goals, the net outcome of interactions and conflicts resulting as an 'aggregate' or component in the final direction or behaviour of the overall system or organization.

This more complex picture is perhaps more realistic: it depends on interaction, communication and perception, as well as the idea that behaviour is a direct response to inputs or stimuli.

Discussion of these various criticisms will help clarify our understanding of organizations and raise a number of questions. Can we expect organizations constantly to maintain equilibrium or will they naturally tend towards chaos, unless controlled? Is conflict endemic, healthy or deviant? How strong are the effects of various factors both internal and external impinging on sub-systems in the organization? Can we understand the problem of *control* by studying the effects of these various factors? Can we use the idea of information flow and perception as a help in explaining the individual's and groups' formation of attitudes and expectations and interpretation of reality in organization?

Introduction to systems theory

What do we mean by a system?

There are many definitions of what constitutes a system. Basically *any group of entities which are functionally interdependent* can be called a system. *Any group of entities which are interrelated so as to perform some function, or reach some goal, can be seen to be acting as a system.*

Let us briefly examine some simple systems concepts, which will be of use in our discussion.

Large systems usually contain *sub-systems*, which ideally work independently towards the final goal of the major system. This picture of a hierarchy of systems and sub-systems represents a *systems model*. By studying the interrelations between sub-systems we can learn something of the nature of the system. Similarly we can identify *components* of the system or sub-system — the next level down in the hierarchy, and we can study the interaction between these. No system is entirely *closed* or self-contained. It must exist in an *environment* and must interact with that environment to some extent. We say that such a system is *open*. We can talk about *inputs* and *outputs* to the system from and to the environment: and we may be able to define the *system's boundary* across which these inputs and outputs pass — that is the boundary between the system and its environment. We can try to define the system's environment by suggesting that it affects the functioning of the system (by constraints or imperatives) but is not *part* of the system — it does not share the system's *goals*. Probably the most popular system concept is, of course, *feedback*. Many systems are structured so that some part of their output response is fed back to become an input. The system monitors its own behaviour through this feedback loop. The feedback concept derives from electrical control systems and has proved an invaluable tool in general systems analysis. These concepts — systems, sub-systems, goal, systems model, input, output, feedback, system boundary and environment — will be followed up in more detail in a later section, dealing with a number of systems models.

The systems approach

Is the systems approach a particular theory or simply a methodology which has much in common with sociological analysis?

I would suggest that the systems approach is a way of thinking which enables us to cope with complex phenomena by identifying their systemic relations. Once we realize that the structure we are studying displays the properties of a system we may be in a position to identify crucial goals, linkages or controlling factors in its structure and functioning. The analytical process typical of systems analysis can lay bare the interrelationships between sub-systems and their inputs and outputs, and may focus our attention on unexpected feedback loops, behavioural lags, delays in response to particular inputs, or crucial interactions between inputs or sub-systems. The systems concept ensures that we look for these linkages since we are aware that the structure we are studying is an interdependent arrangement of sub-systems.

In the next section we will ask specifically what these generalizations about systems structure have to offer us in the study of organizations, and in particular concentrate on two systems' concepts — goals and equilibrium.

1 Organization models

1.1 Organizations as systems

How can organizations be analysed as systems?

Certainly an organization can be thought of as having identifiable goals, with its sub-parts acting in concert to reach these objectives. Parsons defined an organization as a 'special type of social system organized about the primacy of interest in the attainment of a particular type of system goal' (1970 p 76).

The fact that organizations have human components introduces a degree of variety and internal inconsistency to the mechanical model of a functioning system. But the systems approach is, to some extent, capable of coping with this individual variety in organizations, by focusing not on individuals, but on their arrangement in the system. In the strict sense of the word, organizations are arrangements of people or roles. We can study how this system behaves, changes, handles events and processes information. Now such a system can be seen to be arranged for some purpose — it has a goal. Systems analysis however should reveal that there are, in the systems arrangement, sub-systems which may be formally ascribed a different role or may develop, autonomously, different roles — and goals. Sociologists usually label these autonomous developments informal as opposed to formal organization.

So human sub-systems, sub-groups of people, may have goals which differ from or are even contradictory to the stated goal of the major system. And of course the overall system's goals may be complex. The stated goals of the organization may differ from the real operating goals or they may not be consistent in functional terms. It is often suggested that competitive organizations have profit or growth as their major goal, but this is often qualified by the secondary goal of 'benefiting the people who work in the organization and the society which the organization serves'. These two goals are not necessarily adhered to simultaneously — they represent different views of the systems.

Social sub-systems, such as work-groups, office groups, etc., internalize goals in terms of norms which again may or may not be in the interests of the overall system. Industrial sociology provides many examples of restrictive work group norms, developed by the group to defend and advance the group as opposed to the organization.

Albrow identifies some of these latent sub-systems goals:

> It is a characteristic of social action that no objective is 'given' in isolation from other objectives. The limits on the attainment of an objective are set not only by the availability of means but also by criteria which determine what means are acceptable. These criteria frequently stem from goals which are independent of the objective from which the analysis began. Thus managers may well have goals other than high production e.g. profit, industrial peace, the preservation of power and privilege . . .(p 398)
>
> . . . Members of the organizations may put job-security at the very centre of the organizational goal structure, and commitment to any other goal may be regarded as a price to be paid. Alternatively, it may be the case that an organizational goal is treated by the various social groupings in the organization as purely instrumental in obtaining their own purposes. (Albrow 1973 p 406)

Simon (1945) points out that decisions and goals are generated according to the individual's limited perception of reality — rather than in a full, objective knowledge of the situation. Inevitably, the individual can only perceive some part of the system that surrounds him. He must operate within what Simon calls a 'bounded rationality' based on a simplified mental model of the system. It is in terms of this model that the individual makes decisions. One of the objects of the systems approach is to explore — and expand — this mental model.

1.2 Organization goals

System analysis, as applied to mechanical and cybernetic systems, lays strong emphasis on the definition, and preferably quantification, of a precise goal, as an essential first step in any analysis of a system. As we have seen, however, when we try to analyse the more complex *social* systems, such as organizations, this process is not so straightforward, and we may have to adopt 'multiple goal' models, with different goals operating at different levels (Mezarovic *et al* 1973). It is useful, generally, to look at the interaction between the goals at different levels, for example, between the goals of sub-systems and the goals of the system as a whole.

In the case of organizations, goal analysis is well established. Indeed we often define organizations by their goals (as in the quote at the beginning of *section 1.1*). An organization is seen as a co-ordinated body (or system) of individuals (and perhaps machines) arranged to reach some goal or perform some function or service. Etzioni provides a useful summary of this type of systems argument (1970). In this section I will spend some time reviewing the various propositions concerning the goals of organizations and of the individuals in them in order to illustrate the diversity of goals that exist in organizations. Of course we must be careful about what type of organization we are considering. Commercial and industrial organizations are obviously economic organizations and one would expect economic goals to be important for them. However, since all organizations exist in a competitive environment the economic constraints may often be important even though the organization's stated objective is something else.

The traditional economic model of organizations stresses the goal of profit maximization. All other goals are viewed as secondary. However, as Child (1973) points out, the controllers of modern economic organizations have some freedom to choose policies and goals other than those determined by the nature of the market or the technology. Thus, according to Galbraith (1967) the company finds that if it can establish a certain adequate level of profit and if this can be stabilized, then other goals become more significant. A similar denial of 'profit maximization' as the major goal comes from H. Simon, who records the common management view that 'the goal of business is not profit but efficient production of goods and services' (1969 p 162). He suggests that profit maximization is only really possible if one subscribes to the 'economic' model of the omniscient super-rational entrepreneur (Simon 1965). The manager in practice cannot possibly review all possible behaviour alternatives before making a decision. Therefore he must be content with 'satisficing' rather than 'maximizing' and he looks for a course of action that is satisfactory or 'good enough'.

The changing nature of management, as ownership and control are increasingly separated and professional specialization increases, has also been seen as likely to contribute to a lessening in importance of the profit motive. Galbraith suggests that modern corporations are increasingly governed by professional 'technicians' — economists, financiers, systems analysts, technologists, market researchers, who comprise a 'technostructure'. He suggests this new 'class' has the goal of survival, efficiency and control rather than of 'profit maximization'.

In making this type of assertion, we move from the level of the organization to that of the individual. There are both personal goals, dependent on the motivations of the individual, and professional goals, which depend on the organizational roles of the individual. In the vast modern organizations, it is unlikely that the individual will see the company's profit maximization as directly relating to his own welfare — it is a distant goal. Nor is his professional role and decision-making activity directly linked to profit. His personal objectives may be to maximize his own salary, secure his own position and expand his influence. His desire for job security is often a crucial influence on his decision-making. As Burns and Stalker (1961) have mentioned, the efforts expended by executives in business organizations in defence of and advancement of their career prospects are considerable. We might even suggest that successful careerism becomes a goal in itself. Burns and Stalker point out that 'the hierarchical order of rank and power realized in the organization chart, that prevails in all organizations, is both a control system and a career ladder' (1961 p xii). The internal struggles and political intrigue that these career goals involve may of course absorb so much effort as to be dysfunctional (i.e. not in the best interests of the organization).

Thus an organization cannot be viewed on a simple organic or cybernetic model as a unified structure maintaining equilibrium through goal-directed behaviour. The equilibrium of an organization is a result of the balancing and managing of complex internal tensions and conflicts, and its goal is not a unified shared one, but emerges generally as a compromise from the interaction of multiple constraints.

1.3 Equilibrium models

The concept of equilibrium is important to systems thinking. Concepts of equilibrium, however, that draw too heavily on an organic model of a self-adapting, self-equilibrating system can be criticized, for reasons suggested in the previous section, as being inadequate for the purposes of organizational analysis. We will look briefly first at a systems theory drawing heavily on an organic-equilibrium model, before considering some systems concepts and models that revolve more round notions of *managed* rather than natural equilibrium, and that seem more appropriate to organizational analysis.

Parsons' theory of social systems

Parsons has developed a systems theory which has been widely accepted and used in the study both of society in general and of organizations. Parsons' idea of a social system is that it functions so as to constantly adjust itself internally to a state of equilibrium. Any particular input — be it personnel or structural change — is coped with by the sub-systems, and a new equilibrated system evolved.

Parsons talks in terms of behaviour or 'actions' which are either *functional* or *dysfunctional* — that is actions which produce either helpful or unhelpful consequences in terms of the goals of the system. He suggests however that dysfunctional behaviour will inevitably be modified so as not to disrupt the self-equilibrating tendencies of the system. If this does not occur the system will lose all equilibrium and degenerate: 'while parts of the system may not serve the goal (i.e. may be dysfunctional) these will in the long run become modified so as to serve the system or will "disengage" themselves from it. If neither event occurs the system will "degenerate".' (Silverman 1970 p 31)

Parsons tackles the problem of why organized activities in society are stable and continue, despite changes in personnel. His approach leads to a, perhaps, one-sided view that what is central to the 'social system' is its stability — its constant striving towards equilibrium. Hence conflict in society and in organizations is relegated to secondary importance, as is also the phenomenon of change, that so often accompanies conflict.

What Parsons is attempting is a *general* 'theory of society', illustrating how the various parts of the social system function in order to maintain equilibrium. He is attempting to link the ideas of 'normative control', 'shared cultural conditioning', private and public interests, etc., into a 'grand theory' (see Parsons 1970).

Conflict, change and deviance

As we have noted, Parsons' insistence on 'consensus' and 'equilibrium' has been widely criticized for failing to deal with 'change', 'deviance' and 'conflict'.

But we cannot afford to ignore deviant behaviour in our analysis. Thus deviant activities must be included as part of the system and not as residual and dysfunctional. Deviance, and conflict produced by deviance, may be important *functional* components of the systems of organizations: 'Conflict, rather than being disruptive and dissociating may indeed be a means of balancing and hence maintaining a society as a going concern . . .' (Coster 1956 p 137). 'A flexible society benefits from conflict because such behaviour, by helping to create and modify norms, assures its continuance under changed conditions' (p 154).

The idea of equilibrium is still of course retained in this formulation. More radical conflict theorists would suggest that the changes that ensue might totally restructure the organization so that the concept of equilibrium or even of dynamic equilibrium would be inappropriate. We will see in later sections that open systems are characterized by the capability to restructure and adapt themselves in this way continuously in response to changes in their environment. These changes relate not only to straight-forward changes in (for example) market conditions or technological innovations, but also changes in social and cultural values. Open systems theorists, in contrast to Parsonian system theorists, do not see organizational adaptation as being necessarily of a self-equilibrating nature. The way in which an organization adapts to its environment is quite frequently *planned* or *managed* — although of course, unconscious adaptations do also occur, particularly in the sphere of social and cultural values.

1.4 Inputs and outputs

One of the most useful systems' methodologies is to study the inputs and outputs of a system. What are the possible inputs and outputs to and from an organization?

Taking the case of an industrial organization, in summary, the inputs might be:

1 personnel
2 their attitudes and expectations
3 targets, constraints and imperatives from the environment (e.g. the market)
4 raw materials, equipment, techniques.

The obvious output is the product of the organization — be it physical or abstract, i.e. what it does — its function.

But there are other outputs — which feed back to affect the functioning of the system. The *behavioural response* of the people in the organization can be seen as an output. It may be in the form of actual action or it may be simply attitudinal. Adverse attitudes (boredom, dissatisfaction, etc.) may lead to action (strikes, absenteeism, labour turnover, etc.).

Behaviour *in* the system may be determined by both the inputs from the environment and the conditions inside the system. Industrial sociologists talk of technology and job design affecting the behaviour of workers: external market pressures also may affect them. There are many other factors such as the payment system, the strength of the union, etc., that may affect behaviour in the organization.

There are many reservations as to the viability of this type of input/ output model. How can we measure inputs such as community attitudes and worker attitudes? How can we, in any particular situation, identify which input is significant? Can we identify causal links between particular inputs, in an array of inputs, and the various outputs?

There are many techniques of statistical analysis which are of relevance to these problems. For example, if we can produce data on inputs and outputs we can attempt to test for correlations or associations between variations in these data. There are multiple regression techniques which allow us to make some kinds of statistical association between many factors, and test for causal links.

Hence it is, at least in theory, possible to identify links and relationships between inputs and outputs and to make a start at a formal systems analysis. Of course, such analysis is in its infancy and may well be totally unsuccessful. Industrial sociologists have explored many of these possible correlations – for example, between the type of technology and worker attitude or worker behaviour.

One way to try to improve our understanding of the likely impact of and interaction between these factors is to make use of 'systems models' i.e. theoretical pictures of the structure and organization of the system, focusing on key factors and interrelations.

The following sections look at two such models that have been developed by industrial sociologists and systems theorists – the socio-technical model and the open systems model.

1.5 Emergence of the socio-technical model

The work of Elton Mayo at the Hawthorne plant of the Western Electric Company represents an early example of a systems approach to organizations. Like most early systems work, it tended to view systems as closed or isolated groups of interacting subunits, ignoring any inputs that might come in from outside the systems boundary. See for example the works of Mayo's associates, Roethlisberger and Dickson (1970).

In particular they tended to emphasize the concept of equilibrium. The work group was seen as a state sub-system which had both formal and informal interactions. The formal structure depends on the actual task in hand and on the supervisory system. The informal system – which Mayo concentrated on – depends on interpersonal relationships, friendship, group loyalties and group defence. This accent on 'human relations' can be compared with the bias towards task-related interactions typical of the more sophisticated *socio-technical* systems, which incorporated the technological environment of the work group into the model. The prescriptions made by the human relations theorists involved improving communications and consideration of informal group norms and loyalties. The socio-technical school (Emery, Trist *et al*), while not denying the importance of informal group interactions, concentrates on the aspects of these interactions that are in some way determined by and interrelated with the task in hand.

Thus Emery and Trist (1969) see the shop-floor sub-system as being neither a purely technical system nor a purely social system, but as an interdependent socio-technical system. They developed this concept as a result of research into the effects of technological change in coal mines and elsewhere. The essence of the socio-technical approach has been aptly summarized as follows:

> The technological demands place limits on the type of work organization possible, but the work organization has social, psychological properties of its own that are independent of the technology. From this point of view, it makes as little sense to regard social relationships as being determined by the technology as it does to regard the manner in which a job is performed as being determined by the socio-psychological characteristics of the workers. The crucial implication of this theory was that the attainment of optimum conditions for either aspect does not necessarily result in optimum conditions for the system as a whole. Indeed the optimization of the whole may well require a less than optimum state for each separate aspect. (Pugh *et al* 1971 pp 50–1)

Emery and Trist thus denied that socio-technical systems had self-adapting equilibrating tendencies; these systems must be consciously planned and matched if optimization of performance is to be attained. Given a suitable design of socio-technical system, then of course interdependent self-regulation *may* be possible: the system may be self-managing.

1.6 Open systems

The open systems approach attempts to include influences from outside the immediate work-group environment, which the socio-technical approach tends to ignore. It is also used to refer to the effects of inputs, derived from the organization's environment, on the organization as a whole (e.g. a firm).

On this type of model, the system is seen as open — that is sensitive to its environment. This environment also includes other systems which may interact: 'The organization, i.e. the whole complex of interrelated and encapsulated sub-units, groups and individuals, has to adapt to a changing world which includes other groups and organizations such as shareholders, customers, trade unions and governments.' (Lupton 1971 p 122).

Fundamentally, the open system is one in which materials, information, attitudes, etc., are imported and exported across the system's boundary. This boundary can be drawn anywhere for the purpose of analysis. If the system one is studying is the whole organization then the boundary is between the organization and its external environment; if the system being studied is the work-group, then the boundary is between this group and the rest of the organization, which in this case is its environment.

According to the concept of entropy, it is, in fact, impossible for any system to remain *closed*, if it is to survive. Although we can treat some systems as 'closed' for the purpose of analysis, strictly speaking all systems are open. Here we are making an analogy to certain physical systems – usually studied in thermodynamics. It is axiomatic (in physics) that to perform any work a system must import energy, or else it will run down. Similarly, for a social system – such as an organization – it must import both physical materials, human operatives and attitudes, information, expectations and social sanctions.

The organizational system thus relies on its environment to provide its requirements.

This is obvious in mechanical-material terms. It is also true in terms of the need for an enterprise to have its activities accepted (sanctioned) by the community it serves. And again we can see that the motivations and expectations of the work force (the human component of the system) are also generated in and by the 'environment', are 'brought in' to the system, and largely define the behaviour of the 'people in the organization' (see Katz and Kahn 1970).

The modern organization is seen as necessarily open to and aware of its environment, and at the same time it is suggested that it attempts to consciously manage its environment.

As Drucker puts it '. . . managing goes way beyond passive reaction and adaptation. It implies responsibility for attempting to shape the economic environment, for planning, initiating and carrying through changes, for constantly pushing back the limitations of economic circumstances on the enterprise's freedom of action . . .' (Drucker 1955 pp 8–9).

Of course we must be careful not to confuse the organization and the people inside the organization. The statements we have made so far about 'what organizations should or must do' are obviously reifications. Attitudes, expectations and imperatives impinge on individuals or groups and their response in aggregate makes up the organization's behaviour.

In particular we must try to be clear about the difference between these input effects on the controllers, or managers, and the workers. As Child has pointed out, the former group have a certain freedom to make strategic choices, and do not necessarily have to respond directly to economic or technical imperatives: they can manage or cope with the environment (Child 1973). Child's model thus decouples some of the behaviour of actors in the system from the input factors. Nevertheless, many of the predispositions, attitudes, and expectations of both managers and workers are generated, and perhaps determined, by these external influences. Of course, there is much debate as to whether attitudes, etc., are generated inside or outside the organization. It is nevertheless generally accepted that the attitudes and expectations generated in the wider community partially determine behaviour discernible in the organization – or at least are important factors.

Goldthorpe's study (1968) of workers in Luton car plants and their community relations certainly indicates that the 'instrumental attitude' (emphasis on 'expected cash reward' without particular concern for conditions or friendships at work) generated *outside* the workplace dominated behaviour at work, and attitudes to work, for the particular group he studied (although equally one might say the instrumental attitude was adopted as a 'compensation' in that it was perceived as impossible to improve conditions of work).

Quite apart from this type of economic motivation, there are other and more complex factors which impinge on the workers in industrial organizations and which derive from the community – factors relating to the community's history, the degree of working class solidarity, the history of trade unions, the coherence of the community structure, and so on. It is this type of factor that the open systems perspective asks us to consider.

1.7 Open systems and their environments

Katz and Kahn (1970) pioneered this open systems approach to organizations and their management. The modern open systems approach which they describe is currently being pursued with the aim, for example, of providing an understanding of how the managers of modern organizations can deal with and adapt to their fast changing or 'turbulent' environments. Examples of this research are Emery's (1969) work on the 'Causal texture of organizational environments' and Lawrence and Lorsch's (1967) analysis. These studies represent attempts to analyse the structure of the environment in systems terms, to evolve quantitative measures of the rate of change of elements in the environment which affect the organizations. In an attempt to produce a theory of environmental and organizational change, Lawrence and Lorsch (1967) depict three analytically separate segments in the organizational environment (market, research and development, technological) which could change at different rates. This enables a more precise analysis to be made of a generally 'turbulent' environment and of the feedback relationship between this environment and intra-organizational change. For example, the rate of change of scientific developments, as explored by a Research Development department, may be very high 'while at the same time and in the same organization, the rate of change in customers' tastes or competitors' tactics might be low, and the rate of change of product or method very low' (Lupton 1971 p 127).

Earlier attempts to relate organizational structure to environment were made by Woodward (1959) and Burns and Stalker (1961). Essentially these studies highlighted the fact that certain organizational structures were suitable for different types of environment. Woodward concentrated on the technological environment, while Burns and Stalker included such features as types of product market and rates of technological changes. Neither Burns and Stalker, nor Woodward, however, conceive of the relationship between environment and organizational structures as mechanically deterministic. The perception of management, as to what seems to them to be the most suitable form of organization, is still an important mediating factor. Both research teams found organizations attempting to operate with a structure unsuitable to their environment, although they were inevitably less successful than organizations more suitably matched to their environments. The system, therefore, has to be managed — it is not self-adapting or self-equilibrating.

It is precisely because the system is not self-adapting that problems of conflicting goals or strategies at different levels of the organization arise. Management strategy might run counter to the smooth adaptation of a sub-group to its environment and then there may be open conflict or resistance to change. The open system approach can be applied to this phenomenon also by drawing the system boundary round this particular sub-group and analysing this group's reaction to inputs from its surrounding environment, both inside and outside the organization. Lupton and Cunnison (1964) have made contributions in this area.

1.8 Systems modelling

As we have emphasized earlier, both the open systems and the socio-technical approaches have merit. The more recent open systems perspective is an attempt to subsume the socio-technical approach, taking into account interactions with the environment of the shop-floor sub-system and with the environment of the whole organization. Thus the model is expanded to include a multiplicity of factors which impinge on individuals in the sub-system, and does not concentrate on solely individual human factors or task-determined socio-technical factors.

You will have realized by now that there is no *one* thing called systems theory; although there may be a typical systems approach. We have outlined a number of theoretical uses of the systems concept, ranging from Parsons' equilibrium model, to the socio-technical model. Etzioni discusses some further points in his article on 'Two approaches to organizational analysis' (1970). We turn now to the 'cybernetic' system approach.

As we have seen social systems can be modelled verbally, i.e. in words using logical 'argument'.

Some systems – such as mechanical, biological, electronic and operational systems – can be modelled in more formal mathematical terms. This is the basis of cybernetics: the study of systems in terms of information and control, using such physical concepts as feedback, goal-directed behaviour, automatic self-regulation, etc.

Some of these concepts can be used in the study of social systems and organizations, but there are fundamental limits to the analogy between mechanical/physical systems and social systems. Generally, this difference relates to the degree of openness of the system. For example, mechanical systems can be designed to operate relatively independently of their environments: they tend to be closed systems, and they tend to operate according to relatively well defined goals.

Thus, the cybernetic approach, based on drawing analogies between biological, electronic and social systems, has fundamental limitations. These limitations also hold true for the body of thought called general systems theory which attempts to erect general models which can be used to analyse a large range of systems from social organizations to ecological systems.

1.10 Systems, organizations and organisms

The general systems approach amounts to a general taxonomy of behaviour and function across a wide range of diverse areas.

It has much in common with other generalist attempts at unifying our understanding of social, economic, and biological behaviour. So we might expect general laws, applicable for a range of different systems: 'In Cybernetics, organizational forms are studied independently of their carrier, so that, in a certain sense, cybernetic systems constitute common models of systems defined in different, frequently widely remote, scientific disciplines' (Klir and Valach, quoted in Chadwick 1971 p 189).

It has been pointed out that many of these approaches rely on an analogy to natural biological organisms. The state is seen as a vast corporate body – an organism. We use the terms 'organ', 'arm' (of the law), etc., and these functionalist views derive from attempts to produce a model of society based on the analogy of the human body.

There is of course a basic philosophical point here. Why should organizations behave like individuals or organisms? Can we usefully generalize from the behaviour of one component? This type of criticism is similar to that of Herbert Spencer's classic criticism of over-eager analogies between 'organisms' and 'societies': 'The social organism, discrete instead of concrete, asymmetrical instead of symmetrical, sensitive in all its units instead of having a single sensitive centre, is not comparable to any particular type of individual organism, animal or vegetable' (Spencer 1897 p 592).

These critics suggest that one must be wary of reductionist attempts to disregard differences and over-reduce complexities to simple patterns and basic, generalizable models and laws. In particular there seems to be no reason why every system should be reducible to any particular model or analogue. The defenders of the systems approach acknowledge that differences do exist and must not be glossed over, but assert that the systems approach has an important role to play in locating and analysing the precise nature of these differences.

While an organic model or analogy does seem to be implied by systems analysts when they use such terms as 'goal directed behaviour', 'boundary maintenance' and 'purposive behaviour', yet, as we have already indicated, few contemporary systems writers impose a totally organic self-equilibrating model on social systems. Most writers stress that social equilibrium (just as post-Keynesian economic 'equilibrium') is a managed and not a 'natural equilibrium' and that adaptive changes are usually the results of conscious decisions made by groups or individuals who happen to be in a position of power that enables them to make such decisions. Thus it is conceded that there are fundamentally different modes of behaviour for organizations and organisms. The former can restructure themselves internally (either as a result of conscious decisions or unconscious actions) in response to some environmental factor; and this change can occur rapidly. This is not true of organisms or biological systems; their structural adaptability to changing environments is slow and perhaps requires several generations.

Modern system theorists are moving away from a simple organic or deterministic stimulus-response model of change or behaviour. They suggest that it is inadequate simply to identify input factors and related output behaviour (i.e. to study the system as if it were a sealed 'black box'): what is significant is the precise mechanism through which the individual responds to inputs. They are no longer satisfied with an analysis that sees behaviour and attitudes as determined directly, in a stimulus response manner, by inputs.

Buckley, and several other modern systems theorists, insist that we must move past the organic model to a cybernetic model, and deal with the flow of information (which includes ideas, attitudes, etc.). They try to make a fundamental connection with the 'action' perspective, suggesting that the perception of information relies on the meaning the receiver attaches to the information; its meaningfulness depends on him. The study of how people or groups in the system interpret its inputs and how these inputs create systems of meaning can lead to explanations of output behaviour (Buckley 1973).

As Chadwick puts it: 'Human systems are not like mechanical systems ... each person, each group of persons, is a system which adapts and adjusts both to external and internal stimuli ... continually restructuring its perceived world in accordance with information flows received ...' (Chadwick 1971 pp 331-2)

Buckley (1973) attempts to make a bridge between systems theories of behaviour in organizations and the action approach. As we noted earlier, the emphasis moves away from the direct cause-effect model, in which inputs to the system directly determine behaviour, towards a model which includes mediatory process of perception and interpretation. In practice, this suggests that we must study the interaction between inputs of information and meanings, and attempt to understand the mechanism by which meanings and interpretations are generated.

2 Systems theory as a sociological tool

With its emphasis on managed equilibrium, systems theory, as applied to organization, has inevitably found some of its strongest support from managers and management consultants eager to solve problems of 'instability' and 'disequilibrium' in their organizations. Inevitably, therefore, there has been a tendency in systems analyses of organizations to accept as given the managers' notion of what constitutes a satisfactory equilibrium, and to accept the need to control and manage the behaviour of other members of the organization, so as to maintain this equilibrium or status quo. Thus systems analyses rarely contain any adequate examination of the nature of the power structure that confers on certain people in organizations the ability to make fundamental decisions affecting the structure and performance of the organization, and allows their goals to dominate the purposive behaviour of the organization. Systems models are fundamentally descriptions of *how* the system functions: they do not explain *why* — why, for example, there arise fundamental conflicts of interest between sub-groups. For a satisfactory examination of such questions, we would have to return to more mainstream sociology.

In summary, it could be said that the systems perspective describes the structure and functioning of organizations and may reveal the nature and source of the factors determining the behaviour of the system. For example, we might be able to trace particular attitudes or actions of the members of the organization and relate these to economic inputs which impinge on the system from the environment. But, however well the systems approach describes the structure and explains certain behavioural phenomena, it does not explain why the structure, especially its power aspects, is as it is. To illuminate this would require a different approach to organizations.

Section three
Organizational control:
interaction, roles and rules

CHAPTER 5

David R. Weeks

Organizations: interaction and social processes

So far little has been said about 'people' in organizations, that is, those who exercise and suffer the 'control' and practise and maintain the 'ideologies'. In this chapter we begin to redress the balance but in doing so we shall not be offering an 'individual-centred' or 'great man' theory of organizations. As sociologists have realized from their earliest attempts to account for social order, man does not freshly create social organization with each new generation; rather he inherits a vast edifice of traditions, values, habits and potentials which he has the possibility of changing in a variety of ways.

To argue for a stress on 'social structure', however, raises as many problems and difficulties in its own way as are avoided by rejecting an approach in terms of specific 'men'. Whilst we can readily recognize the constraints and influences usually associated with certain social positions within a society or organization, the exact consequences these have for the society or organization remain difficult to specify. The sociologist's endeavour to explain social phenomena in terms of some notion of 'social facts' at base always remains an interpretive one. As Raymond Aron has put it, 'all sociology is a reconstruction that aspires to confer intelligibility on human existences, which like all existences, are confused and obscure', (Aron 1967 p 207). The fundamental problem facing sociologists is how best to identify, collect and explain their raw data.

The extent to which we can 'push men out' and still remain in touch with the social reality of the situation we are describing has its limitations. The point has been well put by Brittan:

> Granted that social facts can be viewed as having a limited autonomy of their own, it must never be forgotten that this autonomy is only relevant within the context of the significance and meaning that men

attach to those facts. Even brute force is never mediated directly. It
always has some symbolic element which has meaning for those who
are exposed to force. The social facts that sociology is concerned
with are symbolic facts. They can only be studied by acknowledging
that the objective world is largely man-made, and that the immediacy
of the empirical world is saturated with the meaning that men
attribute to objects. (Brittan 1973 p 18)

Thus a world made by man can be changed by man. By investigating
the goals men pursue, and the means they employ, we can hope to
understand the dynamics of the construction of social reality which
feed off and add to the 'social facts' which are the basis for systems
analyses, or structural analyses, of organizational functioning.

It is important to point out, however, that analyses which con-
contrate on what might be called 'objective' and 'subjective' aspects of
organizations are not dealing with completely autonomous realms of
social phenomena. In an important sense we cannot have one without
the other. To put the point in more technical terms:

> As Berger has argued, the social is a dialectical process involving the
> interchange between man's externalization of his subjectivity, its
> objectification in symbolic form, and finally, its re-entry into his
> consciousness by the process of internalization.[1] In other words,
> man produces himself – he creates his own social objects, and in so
> doing is not a passive spectator – he is by his very social nature
> forced into an interactive relationship with his world. Of course, the
> outside world exists independently of man as a socious[2] yet its
> significance for man is one which he himself brings to it. (Brittan
> 1973 p 16)

By concentrating on the perceptions and definitions used by the actors
in an organization as a basis for building up an explanation of organizational functioning we may have to give up some of our claims to being
'scientific', for the possibility of testing any theory arrived at in this
manner may well be limited and contaminated by a wide range of
uncontrollable factors. To accept this as a completely damning criticism
is to take a very narrow view of the value and aims of sociology. The
intellectual attraction of the aesthetically appealing abstract and logical

[1] P. Berger (1969) *The Social Reality of Religion*, London, Faber, pp 3–28

[2] 'Socious' has been defined as 'The individual person conceived of as a unit in a
system of social interaction and as a point of convergence of the various social
and cultural patterns of society'. (Theodorson, G. A. and Theodorson, A. G.
(1970) *A Modern Dictionary of Sociology*, London, Methuen, p 406)

argument should not blind us to other desirable qualities such as empirical richness and sympathetic understanding; in other words, to the virtues of a humanistic sociology.

One way of introducing the social action approach is to ask what kind of questions do actors in organizations find themselves asking much of the time, for in this sense we are all social theorists trying to understand and explain why other people act in the way they do. How can we make sense of seemingly irrational and inconsistent behaviour? Why don't organizations operate in the way they are supposed to? Why can't individuals and groups avoid the continual conflicts, rivalries and misunderstandings, and work for the common goals which we often assume they must share simply because they are all members of the same organization?

These kinds of questions land in a middle-ground between theories of organizational functioning which view individuals in terms of playing out well scripted and learned social roles and other theories which focus on personality characteristics as providing the basic driving force behind organizational behaviour. The social action approach attempts to take into account both the enduring features of a social situation, which might be called its culture and distribution of power, and also the specific viewpoints of individuals and groups as they formulate strategies to pursue their own goals and deal with the behaviour of other similar individuals and groups.

The social action perspective

If we are to study the way in which organizations operate from the perspective of the social actions which constitute much of the activity of the organization, then we should begin with a general idea as to what makes an action social. As with much other thinking on organizations, we can turn to Max Weber as our initial guide. Weber defined social action in the following way:

> Action is social in so far as, by virtue of the subjective meaning attached to it by the acting individual (or individuals), it takes account of the behaviour of others and is thereby oriented in its course. (Weber 1964 p 88)

and

> Sociology ... is a science which attempts the interpretive under-

standing of social action in order thereby to arrive at casual explanation of its course and effects. (Weber 1964 p 88)

Thus Weber's general definition emphasizes the subjective meaning
which the actor attaches to his action and the account which he takes
of the behaviour of others. The important point to note here is the
critical role of the interaction between individuals, for it is only through
this interactive process that the social element of action becomes
apparent. This does not imply that social action only occurs when
individuals are in physical contact for the influence of others certainly
does not vanish simply because they are not physically present in a
situation. The essential point is that whenever individuals behave in a
way which they think will influence others they are acting in a way
which has real significance in social terms for them and they are not
simply acting out in a preordained way a facet of a system or a requirement or demand of an organization's structure.

We can relate this important point to the different ways in which the
idea of organizational goal is used in a systems approach compared with
the social action perspective. Many systems theorists make assumptions
about the overall importance of generalized goals which they perceive
as dominating the way the organization functions and which persist
relatively unchanged over time. Rather than accept as 'given' the
nature and consistency of organizational goals as defined by the formal
objectives of organizations, the social action perspective focuses on the
way in which more specific goals (values) are imported into and
generated within organizations by individuals and groups operating at
various points within the organization. The concern in this approach is
to observe the socially generated values, interests and norms which
occur in organizational contexts, and to investigate the processes of
their maintenance and change in relation to internal social interaction
and external environmental changes. Rose describes this general orientation in the following terms:

> Action approaches to industrial behaviour, which I shall refer to
> generally as actionalism, attempt to explore the work-community
> nexus and to incorporate socially generated and distributed aims,
> attitudes and actions in the model of the worker and explanations
> of work behaviour. (Rose 1975 p 227)

By viewing organizational behaviour in this way we can avoid the
tendency to reify organizational structure which tends to ignore the
element of humanly directed social action. Simply because it is possible

to construct a statistically based model of organizational behaviour this does not mean it reflects the actual social intentions and meanings of the actors involved. It may tell you other things about more abstract notions of structure, but it is a poor guide to the organizational actors' thoughts, motives and feelings.

For a more detailed and formalized view of the fundamental assumptions of the social action approach we can turn to the analysis offered by Silverman. He lists the following seven propositions which represent an ideal-type description of social action premises:

1 The social sciences and the natural sciences deal with entirely different orders of subject-matter. While the canons of rigour and scepticism apply to both, one should not expect their perspective to be the same.

2 Sociology is concerned with understanding action rather than with observing behaviour. Action arises out of meanings which define social reality.

3 Meanings are given to men by their society. Shared orientations become institutionalized and are experienced by later generations as social facts.

4 While society defines men, man in turn defines society. Particular constellations of meaning are only sustained by continual reaffirmation in everyday actions.

5 Through their interaction men also modify, change and transform social meanings.

6 It follows that explanations of human actions must take account of the meanings which those concerned assign to their acts; the manner in which the everyday world is socially constructed yet perceived as real and routine becomes a crucial concern of sociological analysis.

7 Positivistic explanations, which assert that action is determined by external and constraining social or non-social forces, are inadmissible.

(Silverman 1970 pp 126–7)

Of particular interest is the second proposition which states that 'sociology is concerned with understanding action rather than with observing behaviour'. By 'understanding' is meant uncovering the subjective meaning the action has for the actor. We must be aware that this is not the whole picture, however, since other actors may interpret the actions of a person differently from the intentions held by the person himself. The consequences of this alternative interpretation may be more significant than the original subjective meaning attached to the action. If the attempts of an organizational member to improve his own efficiency are interpreted by his superior not as helpful and co-operative behaviour, but rather as a threat to the superior's position, the social consequences may not be improved efficiency, but the dismissal or transfer of the subordinate. To understand this turn of events our knowledge of the subordinate's intentions would need to be supplemented by observation of the resulting behaviour of what had occurred according to criteria other than those employed solely by the subordinate himself. We may want to bring in various ideas about the relative positions of power of the individuals involved and the courses of action open to the superior according to his own position in the organization. This is not to say that the subjective meaning of the subordinate is not an important ingredient of the ensuing consequences, but simply to note that it provides insufficient criteria on its own for an understanding of the total set of events.

A further problem arises with regard to the source and scope of subjective meanings and how they may be measured. Clearly individuals do not live their lives in the rather neat and tidy packages into which sociologists tend to divide their existences. Because a man is acting within an organizational context this does not imply that he has not imported important values and habits from outside the organization; as we shall see presently, one attempt to explain the behaviour of factory workers draws heavily on evidence of this kind. We also need to investigate the relative permanence of values, attitudes and motivations as determinants of social behaviour. We cannot assume that the same aspects are paramount in terms of the actor's scale of priorities all the time. These various factors suggest that action theories of organizations may need to be constantly revised in order to keep up with the continual changes in the social action under consideration, a need which is directly derived from the premises of a social action approach. To speak of the typical actor in the typical situation is a problematic statement in terms of the sociologist's ability to identify and measure such typicality in the context of the changing social reality on which such typifications must be based.

Finally, in this section we should emphasize, as hopefully has become clear from the previous paragraph, that the social action approach is not a specific theory, but rather a way of looking at social phenomena. As Silverman puts it, 'The Action approach ... does not, in itself, provide a theory of organizations. It is instead best understood as a method of analysing social relations within organizations' (1970 p 147).

Processes of social action

In attempting to explain any social action we face the problem of how to encompass the variability of such action in terms of concepts which can also reveal the underlying stabilities and patterns involved. We are dealing with social processes and these may be defined as 'any identifiable repetitive pattern of social interaction'. In some systems and structural analyses this problem is overcome by concentrating on what is sometimes called the 'formal structure' of the organization. By assuming that the formal rules and procedures in fact control the way the organization operates, a consistent comparative analysis of organizations is made possible. The social action perspective questions the validity of relying on an uncritical acceptance of the effectiveness of such rules and procedures. As a result a social action analysis is often said to concentrate on the 'informal' workings of the organization, even though the value of segregating 'formal' and 'informal' in this way may be of limited usefulness.[3]

In general terms it is clear that organizational members do not operate within the organization in a purely autonomous fashion. Rather they are constrained by certain rules which are binding not only on themselves, but also on others in varying degrees through the organization. In their adherence to, and adaptation and disregard of, these rules they are probably supported by others in a similar position to themselves. In other words rules develop which determine the operation of the 'official rules'. In circumstances where no official rule exists then various rituals and 'informal' conventions are likely to develop and result in the formation of new social groupings within the organization. This complex social process is worked out in a number of ways. In simple and general terms we can represent it in the following manner.

We can conceive of each individual occupying a social role in terms of his formal contribution to the organization's functioning. These are most commonly designated by job descriptions which to a greater or lesser degree specify exactly what the individual's duties are. These must of course be defined in relation to the tasks and duties of other individuals occupying different or nominally similar social roles. Now knowledge of an individual's role in these terms may or may not be a reliable guide to the individual's actual behaviour. As a rough guide we can say that the more detailed and specific the 'official' role definition, as this is influenced by technology and the distribution of authority, then the more constrained will be the individual in playing out that role. But in times of rapid socal change or social conflict official role

---

[3] For a further discussion of this point see the article by Weeks (1973 pp 375–95).

definitions are likely to be less useful indicators of organizational functioning, as the whole basis of the interlocking relationships on which every individual depends has been disrupted. In this kind of situation previously effective notions of duties and obligations are over-thrown and confusion is likely to ensue until a new set of interrelation-ships has been established and stabilized. One advantage of a social action approach is that by studying the nature of these interrelationships it may be able to predict the likelihood of such breakdown.

Persons occupying nominally similar positions within an organization are likely, given a certain minimum opportunity for communication, to develop a group awareness of their situation which may in turn lead on to the construction of various strategies of action in pursuit of their particular ends. This will not necessarily involve co-operative action in terms of their collective attempt to attain a common goal. What is quite likely is that, whilst they share a common definition of their situation and have developed norms of behaviour which control their actions in an informal sense, they may nevertheless be competing with one another in the pursuit of a common goal. We shall consider this in more detail when we review Blau's work *The Dynamics of Bureaucracy*.

What we have been suggesting is that one basis for forming typifica-tions of social action is in terms of the membership groups which arise as a result of the individual's role in the organization. An important element in the development of such groups is socialization – the way in which individuals are transformed into group members with certain responsibilities, obligations, expectations and values. It is clearly some-what reckless to assume that individuals arrive 'socially naked' in the organization ready to be clothed with the social conventions of their particular work group. Although work is likely to be of considerable importance to the individual, in that it forms an essential basis for the pursuit of many other activities (e.g. by providing money and other resources for leisure activities), non-work derived values and attitudes are also a real source of influence on his interpretation of the work role. In this sense we can talk of the influence of reference groups which are not the individual's work groups (e.g. religious or political affiliations outside of work). The possibilities of a clash of values are, therefore, fairly high both between work and non-work group influences and between different groups of which the individual is a member within the organization. Thus in this way we can see how inconsistencies can develop between different aspects of the worker's behaviour – what is often called role-strain.

The way in which inconsistencies of this kind are dealt with by the individual poses the problem of the formation, change and management of self-identity by the individual. An examination of the way in which the individual adapts the presentation of his self to others, that is, the manner in which he manages the impression he projects towards others, involves a conception of personal characteristics as being rather more free-floating and socially influenced than the view presented by the traditional theories of personality theorists.

It is also important to note that the various levels of social action, influence and identity construction which we have identified are combined in a dynamic interrelationship. As we shall see in the next section it is not always necessary to take into account all of these levels to achieve an understanding of the situation. The concepts which are relevant will depend on the question one is seeking to answer; the broader the question the wider our analytical net must be cast.

A more systematic account of how such ideas can be incorporated into empirical research is provided by Silverman who suggests a 'path along which an Action analysis of organizations might proceed' (p 154). He identifies six major interrelated areas: the role-system and interaction patterns of the organization, the kind of involvements and variety of ends the actors pursue, the actors' definition of their situation and appraisal of the resources they have at their command, the typical actions of different actors and the meaning they attach to their action, the nature and source of the intended and unintended consequences of action, and finally, the changes in the involvement and ends of the actors and in the role system.

Some approaches to the study of social action in organizations

In this section we shall concentrate our attention on four forms of analysis of social action in organizations. They each offer in their different ways examples of the various levels of analysis which we distinguished in the previous section.

In distinguishing between the different approaches we can draw on a distinction suggested by Elger. He writes:

> Among critics of systems perspectives there can be discerned two somewhat distinctive approaches to the analysis of actors' perspectives and their impact on organizational arrangements, each having characteristic theoretical and substantive forms. One approach focuses on the typical 'projects of action' which individuals and groups pursue in the organization – implying an interest in relatively enduring collective aspirations and perspectives founded in common work and community experience. The other traditions attends in particular to the vicissitudes of the 'subjective careers' of organiza-

tion members — with detailed analyses of the transformation of definitions of self and situation as individuals orient themselves amid the
changing circumstances of an organizational career. (Elger 1975 p 100).

The first two of our case studies fall into Elger's first category and the
remaining two into his second.

'The affluent worker' and the 'orientation to work' approach

In their famous study of Luton car and engineering workers (1969),
Goldthorpe, Lockwood, Bechhofer and Platt took the actual objectives
of the workers and their definitions of the situation as of primary
importance in understanding the workers' behaviour. In this way,
as Brown (1973) has pointed out, they avoided the over-narrow conception of many 'human relations' theorists and the over-determinist
approach of theorists concerned with the influence of technology in
shaping workers' behaviour.

Goldthorpe *et al* took account of a wide range of possible influences
and came to the general conclusion that the 'instrumental orientation
to work' revealed by the workers was in large part a reflection of the
more general position that workers held in society. The workers
revealed no general aspiration to the middle-class view of a job as a
career, but rather they saw their work as a means by which they could
attain access to the pleasures and enjoyments of life — a house, a car,
etc. Their recently acquired affluence appeared to have little effect on
their political beliefs and in general there was no evidence of what has
been termed an *embourgeoisement* trend amongst the mass of workers.
Thus in a very significant way extra-organizational values played a
large part in determining attitudes to work.

Although the idea of explaining workers' behaviour in terms of their
orientation to work is a neat and appealing one, it does involve important problems. As Brown has pointed out, once we have discovered a
general orientation to work we must be careful not to assume that this
will serve as a blanket explanation covering all situations. For example,
we still need to consider the consistency with which such views are held
and also their relative endurance or stability. In other words, we must
not discount the possibility of priorities changing as contexts within
which the choices are made change. This will involve change not only in
the individual's non-work life, but also in the organization. Research by
Brown and Brannen (1970) amongst ship-building workers revealed
they had a marked concern for the intrinsic qualities of the work they
were involved in as well as an interest in contributing to the decision-
making processes of the firms. In this case the socialization processes

operating within the organization had a clear effect on any initial attitudes to work derived from outside.

As well as general shifts of this kind it is also important to take into account the context in which such priorities are expressed. Daniel (1973) has suggested that the 'orientation to work' approach as used in *The Affluent Worker* study makes two basic assumptions which may have only a limited validity. The first assumption is that 'the worker does have one overall, ordered, consistent set of needs or priorities in what he wants from a job, and that this set of priorities is manifested in all aspects of his occupational behaviour and choices' (Daniel 1973 p 43). The second assumption is that 'an increase in demands along one dimension must be at the expense of those along another' (Daniel 1973 p 43). If these assumptions are not valid we would expect workers' priorities to change as they encountered different circumstances and it would be quite feasible for workers to campaign for both greater material rewards from their work (Goldthorpe *et al*'s 'instrumental orientation') and for a greater intrinsic satisfaction from their work tasks.

In an analysis of two organizations, Daniel found that at the time of bargaining for a new wage deal the highest priority was allotted to material reward and the worker's relationship to management was seen as basically one of conflict. Nine months later, however, workers in the same firm were more concerned with the intrinsic factors associated with their actual job tasks and the workers' relationship to management was conceived of as co-operative and imbued with the spirit of team-work. The basic message of this research is that the priorities which workers hold are closely linked to the context of their evaluation. In some circumstances extrinsic factors assumed a greater importance whilst at other times intrinsic factors held pride of place.

The general cautionary note that can be drawn from this discussion is that whilst the orientation of the worker is undoubtedly an important factor in explaining organizational behaviour we must be careful not to exclude the influence of intra-organizational factors, nor must we assume that the orientations we identify are valid for all workers under all circumstances.[4]

[4] A contrasting study to that undertaken by Goldthorpe *et al*, (1969) may be found in Huw Beynon's Book *Working for Ford*. Whereas Goldthorpe *et al* base their findings on interview and questionnaire data, Beynon spent a number of years getting to know groups of workers, mainly in one factory. The result is an account of the influences and changes which affected those he studied. Special attention is given to the role of shop steward and Trades Union and little attempt is made to present the kind of sweeping generalizations offered by Goldthorpe *et al*.

A more recent study of a particular worksite, Chemco, is offered by Nichols and Armstrong (1976), and Nichols and Beynon (1977).

In *Workers Divided: A Study in Shopfloor Politics*, Nichols and Armstrong employ the concepts of control, solidarity and ideology to describe the actions of shopfloor workers and foremen and to outline the constraints placed on them by the workings of the wider economic environment and the particular policies of the firm itself. They reveal the complexity of factors influencing employees' attitudes and behaviour and the manner in which contradictions and inconsistencies are generated by the social structure of their situation, for example, by the grading and job assessment scheme introduced as the result of a productivity deal.

The coverage of these issues is extended in *Living with Capitalism: Class Relations and the Modern Factory* (1977), where the roles of management and foremen are considered more fully. Of particular interest are the foremen, split in their ideological commitment between 'traditionals', who are basically on-the-spot job controllers and trouble-shooters, and 'management-men' aspiring to an 'office job'. For the traditionals the new 'participatory' style of management promised with the productivity deal posed a direct threat to their accepted area of authority and in fact stimulated an increase in trade union membership amongst this group.

Of particular significance to us is the major aim underlying both these studies to incorporate the wider influences of the economic system *and* the individual perceptions and actions of workpeople into a single analysis. The result is not without its problems but the attempt is an interesting and worthwhile one.

From this broad concern with extra-organizational influences on social action we can now turn to a study which concentrates on the internal dynamics of organizational functioning.

The Dynamics of Bureaucracy and processes of social exchange

In his book *The Dynamics of Bureaucracy*, Peter Blau offered an action analysis of a Federal Law Enforcement Agency and an account of the interrelationships which developed between the formal rules of the Agency, the actual reaction of the members of the department, and the consequences this had for the social cohesion attained in the department and the exercise of authority. The work performance of the individual agent was estimated in terms of how well he carried out the detailed investigation of particular firms with regard to the complex legislation which it was his duty to enforce. His performance was dependent on the effectiveness and legal accuracy of the decisions he made about his cases. If he found himself in difficulties, facing a problem he could not solve, the official procedure required that he should seek advice from his supervisor. This raised particular problems for the agent, however, as the supervisor was also responsible for awarding his performance rating. As Blau puts it, 'Agents, however, were reluctant to reveal to their supervisor their inability to solve a problem for fear that their ratings would be adversely affected. The need for assistance, and the requirement that it be obtained only from the supervisor, put officials under cross-pressure' (1963 p 127).

The result of this clash of needs and desires resulted in the establishment of an 'unofficial' network of contacts amongst the agents themselves in which advice was sought and offered in informal consultations. Blau suggests that the basis of these consultations can be described and explained in terms of a mechanism of social exchange – an idea he develops from the work of Homans (1958).

> A consultation can be considered an exchange of values; both participants gain something, and both have to pay a price. The questioning agent is enabled to perform better than he could otherwise have done, without exposing his difficulties to the supervisor. By asking for advice, he implicitly pays his respect to the superior proficiency of his colleague. This acknowledgement of inferiority is the cost of receiving assistance. The consultant gains prestige, in return for which he is willing to devote some time to the consultation and permit it to disrupt his own work. (Blau 1963 p 130)

The conception of social interaction implied here is one based on the notion of calculable rewards and costs derived from the social interaction itself. The economic analogy is taken further in that it is predicted that continued interaction between individuals on this basis is likely to involve decreasing marginal rewards to the advisor and increasing costs to the agent seeking the advice. This mechanism of increasing costs to both parties is likely to place limits on the extent of the consultancy arrangement and the agent seeking advice may be eventually forced to seek it elsewhere, perhaps from agents of a lesser competence than his initial advisor. Certain difficulties arise, however, from considering all social interaction as aspects of social exchange. To begin with, the rates of costs and rewards involved will not be determined solely by the ongoing interaction of the participants; broader normative influences are likely to place considerable constraints on the terms of any exchange relationship. In one context an agent may be quite prepared to offer informal advice when no external threat to his own position is present, whereas under more adverse conditions he may withhold such useful information, e.g. when a supervisor is around. The assumption on which the actors make such calculations are, therefore, derived from influences which derive from outside the specific situation. In this way it is a mistake to consider the operation of social exchange outside the historical circumstances which led to the possibility of such interaction. In other words a concentration on the social exchange aspects of social interaction alone cannot account for the normative environment which makes the emergence of exchange relationships a probability.

In his discussion of the effects of the informal consultation system Blau lists seven main consequences, four of which may be considered as beneficial to the organization because they foster social cohesion, and three of which may be considered detrimental to the efficient running of the department. Of the beneficial consequences Blau notes, firstly, that the social cohesion of the group of agents was enhanced and that the co-operative nature of the consultations fostered a feeling of belongingness and unity. Secondly, consultation generally improved the quality of the decisions taken and gave added self-confidence to agents even when they were away from the office. Thirdly, the agents' interest in their work and their knowledge about it were increased. Fourthly, consultations stabilized the relationships in the department and forestalled conflict between agents, especially over the question of promotion.

The three detrimental effects Blau lists as follows. Firstly, the regular patterns of consultation which became established tended to reinforce the competence differentials upon which they were based. Thus the self-confidence of the agents that were consulted tended to increase as a result, whereas the self-confidence of those constantly seeking advice was lessened. Secondly, agents disliked being transferred to another part of the organization or department as they felt a loyalty to their existing group, and because established consultancy relationships would be lost and new ones have to be formed in a new environment. Thus the price of high social cohesion within the work group was a restriction on mobility within the organization. Thirdly, and possibly most important, the practice of informal consulting tended to weaken the authority of the supervisor. Not only was the supervisor consulted less frequently, but respect for his judgement declined when his advice was compared unfavourably with the advice available from the agent's more competent colleagues.

We can now see how an account based simply on the official policy of responsibility and delegation of authority would gloss over many important aspects of the department's functioning which have significant consequences for such wider issues as the job satisfaction of workers and mobility within the organization. We have also noted that, although the notion of social interaction as exchange is a provocative one for explaining the reward/cost basis of some interaction, it is inadequate as a general model of social behaviour since it assumes the existence of normative influences which are not derived directly from the social exchange itself.

Following this analysis of the normative power of work group interaction we can take another step down the analytical ladder to study the kinds of strategies actors are likely to adopt on the basis of the amount of knowledge they have of a situation.

Grounded theory, awareness contexts and the negotiated order

In this and the next case study we are moving into the second category of social action approaches suggested by Elger, that is, those which focus on the subjective careers of organizational members and are concerned with the analysis of 'the transformations of definition of self and situation as individuals orient themselves amid the changing circumstances of an organizational career' (Elger 1975).

Firstly, let us look at the work of Glaser and Strauss and their ideas of grounded theory and awareness contexts. By 'grounded theory' Glaser and Strauss are referring to a process of generating theoretical ideas from the data themselves. They write:

> We suggest as the best approach an initial, systematic discovery of the theory from the data of social research. Then one can be relatively sure that the theory will fit and work. And since the categories are discovered by examination of the data, laymen involved in the area to which the theory applies will usually be able to understand it, while sociologists who work in others areas will recognize an understandable theory linked with the data of a given area. (Glaser and Strauss 1967 pp 3–4)

In their study of the process of dying in a hospital, Glaser and Strauss (1965) developed the idea of 'awareness contexts', which they define in the following way: 'By the term *awareness context* we mean the total combination of what each interactant in a situation knows about the identity of the other and his own identity in the eyes of the other' (Glaser and Strauss 1964 p 670). Thus a dying patient who is aware that he is dying and who knows that others are aware of his impending death (the 'others' may be medical staff or members of his family) is demonstrating an 'open awareness context' with regard to his own situation.

Three other kinds of awareness context are noted by Glaser and Strauss. A 'closed' context exists when an actor does not know either the identity of the other actor or the other actor's view of his identity. A 'suspicion' awareness context is where one actor suspects the true identity of the other or the other's view of his own identity, or both. Lastly a 'pretence' awareness exists when both interactants are fully aware (i.e. as in an 'open' context), but pretend not to be. Using these four categories it is possible to build up a very comprehensive picture of the bases of knowledge from which each actor conducts his behaviour, provided we know each actor's own definition of his situation. The empirical variability which one might expect is affected, as Glaser and Strauss point out, by certain 'structural' constraints which operate to predispose the actors towards the adoption of one particular context. In the dying situation for example, the most usual context is the 'closed' one, and much of the hospital's organization, routine and staff training is geared towards producing and maintaining such a state of affairs.

Should the patient become aware of his true condition, however, then the awareness context will change, and it is one of the appeals of this approach that it is able to cope with, and in some measure account for, the dynamic element inherent in social interaction.

One criticism of this approach is that it does tend to assume that the identities of the interactants are unproblematic to the actors themselves. In many cases one could argue that it is the context which helps to define the individual's own identity when he himself is uncertain, rather than the case of an unambiguous identity being revealed or concealed in an interaction. The case of dying is a particularly clear cut one, a person either is or is not dying; in other words, this situation excludes, to a large extent, the problem of individuals with marginal or uncertain social identities.

Impression management and the negotiation of identity

The influence on self-identity of organizational forces has been a major concern of Erving Goffman, particularly in his studies of total institutions.[5] In a powerful passage he describes the effect on an individual entering the organization from the outside world:

> The recruit comes into the establishment with a conception of himself made possible by certain stable social arrangements in his home world. Upon entrance, he is immediately stripped of the support provided by these arrangements. In the accurate language of some of our oldest total institutions, he begins a series of abasements, degradations, humiliations and profanations of self. His self is systematically, if often unintentionally, mortified. He begins some radical shifts in his *moral career*, a career composed of the progressive changes that occur in the beliefs that he has concerning himself and significant others. (Goffman 1968 p 24)

This process of self-transformation is likely to be particularly severe in a mental hospital which is the reference of the above quotation, but the general tendency suggested by Goffman can be observed in other organizations and this kind of analysis highlights an important area for sociological investigation. As an individual progresses through whatever aspect of life he finds himself engaged in, he will undergo changes of identity in terms of how both he and others define his behaviour. This is not to view the individual as a lump of human clay being moulded by whatever social stamp happens to strike him. The individual has his own resources which he uses to make his own mark, and for Goffman action is an essay in self and impression management, but in a world which the actor must take for granted. Brittan has summed up Goffman's position well:

---

[5] Goffman explains what he means by a 'total institution' in the following passage:

> A basic social arrangement in modern society is that the individual tends to sleep, play, and work in different places, with different co-participants, under different authorities, and without an overall rational plan. The central feature of total institutions can be described as a breakdown of the barriers ordinarily separating these three spheres of life. First, all aspects of life are conducted in the same place and under the same single authority. Second, each phase of the member's daily activity is carried on in the immediate company of a large batch of others, all of whom are treated alike and required to do the same thing together. Third, all phases of the day's activities are tightly scheduled, with one activity leading at a prearranged time onto the next, the whole sequence of activities being imposed from above by a system of explicit formal rulings and a body of officials. Finally, the various enforced activities are brought together into a single rational plan purportedly designed to fulfil the official aims of the institution. (Goffman 1968 p 17)

Examples of total institutions would include orphanages, mental hospitals, prisons, army barracks, boarding schools and monasteries or convents.

Meaningful exchanges are, therefore, conducted in the belief that one's performance is subject to critical evaluation. In short, Goffman's dramatic image presupposes that action is oriented toward the other, so that the other is forced to accept the projected identity at its face — and performed — level. Goffman's image of interaction is presented in a manner which assumes that interaction is 'stabilized' by some form of framework which is accepted by all the parties to the interaction. Dramatic realization consists of making the most out of the possibilities in the given situation, while realizing that underpinning the performance is the intricate net of implicit and tacit rules and assumptions about the limits of interpretation in the role or the encounter. Ultimately, Goffman, while mapping out the intricacies of 'face work' etc., is committed to a view of action which places the actor very much at the mercy of the script. He cannot get beyond the script because, by definition, the script is the total world — the stage on which his performance is validated. (Brittan 1973 p 86)

What individuals make out of the possibilities Goffman discusses in his essay *The Underlife of a Public Institution*. Particularly interesting are what Goffman terms 'secondary adjustments', which 'represent ways in which the individual stands apart from the role and the self that were taken for granted for him by the institution' (Goffman 1968 p 172). Goffman suggests that those lowest down in the organization's structure are most likely to exhibit such behaviour, and he illustrates the way in which patients construct 'make do's' to compensate for missed possessions, and how they 'worked the system' to gain extra food or other luxuries.

Whilst Goffman does not present a view of the self as situationally determined in specific ways, neither does he suggest why some influences are more important than others in terms of a basic unity of personal attributes possessed by the individual. Rather he represents the self as a mixture of social influences which are displayed in different situations according to some scale of unspecified satisfactions which the individual derives from presenting them. This rather remote picture of the self is well expressed by Brittan:

Terms such as performances, fronts, regions, appearance etc. bear all the marks of externality, that is, they are used to refer to the self as perceived in action, they do not refer to the self as reflexive. However, Goffman does not necessarily suggest that this is all there is to the self. Implicit in the notion of impression-management is the belief that the performance will allow the individual to maximize his personal satisfactions and values. Thus the self is presented for consumption in the hope that the consumers will exchange other values which the individual needs to maintain his own identity (at least that identity which is being used as a bargaining issue). In this respect impression-management entails a commitment to fragmented experiences and a fragmented 'self'. (Brittan 1973 pp 147–8)

Thus at the most personal of levels, sociologically speaking, it is not possible, following Goffman's analysis, completely to ground social actions in a consistent and enduring notion of the self. As we have noted throughout the discussion of the various approaches covered in this section, we have always to take special account of the social environment existing prior to the interaction we are studying. Although this environment changes as a result of the interaction which takes place, it is difficult to detail precisely where the major influence originates. In line with the general assumption of a social action approach, the various levels of analysis themselves appear in a dynamic interaction. In some situations, however, the bases of the social realities underlying such action become clearer and the next part is devoted to a consideration of some of those situation.

Change, conflict and the emergence of normative order in organizations

When social change or social conflict arises in an organization it is often a very good indicator of the kinds of social realities which underlie the organization's previous functioning. In the words of Berger and Luckmann, disruption of the normal routine in a major way tends to reveal the different 'symbolic universes' on which that routine was based. Berger and Luckmann define symbolic universe in the following way: 'The symbolic universe provides order for the subjective apprehension of biographical experience. Experiences belonging to different spheres of reality are integrated by incorporation in the same, overarching universe of meaning' (Berger and Luckmann 1967 p 115). Thus within one organization different groups of individuals may subscribe to different symbolic universes although compromising their positions in terms of the practicalities of work. When social change or conflict arises, however, the symbolic differences may be revealed in such a way as to make the original compromise situation difficult to re-establish. The strategies which individuals and groups adopt to protect and retain their own preferred reality will depend on the resources they have at their command and, particularly, on their location in the authority hierarchy of the organization. We can now turn to a number of studies which have focused on the origins and effects of change and conflict to fill out empirically these notions of structure, resources and strategies.

In a well known study entitled *The Management of Innovation*, Burns and Stalker (1966) spell out in some detail the effects of firms changing from a 'mechanistic' to an 'organismic' style of management. In simple terms, the 'organismic' style was a much more flexible arrangement than the more rigid division of labour and distribution of authority of the 'mechanistic' style which it replaced. In many cases the new system was not welcomed by some groups in the organizations who favoured a return to the old familiar system. As Burns and Stalker point out:

> . . . [when] the situation is alive with opportunities for advancement and transfer, [it is] alive also with actual or potential threats to the status, power, chances of success or actual livelihood of some of the members of it. In Mr Blake's firm this was so marked a feature of the organization that one junior manager confessed himself, along with others at his level, reluctant to seek promotion into a position in which he would be more dangerously exposed; he pointed for justification to the very high turnover that had been occurring among the senior management. (Burns and Stalker 1966 p 132)

When opportunities and threats arise in the same situation, Burns (1955) has suggested in another context that two kinds of group develop: one which is endeavouring to gain by any changes (cabals) and the other which favours a stabilization of the situation and a possible return to the old pattern (cliques). Membership of a clique represents a measure of failure in the performance of one's organizational role:

> Cliques in factories, offices and universities; in clubs and societies; among street neighbours, schoolchildren, service units and others are known as cliques only in relation to that specific status . . . the role that involves clique membership is one that accommodates to a degree of failure in the status. The clique in the factory then appears as an organized retreat from occupational status. (Burns 1955 p 474)

Cabals on the other hand exist for success; they differ from cliques in a number of ways:

> The essential points distinguishing cabals from cliques are: (1) there are real status distinctions involved between cabal members. Leadership is important, and proximity to the leader is important; (2) the function of cabal membership is neither to redress occupational failure, nor to gain reassurance, but to promote further occupational

success outside the cabal; (3) the relationship of the cabal to the outer milieu is not one of withdrawal or rejection, but of power, in which the cabal attempts to restructure situations and values in the interests of its members. (Burns 1955 p 480)

Membership of cliques and cabals is likely to be particularly apparent during times of change, and the values and actions of these two kinds of group reflect different strategies based on the resources, both material and social, which the members believe they have at their command.

An interesting study of industrial conflict is offered by Lane and Roberts (1971) in their book, *Strike at Pilkingtons*. Although we cannot hope to do anything more than scratch the surface with regard to the reason for strikes, Lane and Roberts describe in interesting detail how an apparently trivial incident over the miscalculation of a wage payment led to a large-scale industrial dispute. They describe how the various parties involved in the dispute developed their own explanations and strategies in pursuit of their particular ends. The management was concerned to resume normal working as soon as possible, whilst only agreeing to the workers' demands to the minimum extent possible to attain that end.

The workers themselves were 'represented' by two competing groups. Firstly, the Trade Union to which most of the men belonged, the General and Municipal Workers Union, and, secondly, in opposition to this 'official' body there developed a Rank and File Strike Committee who claimed to represent the majority of the workers. The question of which group had the most support is less interesting than the different strategies each adopted in pursuit of its goals. The Rank and File Committee justified its action in terms of the mass support of the workers, whereas the Trade Union played on its position as 'officially appointed' representative of its members. The outcome of the strike was determined by the interaction between these three groups and was also influenced by such outside factors as the mass media.

The dispute not only crystallized attitudes and values held by these large groups of individuals, but it also made some of the strikers aware of the delicate basis on which social order in the organization was founded. This was particularly the case in relation to the exercise of authority in the organization. As Lane and Roberts write:

The modern attitude to authority was well expressed by those workers who, in the act of striking, experienced feelings of elation and liberation. These feelings are, we suspect, extremely common amongst those who spark off a wildcat strike. They are feelings characteristic of those who have momentarily dissolved the shackles of authority. But if these feelings are positive in the situation of striking, they are negative in the longer run for while they are saying 'down with this', they are not at the same time saying 'up with that'. No alternative is being offered, so that when the strike is over they return to the same fundamental system of authority that existed before the strike. (Lane and Roberts 1971 pp 229–30)

Thus mere experience of the possibility of a different form of organization is usually not enough to allow the implementation of permanent changes. The outcome of such clashes when viewed from an action perspective has to take account of the differentials in the exercise of power which in a basic sense define the situation for all concerned in it.

One reaction to a condition of powerlessness may be industrial sabotage. This is considered in an article by Taylor and Walton (1971), 'Industrial sabotage: motives and meanings'. Industrial sabotage is defined as 'that rule-breaking which takes the form of conscious action or inaction directed towards the mutilation or destruction of their work environment' (p 219). Taylor and Walton suggest that there are three basic types of sabotage, each with its own meaning and motives. The first type involves individual and collective attempts to reduce frustration and tension and is usually spontaneous. The second variety attempts to facilitate or ease the work process and, therefore, involves some planning and usually has a highly specific target. The third type can be seen as an attempt to assert control and, therefore, involves a direct challenge to authority and is normally well planned, and/or co-ordinated. Thus although different motives may underlie broadly similar actions we can see the way in which specific behaviours demonstrate particular motives. As C. Wright Mills (1940) puts it, 'stable vocabularies of motives link anticipated consequences and specific actions' (p 906).

Structural circumstances are suggested by Taylor and Walton which are likely to foster the various types of motive which they distinguish. Type one represents the action of a powerless individual or group and is particularly common in a non- or little-unionized plant. The second type is most common where the worker has to 'take on the machine' in order to push up earnings; and the third type usually arises where the organization has a history of militant activity. We can, therefore, see how the resources at the individual's command are linked to the structure of his situation, which in turn tends to channel his activity into one particular form with the appropriate motive.

Conclusion

From what has been said about social action approaches to the study and understanding of organizations we can see that the end result is not a neat and tidy theory about human behaviour, but rather a collection of ideas about why certain things tend to happen in certain situations. This is what one would expect when we remember that a social action analysis of an organization is not so much a theoretical as a methodological perspective. It is a series of prescriptions about studying social phenomena in a certain way. As such new ideas and insights are bound to be required as the conditions under study themselves change.

Neither does the social action approach claim to have a monopoly on the truth. It does suggest that some other approaches involve a misrepresentation of the social reality they are considering, for the reasons given earlier in this chapter. Systems and structural theories have a part to play in the overall analysis of organizational functioning, however, perhaps particularly with regard to pinpointing areas of organizational behaviour of special interest and significance.

The social action approach is not without difficulties itself, however, and we can end this chapter by considering two in particular. The first is concerned with the measurement of actors' perceptions of social situations and the meanings they attribute to those situations. It is one thing to speak of typical actors in typical situations, but it is quite another to clearly establish that you have measured social perceptions and situations accurately. Some of the difficulties involved in this area are discussed by Silverman in the final chapter of his book (1970 pp 215–32).

Following on from that first difficulty is another, which in some ways is a more fundamental one. As was mentioned earlier in the chapter, the subjective intentions of the actors involved in a situation may prove inadequate as criteria for understanding the social significance of that action. As Pivcević (1972) has put it, 'what makes an action a social action is not its subjectively intended meaning, but a set of circumstances in which it is performed. A social action presupposes a *social setting*' (p 346). It is in accounting for the origin of the social setting and in particular the distribution of power within that setting, that the social action approach often falls short of its own goals.

CHAPTER 6

Graeme Salaman

Roles and rules

Introduction

The structuralist perspective argues that organizations have an observable and measurable factual status which need not involve reference to the activities, intentions and points of view of the members (who can, in terms of such a perspective, confidently be disregarded because the regularity is taken as a consequence of, either individuals' conformity with shared norms, or their commitment to an emergent series of negotiated definitions and meanings). This approach obviously needs to explain how and why individual members conform with these definitions, regulations, ordinances or instructions. The concept that is typically used to connect the individual member to the organization's prescriptions and dictates is *role*:

> . . . human beings, as the result of occupying . . . statuses, play such roles as father, mother, factory worker, manager, friend and soldier. All these are separate and well defined roles . . . What makes the role of such importance is the fact that *it largely determines how human beings will act in certain areas* . . . the role of factory worker implies certain duties and certain rewards, certain relationships to management and its representatives, and other relationships to fellow workers. (Schneider 1969 p 14, *my emphasis*.)

But why do social actors follow the prescriptions of their roles? Schneider's answer to this is that role performance is achieved either through the individual internalizing the standards and expectations of a particular role so that he conforms because he personally considers such behaviour as meritorious and proper, or through his exposure to pressure to conform with expectations, backed up by the threat of sanctions. Predictably, in view of their systems orientation, Katz and Kahn give a similar answer to this question. They find the solution to lie in the complex series of relationships in which organizational members are involved and on which they depend for assistance and approval.

> All members of a person's role set depend upon his performance in some fashion; they are rewarded by it, judged in terms of it, or require it in order to perform their own tasks. Because they have a stake in his performance they develop beliefs and attitudes about what he should and should not do as part of his role. The prescriptions and proscriptions held by members of a role set are designated *role expectations*; in the aggregate they help to define his role, the behaviours which are expected of him . . . The crucial point (for our theoretical view) is that the activities which define a role are maintained through the expectations of members of the role set, and that these expectations are communicated or 'sent' to the focal person. (Katz and Kahn 1966 p 175)

> Our first requirement in linking individual and organization is to locate the individual in the total set of ongoing relationships and behaviours comprised by the organization. The key concept for doing this is office . . . Associated with each office is a set of activities, which are defined as potential behaviours. These activities constitute the role to be performed, at least approximately by any person who occupies that office. (Kahn *et al* 1964 p 13)

The concept role is likely to be of relevance in attempts to explain the sort of regularity and patternedness that organizations reveal. In this way the behaviour, say, of a policeman or doctor or bureaucrat can be explained in terms of the nature of their work roles. Certain behaviour is expected of those who fill such positions, and their actions are interpreted in the light of these expectations. In this way an organization *could* be seen as a systematic clustering of official work roles, oriented around the pursuit of some goal. Such a view finds clear expression in Merton's work, when he writes:

> A formal, rationally organized social structure involves clearly defined patterns of activity in which, ideally, every series of actions is functionally related to the purposes of the organization. In such an organization there is integrated a series of offices, of hierarchized statuses, in which inhere a number of obligations and privileges closely defined by limited and specific rules. Each of these offices contains an area of imputed competence and responsibility. (Merton 1952 p 361)

Role is relevant to our understanding of organizations not simply because of the way in which it has been used to explain the claimed regularity which the term organizational structure refers to, but also because, as Hickson remarks, a great deal of structural interest in organizations reveals a marked preoccupation with the degree of role specificity. He argues that underlying the ostensibly discrete and diverse 'plethora' of theories dealing with the nature and determinants of organizational structure there is discernible a convergence of interest in 'the specificity (or precision) of role prescription and its converse, the range of legitimate discretion' (Hickson 1973 p 108). Hickson argues that for many students of organizations, variations in organizational structure have been conceptualized in terms of variations in the content of organizational roles.

An alternative conception of role to the one outlined above (which entails a definition of role in terms of learning and fulfilling the expectations of others) involves an emphasis on the constantly on-going processes of '... negotiation – the processes of give-and-take, of diplomacy, of bargaining – which characterizes organizational life' (Strauss *et al* 1973 p 304). For Strauss and others a role is not simply an acting out of the rules and constraints that operate on a particular hierarchic position, but a constantly changing negotiated product of the interactions of different purposes and priorities within a framework of rules and constraints. Such priorities do not derive simply from the organization, or *its* objectives and goals, but from the personal identities and values of the people involved. The structural view of roles sees them as the result of learning and fulfilling others' expectations and demands. The interactionist view of roles, as represented here by Strauss, sees them as a result of interactions between members' different, and conflicting, interests and capacities.

In short, at a general level the concept role is worthy of consideration and critical scrutiny because it has been employed to explain the ways in which organizational structure is achieved and displayed, and because, through its capacity to mediate between the organization and the individual, it enables the conceptual jump to be made from individual activity to structural regularity.

Some more specific utilizations of the concept in studies of organizations are considered below.

1 Organizational studies employing the concept role

The established use of the concept in organizational studies has already been suggested in the earlier discussion of the structuralist (or systems) view of role. This theoretical approach is particularly liable to focus on what can be called 'official' organizational roles. This view has obvious links with Weber's view of bureaucracy as characterized by a series of hierarchically arranged offices, hedged around with rules and procedures emphasizing, and maintaining, a high level of impersonality, which emerges as a result of members complying with bureaucratic demands and prescriptions rather than following their own, personal whims and impulses.

This 'formal' conception of organizational roles does have the advantage of emphasizing the existence and nature of certain (official) sorts of organizational controls and restrictions which are of undoubted importance in determining the behaviour of organizational members. But obviously these are not the only, or even necessarily the major, constraints to which organizational members are exposed.

However, from such an approach certain issues are likely to be seen as problematic. If a role consists of the formal or official requirements and expectations of people in various organizational positions, then an obvious possibility is that these expectations might be inconsistent, heterogeneous and differentiated. And so the possiblity of role conflict is a natural topic of enquiry for those who see organizational roles in these terms. Studies of role conflict will be discussed later. Another possibility, of course, is that members of the organization as incumbents of organizational positions might not know what is expected of them; in such an exigency the problem is not conflict, but uncertainty and ignorance. This too has constituted a topic for sociological discourse and practical, managerial, concern.

But we have seen that discussions of organizational structure tend to confuse the symbolic, intentional aspects of organizational structure with actual behavioural regularities and patterns, and this distinction is also apparent in discussions of organizational roles. The implication of the approach described above was that roles consisted of the 'formal', official, definitions, descriptions and expectations (with the possibility that such expectations may be conflicting, or that persons may be more or less aware of what was properly expected of them). But an alternative use of role is to consider and analyse the actual behavioural regularities that members of the organization display. For example, Donald Roy (1960) describes certain themes and topics around which regular interaction occurred among the machine operatives he worked with. These constituted the structure of their interaction, which were laden with significance for those involved. Roy notes that the continuation of these interactional themes and topics required, or could be seen as, a

'. . . social structure of statuses and roles. This structure may be discerned in the carrying out of the various informal activities which provide the content of the sub-culture of the group. The times and themes were performed with a system of roles which formed a sort of pecking heirarchy' (Roy 1960 p 218).

The work of Roy and others shows that the so-called informal aspects of organizational activity are by no means lacking in permanence and regularity. Many of the behaviours and attitudes displayed by workers in the factory in which Roy was involved did not derive from any formal or official expectations or demands, but from the work group. Katz says, '. . . considerable structuring of the work situation is done by the workers themselves' (Katz 1973 p 199).

But these regularities that Roy and others claim to have discerned, or classified, although a result of the behaviours and intentions of members of the organization, and their expectations and definitions, are not necessarily seen in these terms by those who produce them. The people concerned were not aware, presumably, that by taking an overall view of their interactions it might be possible to talk of 'window time', or 'banana time', or that the expectations they personally held about another worker's behaviour might be seen as constituting a coherent *role*; they probably thought that 'George (or whoever) was always like that', or that certain things were amusing, interesting, distracting, or fun. However, Rose Giallombardo investigates the nature and determinants of '. . . the informal social structure' (Giallombardo 1970 p 398) of inmates of a women's prison. Giallombardo shows how organizational roles relate to the wider society and may not be understood merely by reference to the isolated, closed organization. She argues that the system of roles observable among the female inmates, although naturally centred upon the problems and conditions of imprisonment, is directly related to extra-organizational sex role definitions. This study is particularly interesting, however, because the roles Giallombardo describes are *also recognized and delineated by the inmates*; the Runyonesque roles she names and describes — squares, jive bitches, boosters, snitchers, and so on — are derived directly from the inmates. She says: 'The social roles distinguished and labelled by the female inmates constitute the basic structure of social relationships formed by the inmates in response to the problems of a prison commitment' (Giallombardo 1970 p 406). This issue will be raised again in a later section of this chapter.

Another way in which the concept role has been employed in studies of organizations stems more from occupational sociology, or the sociology of the professions. This speciality has traditionally shown a great deal of interest in the nature, development and transmission of occupational cultures, knowledge and skills, and thus in the content of occupational, or professional roles. The implications of such an interest for the study of organizations should be apparent: many organizations employ large numbers of expert, professional staff; and some organizations consist, primarily, of professionals (hospitals, universities, architects' or lawyers' offices and so on). All these people are likely to be involved in an occupational role which may conflict with their organizational expectations and demands. This suggestion argues that persons committed to a body of occupational values, expectations and aspirations will routinely experience conflict and frustration within their employing organization. This follows from the contrast between organizational forms and techniques of control and occupational or professional forms of control. Control and regularity among professionals are achieved — in the face of highly non-routine problems and tasks involving complex technology and variable and unstable raw materials — through internalized and shared beliefs and commitments, rather than through bureaucratic control. This employment of the concept focuses attention on some processes that are typically seen as inherent in applications of the concept role, namely socialization and reference group. Gouldner (1970) suggests that position really means identity, and that individuals can have more than one identity, or can be located in more than one system of personally significant expectations. In an organizational context the organizational identity (or position) is predominantly salient — such as personnel officer, or student, or whatever — but this is not to deny that other identities may be relevant and important. So a personnel officer may also be an occupational psychologist and a member of the British Psychological Society, and a student may be coloured, and all these identities will have implications both for the individual and the organization. The point is that by seeing role in terms of expectations attached to identities rather than organizational positions, Gouldner usefully points out the possibility that individuals can see themselves and be seen as having a number of different identities. The problem that follows from this approach is not how the expectations attached to an organizational role may be vague, or unknown, or conflicting, but that the individuals who make up the organizational membership may be involved in numerous conflicting roles.

Not surprisingly therefore, such an approach, by focussing attention on the variety of salient roles that may be filled by a member of an organization at the same time, is particularly concerned with considering and explaining the processes whereby a person becomes acquainted with, knowledgeable about, and committed to a system of expectations and values other than those he is immediately exposed to. Hence the interest in processes of professional socialization, recruitment and control that is typically displayed by studies of professions, or professionals in organizations. Chapter 3 discussed the possibility that conflict between professional and organizational roles may have been somewhat overstated. This is not to deny that professionals or experts may feel unhappy and frustrated, but it is to suggest that the simple notion that professionalism and bureaucracy are in every way incompatible, may have been overemphasized. For one thing it has been argued that professionals need a degree of bureaucratic control to ensure smooth and efficient communications and functioning. In a similar vein Elliott has argued that the traditional idea of conflict between professional and organization may stem from the notion of the professional as a gentleman who was loath to be subordinate, rather than from any actual or necessary professional autonomy. He argues that certain aspects of Weber's criteria of bureaucracy are quite applicable to professionals too, and that not only does non-organizational private professional practice involve the professional in various constraints, but involvement in an organization can be seen as '. . . insulating professionals from pressures they would face in private practice and providing them with the means to perform their professional tasks in relative security' (Elliott 1972 p 99).

But it isn't as though professionals in organizations merely constituted a compliant aggregate of individuals who, albeit unwillingly, were finally amenable to the constraints and regulations that constituted organizational structure. As was noted earlier, Hall's research argues that professionals have a capacity to affect the way in which things are done within organizations — and possibly even to play some part in deciding what should be done, and to whom. This argument is clearly expressed in Strauss *et al*'s article (1973). These authors argue that they discerned negotiative processes occurring among a variety of different professional (rather than organisational) conceptions of proper forms of treatment, the significance of various symptoms, and so on. In other words, as Strauss *et al* put it, '. . . differential professional training, ideology, career and hierarchical position, all affect the negotiation' (Strauss *et al* 1973 p 318).

This difference between role as organizational office and role as the personal identities of organizational personnel as expounded by Strauss can also be seen as reflecting on the one hand a view of organizations as essentially consensual phenomena where, if expectations are known and consistent, conflict should be minimal, and on the other hand, a view of organizations as arenas of constant conflict, negotiation and compromise where individuals attempt, with greater or lesser success depending on their power within the organization and their location within a societal stratification system, to achieve their own ends and priorities, which derive from their extra-organizational identities.

The use of the latter, interactionist conception of role in studies of professionals in organizations is not accidental: the study of employed professionals and of the conflicts between the various expectations and priorities to which they are exposed, leads easily to a view of role that stresses conflict, negotiation and compromise between conflicting values and aspirations. Equally it is likely that the study of ordinary members of organizations – managers and bureaucrats – who are, ostensibly, exposed to a single, organizational, system of expectations and demands leads to a structural conception of role, as outlined earlier.

The formal or official organizational role is used to refer to demands and constraints that derive from senior members of the organization and from the official, and quite often written, organizational specifications and prescriptions. The informal organizational role is used to refer to peers' and colleagues' expectations and demands. The professional or occupational role is used to describe the way in and extent to which some organizational members are controlled by other members of the occupation or profession not present in their employing organization. Typically these different sources of control over organizational members have been seen in terms of different definitions of the concept role, and have led to an interest in different issues.

The concept role then is used in analyses of organizations to refer to the fact that organizational members are controlled through their conformity with the expectations of others. If role is to be used in this sense (rather than merely as another term for organizational position or location) then clearly not every member of an organization has a role, or at least, there is evident a considerable variation in the extent to which organizational members are controlled through learning and obeying others' expectations.

The group for whom these remarks are particularly relevant is, of course, worker members of organizations. These members are frequently controlled directly, for example, through the speed of an assembly line, tight supervision, rigid and explicit rules, bonus schemes, piece work, financial penalties, and so on. This is not to argue that all workers are inevitably controlled in this way: there are important exceptions, for example, skilled workers. However, for many worker members of the organization, control comes not from others' expectations, but directly.

Why is there this difference in forms of organizational control?

Role-type control is less commonly employed with workers in organizations because senior members of organizations (and, possibly, the
workers themselves) see the workers as being in conflict with the goals
and reward system of the enterprise.

When the concept role is used in discussions of organizations there is
at least a suggestion of some degree of willing conformity with organizational, or occupational, expectations and demands; there is some
possibility of the role incumbent choosing between expectations, establishing priorities, or even disobeying. For lower level members of the
organization such 'freedom' is often lacking. The work behaviour of
shop-floor members of many industrial organizations, for example, is
governed not by expectations, or even demands, but by the speed of the
assembly line; and the nature and content of their organizational 'roles'
are determined by negotiations between union and management over
the work study assessments, timings and evaluation.

Variations in autonomy are directly related to the amount of power
individuals and groups manage to achieve and retain within organizations. Discretion and autonomy by definition, if they are genuine,
mean that predictability and regularity are — or may be — reduced. And
it is capacity to cope with the uncertainty that results which is a source
of intra-organizational power as Hickson points out.

The fact that organizational jobs vary in the extent to which they
are prescribed should not be taken, as Katz argues, as meaning that the
work behaviour of managers and workers is necessarily restricted pro-
portionately to the prescriptions to which they are exposed. Even in
the most tightly defined shop floor there is still '. . . a considerable por-
tion of the worker's life within the work organization (which is) *undefined*' (Katz 1973 p 191). In other words the more tightly a job is
defined the more likely it is that workers will develop an informal work
group culture which '. . . is a manifestation of autonomy within the
confines of the organization' (Katz 1973 p 191). This is an interesting
suggestion, and it might be true that workers do sometimes, under
some circumstances, manage to generate a certain culture and pattern
of relationships at work. But this should not be taken as implying that
such work groups are a feature of every work place, or that even when
they do — or can — exist the benefits are such as to outweigh the costs
and deprivations the worker may suffer. In some cases management
may make deliberate efforts to obstruct the development of shop floor
interactions or 'unofficial' organizational roles.

2 Difficulties

Certain points emerge from the previous section. For one thing, it is still not clear exactly what roles are, or how they can be recognized and described. Is a role actual behaviour, as observed, described and categorized (as role behaviour) by some observer/sociologist? But others have used role to refer to the *expectations* that a person is exposed to. This distinction between behaviour and expectation relates to the distinction mentioned earlier between formal and informal structure, or between organizational structure as a symbolic representation of senior organizational members' intentions and purposes, and actual regularities in the behaviours of organizational members.

But what is meant by an expectation? As Dahrendorf has remarked, at least three sorts of role expectation may be distinguished: 'must', 'shall' and 'can' expectations. These differ in the '... degree to which their associated expectations are compulsory' (Dahrendorf 1968 pp 41—2). A further problem is, how do we know what these expectations are that are supposed to be attached to an organizational office? It is unjustifiable to argue that a role exists — or that expectations governing role behaviour exist — merely because the sociologist thinks he can discern some regularity. Behaviour can be predictable and display ordered properties and yet not be in accordance with some moral rule or expectation.

Finally it might be rather difficult to decide when a social position (or organizational office) exists. There is a danger of circularity if it is argued that a role is the expectations attached to a social position and that a social position exists in terms of particular clusters of expectations. As Harding has put it, 'When do human activities become sufficiently distinctive and structured to warrant description in terms of social position and roles? No role analysis has yet developed definitive criteria of what represents a social position' (Bradbury *et al* 1972 p 42).

3 Role as expectation

It is generally considered that a minimal definition of role would refer to the fact that: 'A man's behaviour ... is to be explained at least partly in terms of normative expectations belonging to his social positions' (Bradbury *et al* 1972 p 43). But this too raises difficulties: Who hold these expectations; Is there consensus among the expecters?

The expectations sometimes derive as much from the omniscient sociological observer as from those with whom the role incumbent is likely to come into contact. This is a central element in Cicourel's criticisms of traditional usages of role and norm, which rely, he argues, on a confusion between the *researcher's* framework and the *actor's* interpretative procedures (which are also employed in an unexplicated way by the researcher in his academic description and analysis). But if the focus of attention is on the actor, and what he takes to be, and classifies as, relevant expectations and demands, which expecters are to be considered?

If the idea that the ordered properties of persons' behaviours and interactions follows from their (more or less) conformity with others' expectations it is necessary to consider not only, who are these expecters, but also what is the nature of their expectations and demands, and are they always consistent? Gross *et al* carried out a systematic analysis of the content of a particular organizational role. Taking as their central interest the existence — or extent of — consensus over role expectations in the case of the school superintendent they argue that frequently consensus over role expectations has been assumed rather than demonstrated. Their findings suggest that serious disagreements and conflicts concerning the definition of the appropriate work for school superintendents exists. Consequently the superintendent experiences conflict in coping with, reacting to and resolving these conflicting demands.

In their study of the relationship between role conflict, ambiguity and psychological stress, Kahn *et al* note how a focal person (the role incubent they have chosen to study) is faced with a number of individuals (the role set) whose expectations are salient for his behaviour. Not only is some degree of disagreement over the focal person's behaviour possible, but those holding the expectations might not be competent at communicating their expectations to the role incumbent, or the role incumbent may be unclear as to who has a 'legitimate' right (within the organization) to try and influence his performance (Kahn *et al* 1964).

The crucial question is: who are the people who have the capacity to impose their definitions and expectations on the actor? Certainly Gross *et al* are in error in, as Dahrendorf puts it, '. . . attributing the force of social norms to the uncertain basis of majority opinions', for this makes '. . . the fact of society subject to the arbitrariness of questionnaire responses' (Dahrendorf 1968 p 48).

Pugh (1973) utilizes the distinction Gross *et al* make between what an actor takes to be legitimate and illegitimate expectations that members of his role set have of his behaviour. As well as generally clarifying the discussion of role and its associated concepts, Pugh is also concerned to classify different types of role conflict. The role conflict discussed in this article is 'single role conflict' (Pugh 1973 p 240), but it involves more than just '. . . conflict of expectations concerning a single position due to the differing expectations of members of the social system with whom the individual interacts' (Pugh 1973 p 239). The conflict Pugh describes does not derive from any disagreement over the legitimacy of conflicting role expectations, but from disagreement as to which of a number of perfectly legitimate demands are relevant for the case in hand. This Pugh describes as *role-activation conflict.*

Underlying all the criticisms and anxieties listed above (concerning the nature of expectations, the possibility of people being exposed to conflicting and ambiguous expectations, etc.) there is a more basic difficulty. Too often role is used to describe a process of conformity. Now sophisticated utilizations – such as the interactionist conception of Gross *et al* – note, indeed focus on, the possibility of persons being exposed to conflicting, inconsistent expectations, but the individuals are still seen as very much at the receiving end of – admittedly conflicting – expectations. A hint of an alternative approach is contained in Pugh's article where he suggests the possiblity of actors considering the relevance of rival legitimations. This article moves away from the sort of crude model described by Levinson, and points the way towards a view of roles as involving *creativity* rather than mere *conformity*. This alternative approach, which lies behind the criticisms listed above, sees actors not as conforming with what others expect of them, but as '. . . interpretative and purposive agents within their social world, [thus] role-taking is not only the result of pre-existing social norms, but also provides their source and continuing support' (Urry 1970 p 360). Urry continues: 'Actions do not thus simply follow from the norms and the role expectations associated with a particular group, but depend upon the interpretations made by actors of their experience within their world' (Urry 1970 p 360).

This view of role-taking as a creative exercise which actors or organizational members engage in in terms of their 'experience within their world' avoids the restricted and passive conception of organizational members as displaying in their ordered, regular behaviours, conformity with organizational rules and expectations. Such a view does not deny the importance of organizational rules, others' demands, etc., but neither does it ignore the processes of interpretation, negotiation and compromise that lie behind the production of actions and behaviours. Such performances reveal these demands and rules, and reconstitute them. In this sense although they are external to the individual they are only realized (interpreted or changed) through their application by individuals.

A further advantage of such a conception of organizational role — as referring to the processes of perception, definition and interpretation of expectations and demands in terms of actors' conceptions of their place in, and view of, the world and the organization — is that it permits the introduction of extra-organizational factors and influences. One of the drawbacks with the concept of role when it is simply concerned with describing various sorts of organizational or occupational expectations, is that it is heavily restricted to investigating the 'scripts' supplied by the institution in question, and therefore not only fails to consider how they are used, but also does not consider how such behaviour may be influenced by persons' location in, and experience of, the world. It is unusual to analyse the behaviour of manual worker members of organizations in terms of their organizational role because they are controlled to a considerable extent not through expectations, but through control mechanisms which reveal the managerial assumption that workers are *not* committed to their employing organization, or are not socialized into sharing managerial priorities. Workers' priorities, interests and moralities tend to derive from outside their employing organization.

Conceptions of interest do not derive merely from passively conforming to role expectations and priorities; they also derive from persons' conceptions and experience of their location in the division of labour, or the class system. This notion of organizational members pursuing interests when they interpret and define proper or appropriate behaviour, rather than merely performing roles, has the advantage not only of relating organizational events to larger societal processes, it also draws attention to the possibility of group rather than merely individual (role) conflict. The idea or organizational roles frequently carries the implication of the organization as an integrated, or emergent, production with all members (actors) contributing their bit. This conception is probably particularly attractive to managers or to those who consider non-industrial organizations or the managerial side of industrial organizations. It is far less applicable or attractive to those members or organizations whose work experience leads them to conceptualize the enterprise in terms of conflict rather than co-operation.

As *role* usually draws attention to a certain level of moral consensus and focuses on the processes whereby persons *want* to attend to the expectations of certain others, and plays down the possibility of manipulation, exploitation and conflicting interests, so organizational *rules* are used to overcome 'inadequate' motivation and members' recalcitrance and to achieve some degree of orderliness and predictability when commitment and motivation *cannot* be assumed. But rules do not constitute the only sort of organizational control: they can be seen as a somewhat liberal control mechanism since at least they allow for the luxury of interpretation and discretion in their use, as will be seen. Some forms of organizational control simply eliminate the need for rules by *eliminating any decision-making on the part of organizational personnel.* This can be achieved for example, through automation, mechanization or centralized decision-making. Perrow even argues that hiring professionals is equivalent to mechanization in that both reduce the 'necessity' for organizational rules. He writes:

> Buying and installing machines . . . is one way of reducing the number of rules in an organization. The rules are built into the machine itself, and the organization pays for those rules in the price of the machine. A quite similar means of reducing the number of written rules is to 'buy' personnel who have complex rules built into them. We generally call these people professionals. (Perrow 1972 p 27)

Rules are not simply methods of over-coming recalcitrance. They also include attempts to co-ordinate situations where organizational members lack adequate knowledge of events and processes. Rules are often devised to control behaviour so as to achieve a smooth flow of goods and services between members and departments.

Organizations involve a degree of deliberately created, sustained and monitored regularity. It is this orderliness which in Weber's and other's view gives organizations their distinctive features.

> . . . the purely bureaucratic type of administrative organization (bureaucracy) . . . is from a purely technical point of view, capable of attaining the highest degree of efficiency and is in this sense formally the most rationally known means of carrying out imperative control over human beings. It is superior to any other form in precision, in stability, in the stringency of its discipline, and its reliability. It thus makes possible a particularly high degree of calculability of results. (Weber 1964 p 337)

How is this orderliness possible? How far is it the result of organizational rules? Such questions must be central to any thorough-going analysis of organizations.

4 Structural approach to the study of organizational rules

Structural analyses of organizational rules see organizational rules as the mechanism whereby organizational regularity is achieved. The application of rules within organizations is seen as the crucial feature which not only results in organizational regularity but also is the defining characteristic of an organizationally prevalent type of authority which is based upon legitimacy deriving from '. . . a consistent system of abstract rules which have normally been intentionally established' (Weber 1964 p 330). Weber sees the bureaucratic administration of this rational legal type of authority as characterized by the '. . . continuous organization of official functions bound by rules' (Weber 1964 p 330). It is through this rule-bound quality of organizational activity and the consequent '. . . dominance of a spirit of formalistic impersonality' (Weber 1964 p 340), that organizations achieve their distinguishing feature of calculability.

This suggestion that the existence and application of organizational rules gives organizations their extra-individual quality, can also be seen to relate to Durkheim's insistence that social facts have an existence and influence external to the acting individual. Here lies, it is claimed, the 'reality' or organizations. Hall has put it: 'It does not matter who the particular individual is; the organization has established a system of norms and expectations to be followed regardless of who its personnel happen to be, and it continues to exist regardless of personnel turnover' (Hall 1972 p 13).

Not surprisingly, therefore, in view of the significance attached to organizational rules, researchers have tended to focus attention on the nature, quantity and type of organizational rules (see chapter 3); their relationship to other organizational features; the extent and correlates of formalization of activities within organizations; the extent to which organizational members' decision-making is programmed by their membership of the organization.

The degree of formalization of organizational activities has been seen to relate to other structural qualities, notably the characteristics of the personnel, the routineness of the organizational tasks and the extent of centralization of decision-making within the organization. One recurring theme in analyses of the degree of formalization within organizations is that formalization not only relates to the sorts of tasks that members of the organization are typically involved in (Hage and Aiken 1972), but also relates inversely to other forms of organizational control. Blau and Schoenherr have argued that increase in organizational size creates pressures for the decentralization of organizational decision-making, which tend to be resisted until junior and middle management's decision-making can be seen to be reliable. This reliability is achieved not through the use of rules but through automation and standardized selection which ensure that staff are considered to be reliably trained and qualified and thus reliable. So formalization tends to be inversely related to such training and qualification as are taken to be relevant to job performance: '. . . the presence of a well-trained staff is related to a reduced need for extensive rules and policies' (Hall 1972 p 177). Similarly, but presumably for different reasons, professional forms of control tend to substitute for more 'bureaucratic' forms.

The sort of (structural) analysis outlined above and earlier (which maintains that organizations exhibit regularities of their own which may be discussed without reference to the individuals concerned) adopts a rather formalistic approach to organizational rules, seeing them as measures by which to differentiate one type from another, or as variables to relate to other variables which are considered significant, or as determinants of members' orderly behaviour. Such an approach is not concerned with the actual meaning of organizational rules, or the processes involved in their interpretation and application. The situation described by Hall in the quotation above is generally assumed to have been realized, although of course, the possibility of deviance through conformity with some sub-cultural norm or rule is admitted. But all this means that when an official rule cannot be invoked to explain a behaviour or occurrence, an 'unofficial' one is referred to instead.

But an alternative perspective on organizational rules (and organizations in general) is available and merits treatment.

5 Interactionist approach to the study of organizational rules: causes and consequences of organizational rules

The interactionist approach to organizational rules includes any attempt to describe the relationship between rules and behaviour. A particularly important and interesting study in this tradition is Gouldner's study of a plant owned by the General Gypsum Company. This study deliberately eschewed the sort of approach outlined above in favour of an attempt to describe the '. . . intricately ramified network of consequences many of which are below the waterline of public visibility' (Gouldner 1964 p 26), that are generated by bureaucratic procedures and rules. Rather than simply accept the established orthodoxy that bureaucratic rules create order and regularity, Gouldner queries: 'For whom do the rules make things regular?' and '. . . in terms of whose goals were the rules a rational device?' (1964 p 20).

Gouldner is concerned to investigate the reasons behind bureaucratization, and to consider how attempts to bureaucratize are accepted or rejected. Rather than merely accept the claimed advantages of bureaucracy, Gouldner describes the conditions (or as they will experience them, organizational problems) under which those with power within the organization attempt to impose bureaucratic procedures. In realizing that organizational structure (in this case increased bureaucratization, or more rules) is the result of the decisions and strategies of powerful members of the organization, and in considering organizational structure as a result of negotiations and adjustments between potentially opposed groups, Gouldner anticipates more recent work on the nature and determinants of organizational structure (Salaman and Thompson 1973).

Gouldner, who considers rules only in terms of their disciplining function, suggests that the attempt to impose a rule or to develop a new ruling is a consequence of an organizational member perceiving some other group as failing to fulfil their expectations (roles). Rules '. . . are thus a response to a breakdown in a social relationship' (Gouldner 1964 p 232). Rules are thus a form of control that will be used when alternative forms are no longer possible, and bureaucratization is not simply the rational introduction of a technically efficient, objective organizational structure, but a result of, and a stage in, the conflicting relationships that characterize industrial organizations. He writes, 'In short, bureaucracy was man-made, and more powerful men had a greater hand in making it' (Gouldner 1964 p 240). And, '. . . the degree of bureaucratization is a function of human striving; it is the outcome of a contest between those who want it and those who do not' (Gouldner 1964 p 237). The same point has been made, in somewhat different terms, by Crozier and Hickson. Crozier sees rules as an element in the constant conflict between members of organizations. This conflict is characterized by subordinate members attempting to increase, or retain their areas of discretion, and hence their organizational power, and by senior members' attempts to reduce the uncertainty caused by this discretion through the creation and imposition of rules.

Gouldner argues that the imposition of rules should be seen in terms of the systems of meanings, definitions and expectations that exist within the organization and the existing conflicts of interest; that the imposition of rules follows from certain experienced 'problems' and difficulties, rather than as an inevitable corollary of any attempt to establish an organization, and that the consequences of these rules will depend on the way in which those who are subject to them define them and are prepared to commit themselves to them. This then leads to an emphasis upon the culture of the organization within which various groups are distinguished, defined and evaluated, and which contains conceptions of proper, fair, legitimate inter-group behaviour and relations, as well as generally accepted explanatory models of the behaviour of other groups.

An interest in the 'unanticipated' consequences of rules and how their actual concrete utilization by organizational members in the execution of their work duties (and the consequences of such utilization) occurs within a context of existing group structures and relationships also characterizes the work of Peter Blau. Blau's study of two government agencies supplies additional evidence of the ways in which rules and procedures set up to achieve a certain effect, can produce unexpected — and possibly, to some, undesirable — consequences.

Blau describes the consequences that followed the utilization of statistical performance records. He notes how this type of work performance assessment served not only as a new form of control, it also produced unexpected and, for some, undesirable consequences. For example, despite the desirable repercussions, the statistical performance records also produced what he calls a displacement of goals; that is, they induced the interviewers to orient their activities towards new priorities. Blau writes, 'An instrument intended to further the achievement of organizational objectives, statistical records, constrained interviewers to think of maximizing the indices as their major goal, sometimes at the expense of these very objectives' (Blau 1963 p 46). Furthermore, Blau argues that the introduction of statistical records caused a reduction in co-operation and an increase in competitiveness within the work groups. But once again it is maintained that the observed consequences of introducing a new bureaucratic procedure depends crucially upon the culture of the group. In one case where the records did not have the consequences described above, Blau argues that this was because the group had developed a work/professional code of its own which stressed the importance of client assistance and denigrated the goal of maximizing productivity since it was seen to conflict with the 'proper' goals. (Interestingly, then, the group that was most concerned with productivity was less productive than the group that stressed client service: this is because, Blau claims, a concern for increased productivity serves, finally, to weaken group cohesion, which results in reduced efficiency.)

3 Rule use or application

A major element of lay criticisms of organizations or bureaucracies is

that the rules serve purposes other than those that can be subsumed
under the officially acknowledged organizational goal. The issue of what
organizational rules mean to those who are employed to implement
them has fascinated many who study organizations. Blau and others
have noted, for example, how the inevitably abstract and general
nature of rules means that to apply a rule requires more than mere
knowledge of it: it requires some degree of adjustment, adaptation and
interpretation in the light of particular situational contingencies. Blau
writes:

> A bureaucratic procedure can be defined as a course of action
> prescribed by a set of rules designed to achieve a given objective
> uniformly. Agency-wide rules must be abstract in order to guide the
> different courses of action necessary for the accomplishment of an
> objective in diverse situations. (Blau 1963 p 23)

Blau isolated three interrelated types of rule modification in the light of
actual situations: 'adjustment, redefinition and amplification of procedures' (1963 p 27). These processes are possible because of the general,
abstract nature of the organizational rules. They also follow the fact
that officials in question, interviewers, found themselves faced by and
required to cope with immediate, situational demands and difficulties,
and their own priorities and objectives. Blau writes, '. . . the officials in
actual contact with clients re-defined abstract procedures in terms of
the exigencies of the situation and of the dominant objectives of their
task' (Blau 1963 p 29). But what are these objectives? Are they the
same as 'organizational goals'? Blau concedes that these objectives, in
the light of which rules are interpreted and modified, are derived as
much from the difficulties and aspirations of those *members* of the
organization who face the public, as from any overreaching *organizational* goal. He writes, 'Officials in actual contact with clients . . .
redefined procedures in accordance with some immediate objective,
such as maintaining good public relations and work satisfaction by
acceding to the demands of clients' (Blau 1963 p 34). These modifications may defeat the original purpose of the procedure.

However, Blau still sees the rule modifications and re-definitions he
describes, as essentially functional; he says, 'It is hardly surprising that
operations in the employment agency were *adjusted* to conditions in
the industrial community in which, and *for which*, it worked. If this
had not been so, the organization *could not have served the employment needs* of the community.' (Blau 1963 p 35. My emphasis). It
might be asked what evidence there is that the organization does serve

the employment needs of the community. But Blau's assertion follows temptingly from a perspective which views organizations as goal attaining structures.

Rules can be used not simply to control and make orderly the behaviour of members of organizations, or to achieve co-ordination and interdependence, but as resources, or stakes, in the constant intra-organizational negotiation and bargaining that underlies the display of regular, organizational features. Gouldner has remarked that just as rules define minimum levels of performance, so from the point of view of the worker they inform him of what will constitute an acceptable output: 'The rules served as a specification of a minimum level of acceptable performance. It was, therefore, possible for the worker to *remain* apathetic, for he now knew just how little he could do and still remain secure' (Gouldner 1946 pp 174–5). Enforcement of the rules was used as a threat in the constant bargaining between supervisors and men. When things were going well the men might be rewarded by a temporary non-enforcement of the rules concerning, for example, smoking or chatting. But if things were felt to be getting lax, then the rules would be rigorously enforced. Gouldner says, '. . . *formal* rules gave supervisors something with which they could 'bargain' in order to secure *informal* co-operation from workers' (1964 p 173).

Rules can serve to protect interests, and within an organization rule design, enforcement and adjustment can be seen as negotiations between conflicting interest groups as they attempt to control or influence each other's behaviour, or to extend their area of influence. Perrow writes, '. . . rules protect those who are subject to them. Rules are means of preserving group autonomy and freedom' (1972 p 30). This can be seen in the phenomenon of 'working to rule', where, ironically, the unwritten basis of everyday assumptions that necessarily underlies the production of behaviour that complies with a rule, is suspended. Behaviour under these conditions conforms with the rules, but not with the intentions known to inspire them. Working to rule is thus a feature of industrial conflict. The political nature of organizational rules is also the main theme in Strauss *et al*'s analysis of a psychiatric hospital (1973).

Strauss *et al* note that within the hospital they studied, the rules were vague, general, '. . . far from extensive, . . . or clearly binding' (1973 p 306). Furthermore, '. . . hardly anyone knows all the extant rules, much less exactly what situations they apply to, or for whom and with what sanctions' (Strauss *et al* 1973 p 306). The authors discerned the same irregularity of rule promulgation and enforcement that Gouldner described: sometimes the rules were enforced, sometimes forgotten.

In this situation the different occupational groups used the rules not to determine their behaviour, but to achieve their particular priorities, or to obstruct other groups. The rules thus become a sort of organizational resource employed by the members of the psychiatric hospital in their inter-professional negotiations and conflicts. The authors also argue that even the small number of '. . . clearly enunciated rules . . . can be stretched, negotiated, argued, as well as ignored or applied at convenient moments' (Strauss *et al* 1973 p 308). Such a possibility follows from the fact that, '. . . here as elswhere [rules] fail to be universal prescriptions' (1973 p 308). The objectives that members of the hospital attempt to attain can, in very general terms, be seen in terms of the overarching organizational symbol: '. . . to return patients to the outside world in better shape' (Strauss *et al* 1973 p 308), but this goal is so vague as to be programmatically inadequate. When it comes to any particular case disagreements arise as a result of different psychiatric ideologies, different professional interests, different career routes and aspirations and past negotiations and policies.

The work of those authors mentioned in this section is an attempt to emphasize that the relationship between formal, written rules and actual behaviour, and between such behaviour and the objectives that lay behind the rules, *cannot always be assumed, but must be investigated empirically*. But this does not (or should not) mean that official rules and procedures are overlooked. Crozier in his comments on Dalton's book has made this point neatly:

> He [Dalton] is so haunted by the fear of being misled by the formal structure and the formal definitions of the roles that, in his analysis of the way managers really behave, he reports only irregularities, backdoor deals and subtle blackmail. Dalton's description is extremely suggestive . . . but he forgets the rational side of the organization and the series of social controls that prevent people from taking too much advantage of their own strategic situation. No organization could survive if it were run solely by individual and clique backdoor deals. (Crozier 1964 p 166)

But another approach to rules (whether organizational or societal) has recently been developed and can usefully be treated here. It was noted above, for example, by Strauss *et al* and the others, that rules were to some variable extent abstract, vague and general in nature. This point has been emphasized by Douglas, who has argued strongly for a consideration of the situational, in-use, concrete applications of rules. He maintains that with respect to social (or organizational) rules, 'Abstract definitions and arguments have done little to advance our knowledge of social rules and their relations to social action and social order' (Douglas 1971 p 133). This is not to say that these abstract rules are unimportant, for as Douglas notes (and as Strauss *et al* support) such rules and moralities serve as resources to be drawn upon in the construction of definitions and strategies in particular situations. They supply, as it were, vocabularies that actors use with reference to particular situations. But Douglas (and others) suggest that it is unwarranted to *assume* from a sociological 'knowledge' of a rule, that certain behaviours, sanctions, etc., will occur, for all rules must be used selectively with reference to actors' knowledge of the situation, and the practical contingencies they face. He writes, 'Anyone who starts with the abstract rules and hypothesizes what the concrete, situational uses will be, or what the social actions of those expressing the abstract rules will be, is almost certainly going to be wrong' (Douglas 1971 p 171). The answer then, is to '. . . concentrate on studying rules in use if we want to see what the rules mean to members in their everyday lives' (Douglas 1971 p 139). As the previous discussion of Blau and Gouldner made clear, there is some truth in what Douglas says. Equally obviously, however, the extreme position he takes when he says abstract rules have no predictive value is untenable. We can, and do predict events on the basis of knowing rules all the time. (Although such predictions are certainly based on taken for granted knowledge about the situational meaning and application of the words and expressions used in the statement of the rule.) Yet despite the fact that people act as though rules determined behaviour (which means of course that in a sense they do) and are able to predict behaviour on the basis of knowing a rule, Douglas is concerned to discover exactly what is involved in 'knowing', 'obeying' or 'deviating from' a rule.

Many other investigations of government, federal or public administrative agencies have also been conducted (some of them are excerpted in Salaman and Thompson 1973) which focus on the situational meanings and interpretations of organizational rules in terms of the practical contingencies faced by organizational personnel. Such procedures typically involve some sort of classification of persons, events and circumstances into 'cases' which can be treated in certain ways in terms of what is 'known' about them and the practical 'purposes at hand', the practical contingencies they face, as policemen, lawyers, employment agency interviewers and so on. Just as the rules are used in terms of knowledge about types of clients or victims, so the application is explained and justified to relevant, competent others in terms of what are taken to be priorities and objectives and knowledge about the nature of the person concerned.

Rules vary in their ambiguity and generality. Katz has suggested, and there seems every reason to accept his argument, that within industrial organizations there is discernible a considerable degree of variation in the specificity of rules relating to organizational tasks and duties, and individual members of organizations may well find themselves subject to quite tightly defined expectations and definitions. Crozier writes: '. . . it is impossible, whatever the effort, to eliminate all sources of uncertainty within an oranization by multiplying impersonal rules and developing centralization' (Crozier 1964 p 192). However the tightest job description of rules necessarily involves some degree of ambiguity, and is still problematically related to actual events and behaviour. All rules require some degree of interpretation, knowledge and utilization. Rules are composed of words and are 'known' and applied in social situations. All Douglas is doing is focusing on the processes of situational and therefore, variable, interpretation that results in words (rules) being applied to behaviours to the satisfaction of those concerned that rules are being 'properly' followed and applied.

Similar interests, emphases and convictions are apparent in some of the studies excerpted in Salaman and Thompson (1973). Bittner, for example, in his piece on 'The police on skid-row', shows how the policemen use the rules and procedures not to determine their behaviour, but as resources to employ in the achievement of the situational purposes at hand – the maintenance of peace, quiet and safety in skid-row (plus certain other personal priorities like preserving face, and so on). The rules are used and the situations are defined in terms of policemen's knowledge of the inhabitants of skid-row, and the nature of life there. Bittner describes just how skid-row inhabitants and skid-row life are known to the policemen who service the area. As he says, in the attempts to achieve what they take to be the purposes at hand the '. . . patrolmen do not really enforce the law, even when they do invoke it, but merely use it as a resource to solve certain pressing practical problems in keeping the peace' (Bittner 1973b pp 337–8). The *ad hoc* nature of patrolmen's decision-making must be seen, Bittner argues, in terms of their attempts to keep the peace when faced with a world that they know and define in certain ways: their decisions do not flow from some generalized occupational mandate or procedure. To summarize, '. . . the basic routine of keeping the peace on skid-row involves a process of matching the resources of control with situational exigencies' (Bittner 1973b pp 341–2).

This chapter has attempted a consideration of sociological approaches to organizational rules, and their significance within the organization. Once again it has been remarked that different sociological perspectives on organizations give rise to different conceptions of organizational rules. While some consider rules as the means whereby organizational orderliness is directly achieved, others consider the origins and consequences of organizational rules with an emphasis on the policital implications of rule design, enforcement and application. Such a view too, sees rules as concerned with organizational structure, but in this case as a result of the negotiations, interpretations and modifications that produce a constantly changing orderliness.

CHAPTER 7

Hedy Brown

The individual in the organization

Introduction

What kind of questions come to mind when one thinks of motivation and work? To begin with one might ask why people work at all and one answer might be that they have no choice. If that is so, questions about motivation and work can be seen to concern the fundamental relationships of the individual with his society. One might then ask what expectations do people have about work? Are they expecting happiness and fulfilment or drudgery? Do they go to work with some notion as to what constitutes a fair reward for effort, a fair day's work for a fair day's pay? Can we ask such questions in general or only in relation to particular groups of workers? In other words, does it matter that the history, technology, nature and conditions of work are very different in, say, coal-mining, dock work, car factories, the catering industry or the professions? Indeed, are there cross-cultural differences and do British, Chinese, American, Japanese or any other workers differ from each other in their attitudes to work? In posing such questions we are essentially concerned with discovering whether we can focus on the individual worker and his motivation or whether people can only be studied by taking their historical and contemporary social contexts into account. Next we might turn to a quite different set of questions concerning ideology and control, the theme of this book. Do the questions one asks about motivation and work depend on whether one is an employer or an employee? If questions are asked mainly from the point of view of the employer, is the resulting knowledge unbiased or tainted? And can an understanding of motivation be used as a tool of control, for instance, by devising incentives which will elicit the required behaviour?

Social scientists differ from one another in their emphases and theories. In this book, a number of standpoints within sociology are explored and all share a primary interest in the determinants of behaviour and experience which are at the *societal* level – social structure, social class and power relationships within society. Even where they address themselves to the individual actor they see him as the product of societal forces. Social psychologists work within a broader framework. They appreciate that psychological phenomena, such as a person's motivation or attitudes, are in part the product of sociological factors and that an individual cannot be fully understood except in the context of his history, his immediate social situation and the society of which he is a member. *But*, as psychologists, they also pay attention to factors or issues which would be ignored by the sociologist as irrelevant or unproblematic. In exploring motivation, for instance, psychologists address themselves to the question of the possible innate or biological origins as well as to the social influences on motivation. Primarily, however, sociologists and social psychologists differ in whether psychological phenomena, whatever their origins or history of development, should and can be studied as phenomena in their own right (and be treated as independent variables) or whether they should be regarded as the outcomes or products of societal processes (and be viewed as dependent variables).

In reviewing the main currents of psychological research in relation to motivation and work we will see that there have been shifts in what has been seen as problematic. New questions have been asked and new solutions have been sought.

First of all, the *efficiency of organizations* was and is a major focus of studies. Utilizing a psychological perspective we can question how to raise the productivity and efficiency of the members of an organization – be they workers, supervisors or managers. What is their motivation at work, how can it be elicited and used towards the achievement of given organizational goals? What is the contribution to organizational efficiency of careful selection and training of staff, the design of tasks, machines and systems, the use of financial and other incentives?

Secondly, there has been an increasing concern with the *satisfaction of the worker*. Most fundamentally we may question whether industrial and other organizations alienate man from himself and from more 'natural' surroundings. On a more immediately practical level a considerable amount of thought and research has gone into exploring whether some organizational arrangements (such as 'flat' hierarchies, participative styles of management or good personnel policies) are more conducive to the fulfilment of various psychological needs such as man's need for psychological growth and self-actualization. This focus on the individual's satisfaction, rather than merely his efficiency and on eliciting co-operation rather than relying on punitive controls, embodies a more complex view of human motivation than did the earlier 'carrot and stick' approach. At the same time, it is not necessarily a sign of more ethical concerns since satisfaction is, in this context, seldom seen as an end in itself. Nor is the legitimacy of the structure of society and its division into classes with unequal life chances questioned or challenged.

The interest in the individual's psychological well-being rests, and this forms our third category of questions, on a presumed *link between satisfaction and productivity*. This link has not been established but the idea of its possible existence has influenced the choice of research areas as well as management thinking and management styles. The efficient use of resources does not, of course, only depend on the willing co-operation of employees but also on the quality of the decisions taken, the technology of production, payment systems, levels of skill, agreements with unions, and so on. Nevertheless, a lack of co-operation (possibly because of lack of personal satisfaction at work) may lead to under-use of machinery, overmanning, absenteeism, accidents and labour turnover and may hence frustrate the goals of the top decision-makers. A firm which does not have a good reputation with its employees also usually is unable to attract the desired quantity and quality of job applicants. A good deal of social psychological work has, therefore, focussed on exploring the relationships between the nature of work and its surrounding conditions and their influence on the attitudes employees develop, the satisfactions they gain and their productivity. The commonsense assumption that an individual is more likely to be effective in his job if he likes his work, his fellow workers, supervisors and the policies of the firm he works for and has no great personal worries has, however, not necessarily been borne out.

Reflections on the nature of work

Why do we work? What needs are satisfied through work? On reflection, it is not possible to give a simple (or generally accepted) answer to such questions. In a slave society only slaves do what in that society is defined as work and they are seen to work so as to avoid punishment. In other societies work is more often viewed as an essential and significant link between man and his social world, defining his status, his interests, his income and providing (or failing to provide) some of his satisfactions. There is no evidence at all that work in itself is experienced as nasty and to be avoided (and hence that the only thing to do is to camouflage the nastiness a bit). Where it is experienced as such this is likely to be due to the economic, physical, psychological or social conditions of the particular job – low pay, excessive division of labour (resulting in repetitive, meaningless fragmentation), lack of responsibility, bad working conditions, and so on. Such negative aspects influence motivation in two ways. Over and above their direct effects they are important also because they relay to the individual the low opinion society or a particular management extends to him. Similarly, unemployment damages one's self-esteem. Bakke (1934) and Jahoda *et al* 1966) pointed to the devastating psychological consequences of prolonged unemployment in the 1920s and '30s which led to apathy, depression and resignation in the communities they studied (though, in other circumstances the effects might be the reverse – bitterness, aggression or revolution). Today, the *financial effects* of unemployment are less severe than in earlier times (though the experience of economic deprivation is always relative to what others in well paid jobs, who serve as a point of reference for one's judgements, can afford). We may also speculate on whether the *psychological effects* are as extreme as in the '20s and '30s though they will still be painful to bear and individuals will differ greatly in how they are affected. Three reasons for such speculation suggest themselves. One, the idea that hard work is honourable (the protestant work ethic) does not have the hold on us it used to have. Two, we understand more readily that unemployment is due to 'structural' factors rather than an individual's shortcomings (and hence an unemployed person's feelings of guilt are reduced and his neighbours and family show more understanding of his situation). Three, the roles of husbands and wives are undergoing changes. More women, including mothers, are going out to work and men are moving into the home, taking an active part in child-rearing and in domestic work (Brown 1979). The role differentiation between the male breadwinner whose sphere of influence and significance is outside the home and that of the female partner whose influence and significance is in the home and with the children becomes blurred. The point of stating this here is that a man's satisfactions are in consequence not so completely bound up with his economic role as they might have been in earlier industrial periods and hence his psychological isolation by being out of work may be lessened. Nevertheless, not only unemployment but also retirement is seen as a social problem as both may rob the individual of his most important social nexus.

Maslow's views on motivation

Many human needs have been learnt in particular cultural and societal contexts. There have, nevertheless, been attempts to establish the existence of 'constant fundamental needs' which are 'independent of the particular situation in which the organism finds itself' (Maslow 1954 p 74). Maslow drew on many thoretical approaches in psychology and attempted a 'holistic-dynamic' synthesis which would do justice to man's potentialities and virtues rather than dwell on his shortcomings. His theory of motivation is here introduced since it has become extrapolated and applied to organizations. Maslow suggests that needs exist in an *innate hierarchy* in which the lower needs have to be satisfied to a considerable extent before the higher needs emerge to motivate the individual's behaviour. His theory of motivation contains five levels:

1 physiological needs
2 safety needs
3 belongingness and love needs
4 esteem needs
5 the need for self-actualization

It is difficult to decide how far Maslow' theory represents a *correct* picture of human motivation. It is easy to show that there are apparent reversals of the levels in the hierarchy. People may go short of food to share with friends or even go on hunger-strike to demonstrate their allegiance to a political ideal and in this way may fulfil love and ego needs. On the other hand, Maslow's theory of the 'prepotency' of the physiological needs is supported by accounts of civilized people turning to cannibalism in circumstances of extreme deprivation, e.g., the survivors of an air crash in the Andes eventually ate parts of their dead comrades to survive. Other examples of reversals of need levels are people who neglect safety needs or incur risks or dangers, again to fulfil higher needs for achievement or status. But, another source of support for Maslow's views are the observations of historians that revolutionary movements may gain momentum at a time when the physical conditions of people have improved (those of the French peasants before the French Revolution and those of the Russian peasants before the Russian Revolution) and such examples may possibly illustrate that when lower needs are met a desire for higher, self-actualizing needs is freed or activated. Nevertheless such examples are merely suggestive of support for Maslow's views. Complex social phenomena like revolutions can never be explained solely by reference to the motivation of individuals.

The reason why Maslow's theory has been introduced here is that it had a considerable effect on psychologists interested in the human potential, on management consultants, management teachers and possibly on managements as well. Its assumptions and beliefs about human nature fitted the changing social climate of the years after the Second World War. In industry, controlling employees through their greed and fears became unfashionable as well as frequently unworkable and earlier theorists, such as Taylor (1911, reprinted 1947), who developed management strategies from these assumptions lost some of their credence. The implications of Maslow's views for industry are that once basic needs have been met (as they are assumed to have been in times of full employment and with the safety net of welfare services) the higher psychological needs of workers will be activated and they will put forward claims which meet their needs for security, status, significance or self-fulfilment. In these circumstances, pay tends to be only one of a number of issues in negotiations between employers and employees.

The theory, of course, is in the nature of an explanatory rather than a strictly testable model. It was never intended to serve as the basis for management policies and it certainly does not stand up to a critical evaluation from that point of view.

In the first place, its applicability to industry is not supported. For instance, Hall and Nougaim (1968) followed management trainees for five years to study whether their needs emerged in the kind of sequential pattern suggested by Maslow. If the theory were correct then one would expect the more successful managers to exhibit higher-level needs (having already satisfied their lower level needs). However, both the successful and unsuccessful managers decreased their concern for the two lower level needs and increased their higher level needs. The hierarchical model is not supported in this study in that it would be incorrect to infer that the gratification of lower-level needs *causes* the higher needs to emerge. The authors suggest that the *salience* of needs may vary, not because of their satisfaction or lack of satisfaction but because of the influence of changing roles and increasing age.

Secondly, there is no automatic reason for assuming that a man must look for the satisfaction of his higher needs *within* the firm (or even his lower ones if he is prepared to live on social security or his wife's earnings). Indeed, in so far as he does satisfy his higher needs at work he may do so by resisting management control and asserting his independence. We all know that men can stand up against management pressures by group solidarity (whether in the face-to-face group or through union membership) or that people can seek satisfactions for their needs for affection, esteem and self-fulfilment in their family life, in the pursuit of non-work interests of all kinds, from hobbies to public service or through education or travel. Indeed, Goldthorpe *et al* (1968 and 1969) reported in *The Affluent Worker* that the car workers they had studied adopted what they called an *instrumental* attitude to work — they did not expect to get satisfaction or interest from their jobs. Instead, their high earnings on the conveyor belt production line was merely a means to obtain satisfaction outside their working lives. It can be argued that this instrumental orientation is a conscious or unconscious defence mechanism which shields the worker from the full psychological impact of intolerable working conditions — repetitiveness, boredom, danger, dirt, lack of discretion and control — and his low status. Alternatively we can see it as the successful internalization of the values of the 'consumer society'. Interviews with these workers also revealed that they were attracted to extrinsic and economic rewards in *compensation* for the lack of intrinsic satisfactions, not that they did not value the latter. Cotgrove *et al* (1971) also found that the nylon spinners they studied *tolerated* noise, heat, boredom and shiftwork (all major sources of complaints) only because pay was high. Workers often have a realistic appreciation of the limits of intrinsic satisfaction available to them at work and that is quite different from saying they would not prefer to have more challenging and autonomous jobs.

Maslow's hierarchical model of human needs does not seem to reflect readily the realities of motivation at work. However, we could use his terminology to assert that, on the whole, skilled workers, professional people, managers and, in general, members of the middle class (who may start off with more of their basic levels of need satisfied) have both more job choices open to them and are more intent on taking jobs which permit self-actualization at work. They usually also earn more and have better conditions of work; hence they gain 'intrinsic' satisfactions at work and have the income necessary to obtain 'extrinsic' satisfactions as well.

Maslow's model, in spite of its apparent shortcomings for enhancing our understanding of motivation at work, has had an impact on managerial thinking. There are two reasons for this. One, as has already been mentioned, his view that man had great potential which he should be allowed to develop fitted the social climate of the post-war world. Two, his ideas were taken up by a number of social scientists and management consultants such as McGregor (1960), Likert (1967) and Argyris (1957 and 1962), all of whom saw a clash between the individual's psychological aspirations and needs and contemporary organizational structures and management styles. To reduce this lack of congruence between individual and organizational needs and to secure the workers' commitment as well as to provide satisfaction they advocated various remedies such as group decision-making and participatory styles of leadership.

Herzberg's theory

Perhaps the most spectacular impact on managerial thinking was made by Herzberg (1968a and b) who based his postulates on Maslow's model of the hierarchy of needs. Briefly, Herzberg and his collaborators suggested that the factors which produce job *satisfaction* (and which therefore would elicit motivation to gain such satisfaction) are separate and distinct from the factors leading to *dissatisfaction* and that they are not opposites of each other. Within our society those who are employed and earning their living are presumed to have satisfied what are in Maslow's hierarchy their 'lower' needs. However, whilst failure to have these needs met will inevitably produce dissatisfaction, the reverse does not hold. Employees do not feel satisfaction merely by having their basic needs met. For a job to be satisfying it must also meet the higher-order self-actualizing needs. Herzberg, therefore, proposed what he calls the two-factor theory of job satisfaction. He sees job satisfaction as a function of challenging, stimulating work activities or work *content* and these he calls 'motivator' factors since they would call forth extra effort from employees and lead to superior job performance. These motivator factors are intrinsic to the job and include achievement, recognition for achievement, the work itself, responsibility and growth or advancement. Factors leading to dissatisfaction are called 'hygiene' factors, are extrinsic to the job and refer to the job *context*. They are aspects such as company policy and administration, supervision, interpersonal relationships, working conditions, salary, status and security.

One may well think that these work context factors affect the work content factors (or your attitude towards them) to such an extent that this distinction is not very meaningful. Herzberg, by emphasizing the importance of work content factors, looks to the motivation and satisfaction of the individual in isolation whilst people's expectations are very much affected by both past social experiences and learning and by present social cues and interactions. However, Herzberg makes some very interesting propositions on how to strengthen the 'motivator' factors (see, for example, Herzberg 1968). He is against what he calls *horizontal* job enlargement (adding one more meaningless task) or job rotation (exchanging one dull job temporarily for another dull one). He advocates what he calls *vertical* job enlargement providing a genuinely enriched job with more responsibility, achievement and recognition.

Psychological research (for example by Berlyne 1960) has shown that people (and some animals) have strong curiosity or exploratory motives and that they prefer a degree of variation and change in their environment. Highly repetitive jobs are unlikely to provide the desired level of stimulation. But, contrary to what Herzberg says, 'horizontal' integration of jobs may, nevertheless, create some satisfaction by providing such variation. Frequently, of course, workers will create their own stimulation by exercizing ingenuity in restricting output. However, from a management point of view, their energies would not then be directed towards useful ends.

Herzberg's work has stimulated a considerable body of research. Herzberg and his collaborators had originally asked their respondents what aspects of their work and work situation had led to either extreme satisfaction or to extreme dissatisfaction. On coding the answers they found that job satisfaction tended to be associated with job content factors and job dissatisfaction with job context factors. However, this may in part be due to people's inclination to express satisfaction about something they themselves are contributing to, that is, the job activity or job content whilst the dissatisfying experiences are seen as someone else's responsibility, that is, they are seen as caused by the supervisors, fellow-workers or by other aspects of the job context. In the same way, of course, managements, too, locate the causes of what they see as the undesirable attitudes or behaviour of workers anywhere but in their own policies.

A British study undertaken by Wall, Stephenson and Skidmore (1971) showed that job *applicants* in a formal and ego-involving selection interview on the whole attributed their highly satisfying past experiences to those factors which Herzberg called 'motivator' factors and their highly dissatisfying past experiences to those Herzberg labelled 'hygiene' factors. However, matched individuals interviewed in an informal situation by an independent researcher, and when the need to give socially acceptable answers was minimized, failed in their responses to the same questions to support Herzberg's hypothesis. Dunnette, Campbell and Hakel (1967), on the basis of their own research on members of six occupational groups and through their review of research which did not have some of the methodological weaknesses of the original study, came to the conclusion that Herzberg's dual factor theory was a gross oversimplification and that the same factors can contribute to both satisfaction and dissatisfaction and can originate in job content or job context factors or in both jointly. They nevertheless stressed that the 'motivators' in Herzberg's terms are the most important overall and the 'hygiene' factors least important.

Centers and Bugental (1966), among others, have found that there are systematic differences between different socio-economic classes as to what are considered good or poor jobs. Thus, white-collar workers consistently placed a higher value on intrinsic sources of job satisfaction than did blue-collar workers. Turner and Lawrence (1967) report that urban workers were more satisfied with non-involving work than were those situated in rural areas. Blood and Hulin (1967) and Hulin and Blood (1968) argued that rural workers had not been alienated from middle-class 'protestant ethic' work norms whilst those in large, industrialized communities formed a separate cultural sub-group with different norms. It is interesting to speculate whether the Luton car workers studied by Goldthorpe *et al* (1968) mentioned earlier in this chapter would have developed different attitudes and expectations if the management had been aware of and made use of Herzberg's ideas. This is doubtful as the nature of the production line in car manufacture does not readily allow for the kind of vertical job integration advocated by Herzberg unless a great deal is invested in new technologies. (There are experiments in progress in Italy and Sweden where production lines in car factories have been designed to allow for vertical job integration). Reports from different kinds of factories also suggest that jobs have remained boring there in spite of attempts at job enrichment, increased flexibility in moving between jobs and in choice of work (see, for instance, Cotgrove *et al* 1971). These researchers also point out that in the organization they studied, the switch from work study and the use of financial incentives (which involve problems and disputes over rate-fixing) to job enrichment (with less supervision and more responsibility for the individual worker) was accompanied by increased pay. It is, therefore, difficult to assess the consequences of job enrichment alone and, also , how long any satisfaction it brings to the worker might continue. They note that workers were initially attracted to the scheme by higher pay but they also point to the emergence of latent needs for self-actualization when circumstances made such aspirations possible.

Motivation and the problems of management

As has been pointed out, the interest of managements in exploring the psychological needs of their workers does not arise from purely altruistic concerns but is based on the supposed link between productivity and job satisfaction. However, it is not self-evident which way round causality works. Are satisfied workers more productive or does high productivity lead to satisfaction through the exercise of skill and the overcoming of obstacles, through increased earnings or through social approval from colleagues or supervision?

The idea that satisfaction and productivity are linked was probably first articulated as a result of the now historic researches at the Hawthorne works of the Western Electric Company in the late 1920s. There an experimental group was set up in the Relay Assembly Test Room which worked under a variety of new conditions. Eventually it was demonstrated that the close contact with a friendly researcher and the relaxed atmosphere improved their 'morale' (that is, their satisfaction) and it was this rather than the better pay and rest pauses, which had led to increased productivity. An already established group was subsequently observed whilst working under its usual and unchanged conditions in the Bank Wiring Observation Room. The workers in this group were less well satisfied and restricted their output to fairly low levels (Roethlisberger and Dickson 1964).

A great deal of research has been carried out since those early years but there is still no complete agreement on the relationships between satisfaction and productivity. Brayfield and Crockett (1955) concluded that productivity on the one hand and job attitudes and satisfaction on the other are not appreciably related. Herzberg *et al* (1957), however, in reviewing a somewhat different selection of studies, concluded that such a relationship did exist but that in many cases the correlations were low.

Interestingly, these reviews found that lack of job satisfaction led to both *absenteeism* and *labour turnover*. In England, Hill and Trist (1953) similarly demonstrated the functional equivalence of *absenteeism* and *accidents* as a means of withdrawal from the work situation. All these factors are, of course, a cost to management: in the case of absenteeism in having idle machines or in using management time to make new dispositions of staff; in the case of labour turnover, there are the costs of recruitment, training, placing, and so on. Accidents may involve all these costs as well as compensation payments. The results one obtains in comparing 'satisfaction' and 'productivity' depend, therefore, a little on how performance or productivity is defined and the time span taken.

There is also the problem of how one defines satisfaction. Are we concerned with satisfaction with work, pay, promotion prospects; security of employment, supervisors, fellow-workers or what? The same factors may have contradictory consequences in meeting some needs and thwarting others. Thus, increased supervisory pressure may lead to dissatisfaction and at the same time may strengthen group cohesiveness which tends to be experienced as satisfying. On the whole, the evidence shows a low but fairly consistent relationship between satisfaction (variously defined or undefined) and performance. *It is, however, not clear why this relationship exists*. Did satisfaction with the job *cause* the performance? Or did performance *cause* satisfaction? Vroom (1964) pointed out that job satisfaction and job performance are caused by quite different things: job satisfaction is seen to be closely affected by the amounts of rewards people derive from their jobs. Level of performance is closely affected by the basis of the attainment of rewards. Thus, although job satisfaction and job performance are caused by different things they do bear some relationship to each other. Lawler and Porter (1967) put this as follows:

> If we assume that rewards cause satisfaction and that in some cases performance produces rewards, then it is possible that the relationship found between satisfaction and performance comes about through the action of a third variable – rewards. (p 23)

For rewards to have this effect (of linking satisfaction and effort) a number of conditions must be met. Workers must be aware of the basis of their remuneration; they must recognize and accept the link between increased efforts and increased rewards; most importantly, they must perceive these rewards as both equitable and desirable or else they will not give satisfaction nor will they elicit the desired effort. There are then great difficulties for managements in establishing acceptable and workable, if imperfect, connections between effort, reward and the resulting satisfaction.

In what ways are these views of Lawler and Porter different from those of Herzberg? Herzberg and his collaborators distinguished between factors causing satisfaction and those causing dissatisfaction at work and they thought that satisfaction of 'higher' needs leads to better performance. However, they stressed that the experience of achievement and recognition for successful job performance are themselves 'motivator' factors. One can reasonably say, therefore, that this might imply that performance can precede rather than follow satisfaction. Thus their position can be reconciled to some extent with that taken by Lawler and Porter who proposed that performance leads to satisfaction and that they are linked through the mediation of rewards. The generally low performance-satisfaction relationships found in empirical research can then be seen as the result of rewards which cannot be or are not closely tied to performance. These rewards may depend on membership in the organization or on having a particular job, rather than on individual effort. A practical implication of the Lawler and Porter model is that increasing the performance of employees (through selection, training, placement, feedback on performance, suitable equitable incentives, good equipment and organizational efficiency) also increases satisfaction, other things being equal. But, according to Herzberg, some other things are not equal in that some jobs are more satisfying than others and, indeed, the initial attitude and expectations of the people involved also affect the issue.

Other models have been proposed which include intervening or mediating variables between performance and satisfaction. Triandis (1959), for instance, suggested that *organizational pressure for high production* influences both satisfaction and performance but not in the same way. As pressure increases, job satisfaction is hypothesized as decreasing, irrespective of the concomitant variation in performance. Furthermore performance in the Triandis model is hypothesized as being curvilinearly related to pressure for increased production. High pressure is seen to be self-defeating and not as leading to increased performance.

We are, then, it would seem, left with a number of models none of which can account for all the complexities of the relationships between satisfaction and performance, particularly over a period of time when rewards may pale because of their familiarity and hence cease to be 'motivators'. It must also be remembered that by focusing on the relationship between satisfaction and performance one examines the relationship of only two co- or interacting variables. People may be high producers (or go to highly paid jobs) because of hire purchase commitments or for other instrumental reasons. There are 'costs' to organizations which are associated with dissatisfaction or low levels of satisfaction — low productivity, absenteeism, labour turnover, accidents and sickness. But are there also psychological 'costs' to the individual (to say nothing of the 'cost' to him of low earnings)? These psychological costs may include lack of self-esteem, lack of self-actualization, or, in stressful jobs, psychosomatic illnesses like ulcers or high blood pressure. But where a job is satisfying (financially and psychologically) are there still other costs to be incurred? For example, is the satisfied (but hard pressed) manager damaging his family life and his marriage? J. M. and R. G. Pahl (1972) suggested that the current generation of managers and their wives are, and will be, concerned much more with the quality of their personal relationships than with an affluent and materialistic style of life. These husbands, therefore, are likely to be rather less willing slaves of their organizations. It is important to point out that the motivation of managers, too, is likely to be subject to changing assumptions about values and priorities in their lives. Most of the debate on job satisfaction and performance has focused on 'the worker' whilst taking for granted that the self-actualizing nature of the manager's work and his high rewards left him free of problems but we need to question whether this distinction is quite so clear cut.

Conclusions

Are we then in a better position to answer the questions raised at the beginning of this chapter? I think some light has been thrown on some of them but others have not figured in the psychological literature about motivation and work. I have tried to explain that this is, in part, the result of psychologists (and other social scientists) working within given theoretical and empirical traditions but it is also due to their researching applied problems very much in the way they have been presented to them by those who pay for the research, in this case managements or governments rather than unions. If the latter had sponsored research, they might have taken the manager and his attitudes and behaviour as problematic and in need of explanation rather than the worker who tends to be the focus of research at present. Nevertheless it is important for the worker as well as the manager to explore how productivity can be increased (if, as is the case, some British industries are less effective than similarly equipped industries elsewhere and yet we aim at a comfortable standard of living). But one sometimes also gets the impression that psychologists have lost a feeling for the wider fabric of society, the sense of what the layman feels are the real issues and that they have omitted to ask more general questions. There is a real neglect of cross-cultural comparisons in the literature and our knowledge of the differences between the British and the German or Japanese worker or manager and their motivation, for instance, is virtually derived from untested popular stereotypes. Most of the psycholgoical literature, too, addresses itself to issues concerned with the male industrial worker. There is also little or no evaluation of the historical meaning of work (which would show which psychological facets are the outcome of class society and capitalism and which are present in all kinds of societies).

In order to understand motivation at work one needs to study also past and current attitudes and the values our educational system and society at large place on entrepreneurship or skill. We may want a high standard of living (including a national health service, education, pensions, street lighting, rubbish collection, and so on) but the ethos and thrust of the educational system is at present hostile to industry and manufacture and the fiscal system is hemming in enterprise and skill.

Much research on motivation in relation to work has focussed on the individual in the here and now and as if it were meaningful to study him in isolation and yet his attitudes derive from society. It has also looked on organizations as if they were closed systems. However, stresses and tensions there reflect those in the wider society (as is demonstrated in other parts of this book) and are rarely merely due to the circumstances or mismanagement within an organization. Much work has been done by social scientists on the connections between the technology of production, the organizational structure and the pattern and quality of human relationships in an organization. All these affect motivation but such work has rarely included specifically the study of motivation. We need to be aware, then, that when we review the literature on motivation we isolate a segment of a global subject. Nevertheless such a focus is justified (so long as its limitations are appreciated) since there is a psychological level of reality and each society has the problem of motivating its members. Whatever changes are brought about at the societal or political level and even where such changes are dramatic as in a revolution or by gaining independence from colonial status these psychological problems of satisfying human needs remain. As this chapter has shown these needs (which elicit motivation) have their springs in the individual but are largely derived from society and whatever their precise articulation go beyond the fulfilment of economic criteria.

CHAPTER 8

Hedy Brown

Work groups

The re-discovery of groups in organizations

Attitudes, values and behaviour are learned in social contexts. Social psychologists have, in particular, studied the social context provided by *group membership* and this is the focus of this chapter. A group is not merely a collection of people. The word refers to the *psychological* bonds people tend to develop when they associate with each other over a period of time in face-to-face relationships. Typical groups are the family, the work group, a sports team or a neighbourhood gang. A great deal of psychological research has delineated such aspects of groups as their evolving norms, and the circumstances in which members conform to such norms, their patterns of communications, the effect of individual differences and status relationships. The result of association in groups is a certain merging of views and attitudes; at the same time they enhance the individual's identity and self-image by the reflections of himself he gets from others in the group. This process of creating an identity, for the individual and the group, is also strengthened when one group sets itself off against another. Groups can resist managements and the psychological satisfactions an individual may gain from his group membership may be more potent than the rewards (or threats) the management can hold out. From a management point of view an important question, therefore, is whether and how attitudes can be generated which are favourable to meeting management objectives.

The Hawthorne Studies were the starting-point for a great deal of research and for the emergence of a school of thought, indeed a managerial ideology, which emphasized the crucial importance of 'human relations' in industry. Research focussed initially on communications and participation in decision-making (e.g. Lewin 1947; Coch and French 1948; Jacques 1951) and the influence on productivity and satisfaction of different supervisory styles (Lewin *et al* 1939; Likert 1961; McGregor 1960). This emphasis on the internal human relations of organizations has been criticized almost ferociously by sociologists who point, quite correctly, to the artificiality of looking at organizations as if they were microcosms existing in a vacuum. As sociologists, their own focus of explanation is elsewhere, in the social structure of society as a whole. (Mayo, too, paid attention to the wider context in his book *The Social Problems of an Industrial Civilization* 1949.) Sociologists deny the validity of an approach which seeks the causes of dissatisfaction of employees *within* an organization and as arising from inadequate social relations and which, furthermore, ignores the conflict of interest which may exist (and some would say inevitably exists) between workers and managements.

Social comparison processes

I should like to turn now to a consideration of some concepts and theories which are echoed in other parts of this book and which may throw a light on behaviour and experience in organizations. These theories explore the way in which both individuals and groups may adopt standards of behaviour and articulate their expectations by comparing themselves to those other individuals or groups who constitute, in their estimation, relevant points of reference. Hence, both satisfaction and a feeling of deprivation are relative to one's expectations which are defined by one's reference group. Such a group need not be one's current membership group. A person may well adopt the values of a group to which he aspires but of which he is not a member.

Stouffer *et al* (1949) in their study of *The American Soldier* used the concept of 'relative deprivation' to describe the mismatch between expectations and rewards which may arise in consequence. They showed that satisfaction with status and work depended on a person's subjective expectation as to what was his just due. Thus, even though soldiers with high school education had better opportunities for promotion than those who were less well educated, they were nevertheless more dissatisfied with the status they had achieved in the army since they had expected *more* advancement. Another example in *The American Soldier* showed that men in the Army Air Corps were less well satisfied with promotion opportunities than were those in the Military Police even though the actual opportunities for promotion in the former branch of the army were far greater than in the latter. But the very existence of the possibility of advancement and the comparisons with other members of the Army Air Corps created expectations and aspirations which in the event had not been fulfilled – hence the subjective experience of 'relative deprivation'. This concept was invented by Stouffer and his colleagues *ex post facto* to explain their findings. Since then, however, interesting experimental work and other research has confirmed the existence of a sense of deprivation or injustice when expectations are violated. Furthermore, the likely *behavioural consequences* of this psychological experience have been investigated. Homans (1961) and Blau (1964) developed some interesting theories which have already been referred to in Chapter 5.

Homans used the notion of *distributive justice* which he saw as existing among people involved in an exchange relationship when first, the *profits* of each person are proportional to his investment and secondly,

$$\frac{\text{A's rewards less A's costs}}{\text{A's investments}} = \frac{\text{B's rewards less B's costs}}{\text{B's investments}}$$

In other words, it is the inequality between ratios of profit (reward less costs) and investments which lead to a feeling of injustice and relative deprivation in the person for whom the ratio of profits to investment is the smaller. If a person has higher outcomes but is seen to 'deserve' them because of his higher inputs then distributive justice is achieved. Thus, *if* in a given society being of the male sex is considered superior (that is, a man's input is higher) than a woman who is paid less in the same job will not feel unjustly treated. The utility of this kind of formulation rests on the realization that for so many aspects of life no absolute standards exist. How much a person is 'worth' depends on how much other people are 'worth' with similar attributes, achievements and costs. But the problem with this kind of formulation is that just what people count as their costs, profits or investments is partly again arrived at by comparisons with others, partly by a subjective and personal choice and interpretation of relevant variables. A feeling of inequity can arise when a person's own ratio between (perceived) inputs and outcomes is not balanced *or* when his own ratio is not equal to that of his comparison group or person.

The 'investments' a person brings to a situation normally includes some or all of the following: age, sex, seniority, skill, education, ethnic background, effort. His 'rewards' are what he receives in pay, status, job satisfaction, fringe benefits, security and comradeship and appreciation from others. But what about 'responsibility' – is it a 'cost' or a 'reward'?

One may well feel responsibility is a cost due to the anxiety and worry it may cause but it may also be valued as an index of advancement or appreciation by management and hence is a reward. Homans (1961) makes an interesting point. He uses the concept of *status congruency* which is said to exist when the responsibility of a job is congruent with its superiority in other respects, e.g. pay. The costs one incurs by carrying responsibility are of a kind one's inferiors cannot incur and these costs in themselves therefore imply superiority. As I mentioned above, it is not the absolute difference in outcomes or profits which determines the subjective equity of the exchange, it is the ratio between inputs and outcomes which has to be in balance with those of the comparison group or individual. Status incongruence has interesting psychological consequences. A person who has, say, a great deal of responsibility but no higher pay than others in an exchange relationship with him presents conflicting or ambiguous stimuli. Those who interact with him, therefore, have the additional 'cost' of not knowing how to behave towards him – whether to treat him as an equal or a superior. The person himself, if he is aware of his own status incongruence, may suffer from a feeling of injustice (the term used by Homans 1961) or a sense of inequity (the term used by Adams 1965). The more indices there are in a society for denoting status the greater is the possibility of confusion. Lack of 'social certitude', or status incongruence, exists when a person has high status in one aspect of his life and low status in another. Examples might be a rich but uneducated man in a society which values both wealth and education, or a Negro doctor in a society which accords status to the doctor but not to the Negro.

What are the behavioural consequences of status incongruence, injustice or inequity? Perhaps the best known example in the literature concerning the manipulation of perceived status incongruence is Homans' (1961) interpretation of Whyte's (1948) study of *Human Relations in the Restaurant Industry*. In American restaurants, cooks tend to be male, older, more skilled, senior and more highly paid than the waitresses who in addition to being younger, less skilled, less well paid, less senior also have the low ascribed status of being female. Yet the waitresses must pass the customers' orders to the cooks and hence control what the cooks do. The cooks and waitresses are, therefore, in an incongruent status relationship and as a process of probably unconscious adaptation various psychological and physical barriers have been erected to reduce the actual interaction of the two sets of workers. Orders may be passed in writing, or are spoken through a small window or over a high partition.

An interesting example from recent British industrial race relations is the alleged reservation of skilled jobs for white workers in some textile mills. If being white is perceived as being a higher attribute, then it would be congruent if 'good' jobs (where some of the costs and rewards are those an 'inferior' cannot incur) are reserved for white workers. When Pakistani or other immigrants do not share this view of the relative statuses of the two groups they will seek to remedy the situation by demanding the 'right' to the more skilled jobs. I do not wish to give the impression that one should explain this kind of phenomenon in these psychological terms; a much simpler explanation in terms of economic motivation is quite appropriate and sufficient. But it is, to me, interesting that such a situation *can* be explained also in terms of a fairly sophisticated psychological theory of status congruence and balanced exchange relationships.

Status congruence may also lead to a feeling of 'social ease' which may be important when people have to co-operate actively with each other. An interesting example of the implications of status congruence for efficiency is provided by Adams (1953) in his studies of the variations in the effectiveness of U.S. Army bomber crews. Adams identified what were the significant status hierarchies in the groups under investigation. The most significant of these were age, military rank, amount of flying time, education, reputed ability, popularity, length of service, combat time and position importance. Group congruence obtains when individuals in the group stand in exactly the same rank order in all effective status hierarchies in the group. Adams found that crews with moderate degrees of status incongruence were superior in technical performance.

Low status congruence reduced the efficiency of crews (in hitting targets during bombing practice). A possible explanation is that inconsistency in statuses leads to only minimal communication, restricted to technical requirements, and this reduces the cohesion and efficiency of the group. Status incongruence may also adversely affect individual motivation. More interestingly, Adams also found that high status congruence was associated with low levels of performance. One may hazard the explanation that high congruence leads to a feeling of social ease, with less concentration on the task, and the close integration of the crew provides security against the pressures of outside authority. High status congruence appears to lead to the emergence of what is sometimes referred to as the *social leader* whilst low congruence seems to produce the *task-orientated leader*. The 'interaction process analysis' developed by Bales (1950, 1953) indicates that groups need both kinds of leader, and the right balance between meeting task and socio-emotional needs may have been reached in the groups with moderate status congruence.

One of the problems of formulations based on exchange theory is that both inputs and outcomes are subjectively evaluated. Where a number of people are involved in an exchange with a third person (e.g. workers with an employer) there may be different views among them (particularly if they are divided into different occupational groups) as to the relative weight to be given to different inputs (such as skill in comparison with seniority) and it will be impossible to satisfy everyone. The same applies to a person's outcomes, some of which, in addition, might be negative ones, such as poor working conditions or monotonous work. Nevertheless there exist normative expectations as to what constitute 'fair' relations between inputs and outcomes and these expectations are learned through socialization and are validated by reference to the input and outcomes of comparison groups. Adams (1965) discussed the cognitive and behavioural consequences of perceived inequity. In following Festinger's cognitive dissonance theory (Festinger 1957) he suggests that the experience of inequity creates tension in a person and that this tension will motivate him to reduce or eliminate it. The strength of motivation, it is suggested, will vary directly with the magnitude of the inequity experienced. Inequity can be reduced by a person altering his or her inputs by working less hard. A number of other studies (Adams and Rosenbaum 1962; Adams and Jacobson 1964) tested this hypothesis by focusing on how inequity due to over-payment affects the quality and quantity of work. Thus students hired to proofread galley pages who were induced to believe that they were unqualified (low inputs) for the job but were paid the standard rate worked harder than those in whom an identical perception of their inadequacy was induced but who were paid less than the standard rate. In Britain, Jacques (1961) found that perceived injustice provoked dissatisfaction among workers. But, perhaps more interestingly, he found that workers who felt relatively overpaid also showed feelings of unease.

The insistence on 'differentials' in pay by skilled workers, particularly in comparison with less skilled workers in the same industry, is probably, in part, also an attempt to achieve equity between their own perceived inputs and their outcomes. Similarly, the insistence by the professions on qualifications and other entrance standards and on codes of conduct raises their (and other people's) perception of the value of their members' inputs which then 'deserve' corresponding outcomes. (The same measures, of course, also effectively restrict entry to the professions and thus the relatively scarce supply may also bring a more favourable outcome to the individual).

A person may further reduce inequity by cognitively distorting or re-evaluating his inputs and outcomes. He may emphasize security of employment if he fails to gain promotion, or the interest or social value of his work if he is relatively underpaid, and so on. People also can change their reference or comparison group and thus reduce the experience of inequity. A person can also leave his job if he is dissatisfied and high rates of labour turnover (in comparison to the rates of similar firms in the same location or between departments in the same firm) might be taken as evidence of a sense of relative deprivation in those who leave.

The problem with theories such as exchange theory, or the theory of inequity, is the difficulty of predicting how a person will evaluate his inputs or outcomes and how he will bring them into a more balanced state. Similarly, the problem with cognitive dissonance theory is to predict how an individual will choose to reduce his cognitive dissonance. It is in the nature of such theories that precise predictions are an unobtainable goal. Such theories are conceptual models, that is, they provide a broad framework indicating possible relationships between a number of variables. (For a full review of research in this area consult Pritchard (1969); Pritchard *et al* (1972) and Walster *et al* 1978).

The same kind of criticism can be made of social comparison processes: the problem here is to identify the groups or individuals who are taken as reference points for particular aspects of another person's or group's behaviour or values.

The interesting idea in Adam's equity theory (and Homans' exchange theory formulation), however, is the suggestion that people try to balance inputs and outcomes rather than that they *maximize* outcomes as other psychological theorists (as well as economists) have supposed. The other point to emphasize is the topicality of the theme of distributive justice. Concern with equity, with getting one's subjectively perceived 'due' leads to two very distinct and not easily reconciled positions. The more highly paid and more skilled workers wish to achieve their 'due' by maintaining wage or salary differentials between themselves and those of less skills or those who for other reasons are seen as less deserving. Thus, differentials are often based on traditions which have no present reality – they may reflect past scarcity or past but not present inequalities in skills and knowledge. By contrast, low wage-earners see themselves and are seen by the government and some of the unions as 'relatively deprived' and therefore a 'just' policy would seek to improve their income, both absolutely and relatively. The 1973 wage restraint formula of limiting wage increases to £1 plus four per cent of the current wage or salary (with an annual maximum increase of £250) tipped the balance slightly towards the lower income earners whilst subsequent wage policies of straight percentage increases emphasized differentials.

Control through group membership

Individuals then relate their attitudes and behaviour to those with whom they are closely involved and, in certain circumstances, they respond to perceived expectations and pressures from others. To a certain extent, too, a person's self-image depends on the response to himself he gets from others. This need for support from other people has been manipulated to influence individuals towards adopting attitudes and thoughts they might not otherwise have espoused. We have seen, elsewhere in this book, that mental patients (and others), robbed of their customary surroundings and props to their identity, have difficulty in maintaining their previous self-image. These techniques of isolating people and subjecting them to new information and group pressures have also been used in indoctrinating prisoners of war. Quite generally, membership of institutions, whether voluntary or forced, such as military academies, convents or public schools usually implies a break away from previous surroundings and immersion into new groupings with a defined outlook and standards which it is intended the newcomer should make his own. The eventual effect on a group member depends on the interaction of three aspects: first, the individual's present attitudes and his susceptibility to succumb to group pressures; secondly, the extremity of the measures employed in isolating an individual from his normal group memberships and sources of information; and thirdly, the 'fit' between any new views he may have adopted during this indoctrination and those current in the larger society of which he is a part or to which he returns. Industrial organizations, too, use a variety of training strategies to develop relevant skills and attitudes in their members, some of which operate through the medium of intra-group influences on members. It is sometimes suggested that organizations have a new powerful tool at their disposal for influencing their members by encouraging them to participate in so-called T- (for training) groups. The aim of such groups is to increase the sensitivity of members towards each other, for each member to arrive at a better understanding of how others see him and to gain some insight into his own motives, feelings and inter-personal strategies. The implication is that, if some progress is made in these directions, then the trainee will emerge a better manager. Such T-groups are also known as 'laboratory' groups (because they provide an opportunity for participants to explore their own behaviour or that of others and to experiment with new forms of behaviour and observe their effect) or else they are categorized in terms of the processes which they stimulate as 'encounter' or 'sensitivity training' groups. Although such labels are often used interchangeably, encounter groups usually encourage a wider range of expressive behaviour, for example, touching or weeping.

T-groups have their origin in the practice of group psychotherapy. Psychotherapy is based on the notion that neurosis (as well as normal behaviour) can be explained in terms of the conflict between primitive emotions in the unconscious mind and the more civilized and learned tendencies in the conscious mind. In *directive* psychotherapy the psychiatrist uses interviews and psychological tests to arrive at an interpretation of his patient's basic problems so that he can help him bring his self-concept into harmony with 'objective' reality. In *non-directive* therapy the psychiatrist makes no attempt to interpret the patient's emotions for him. He tries instead to make him feel accepted and understood so that the patient can himself work towards changing his view of himself and of his relations with others.

Group Psychotherapy is based mainly on the non-directive approach but it brings a number of patients together. It was first developed during the Second World War, initially in order to utilize scarce psychiatric manpower to better effect. But it became quickly apparent that membership of a group in itself is beneficial. Patients in such groups are comforted by realizing that they do not suffer alone, that they can discuss their common problems and that they can learn from each other how to live with their psychological disabilities.

Psychiatrists vary in the extent to which they intervene and interpret their patients' problems and interactions in the group. Some groups also act out their problems (this may produce a 'catharsis' and it also helps patients ill-at-ease in expressing themselves in words) or they may use the free-association techniques of psychoanalysis.

You may wonder how a psychiatric method of healing mental patients came to be transformed into a technique for management training. Briefly, group psychotherapy as well as the interest aroused by Second World War group selection methods for officer cadets (referred to earlier in this chapter) stimulated a great deal of research into relationships in groups, particularly in so-called 'leader-less' groups where people met together without a chairman or leader and without a particular purpose or agenda (other than that of gaining insight into group dynamics). This early post-war work is associated in the USA particularly with the National Training Laboratories at Bethal, Maine, and in Britain with the Tavistock Institute of Human Relations in London. Participation in such T-groups (as they began to be called) can be a very harrowing experience. To begin with it is a novel and somewhat embarrassing situation to come together for an evening or a week's stay without any pre-arranged task and with members uncertain as to what is required of them. At times the participants are indeed set a task, such as finding a solution to a problem of interest to the members, but even then the 'real' learning centres not on the task area but on the social and emotional problems of arriving at an agreed solution which is acceptable to the group as a whole.

A trained observer is with the group, who helps members to understand the conflicts, emotions and tensions generated in the group and these new insights and the new experiences a person has of himself and others constitute the learning process in the T-group.

Are T-groups effective as a method of *management* training? Do they achieve the increase in inter-personal sensitivity which is their aim? Do they affect some participants adversely? No definite answers can be given and T-groups have created considerable controversy. Both group psychotherapy and T-groups aim at breaking down barriers between the unconscious and the conscious mind on the grounds that overt, conscious actions often arise from unconscious motivation and that awareness of the hidden springs of his actions or thoughts will make a man more rational in his behaviour and in his thinking as well as more at ease with himself. Whether or not it has these effects, the process of introspection and of being exposed to the views which others in the group express of oneself often causes intolerable levels of anxiety. A private individual may well decide to take the risk of psychological discomfort (or worse) for the benefit he hopes to gain by joining such a group. But should organizations (as they often do) arrange for T-group sessions and encourage their managers to attend? Can attendance be truly voluntary in such circumstances?

Another problem is the competence of trainers or observers to deal with the anxiety states created in some participants. The trainer, after all, uses a psychiatric technique without being himself a psychiatrist. Furthermore, psychiatrists tend to select the patients who they think may benefit from group psychotherapy and they use different methods for other patients (or refer them to those who practise such other methods). Normally, members of T-groups are not screened for their ability to avoid breakdown in such groups and it is a convenient, but not necessarily true, myth that the skill of the leader is not so crucial since the group as a whole will give support to a distressed member.

The other controversy which surrounds the use of T-groups is not based on ethical considerations of possibly harmful effects but on the extent to which they prove beneficial. Here, the picture is divided, some evaluation studies reporting favourable changes in participants such as an increase in listening, tolerance and flexibility. (But according to Fiedler (whose work is discussed below), a directing, controlling or, if you like, autocratic leader does well in certain circumstances.) Evaluation of other groups shows no effects or negative effects, such as an increase in tension and irritability (see for example House 1967; Campbell and Dunnette 1968; Cooper and Maugham 1971).

It is not surprising that the effects of T-groups can be so different for different participants. If one accepts the notion that the unconscious mind contains thoughts, memories or impulses which have been repressed because they are unpalatable to the conscious mind then it follows that the conscious mind will try and keep them there. Resistance to breaking down the barriers between the conscious and unconscious mind will be strong and man's ingenuity in shielding himself from unwelcome insight is very great. Some people, therefore, will be unaffected by the experience, for some it will produce great anxieties, whilst some, no doubt, will grow in maturity and sensitivity through going through the process of uncovering hidden aspects of their personalities. Perhaps successful T-groups presuppose an openness to change and a willingness to reflect on relationships which is not very common.

A further question, of course, is: what happens to the trainee when he returns to his organization and the same constraints and pressures as before? Assuming that he has gained new insights and was not over-whelmed by the experience, will he be allowed to act on them? This is doubtful even where organization-wide T-group training is in operation. Much might depend on whether the T-groups in such a case are unstructured or whether they focus on defined problem areas for which participants try to find practical and creative solutions whilst they learn to become aware of their own attitudes and inter-personal strategies. T-group training is different in degree, if not always entirely in kind, from 'normal' management training. The latter aims to increase competence by imparting new knowledge and to give experience in practising new techniques. Thus, managers might go on a course to learn about computers, or a new system of financial control or they may come to learn how to conduct selection interviews. However, such training is often also intended to affect a participant's attitudes, be it towards technological change or towards employees. Attitudinal change is thought to follow in the wake of new information, through involvement and discussion with others or through overt role playing. However, as we have seen, T-groups aim at more fundamental changes in tapping normally hidden aspects of the participants' personalities.

T-group training is not, on the whole, as is sometimes suggested, a sinister method of controlling or manipulating managers. This conclusion is based on the fact that such training is not, in general, very effective in changing participants or their relationships with each other. But T-groups, particularly where attendance is not wholly voluntary and unconnected with the organization in which a person works, may pose ethical problems of intrusion into privacy and of turning some participants into psychological casualties.

Control through leadership

Leadership, too, can be viewed as a social exchange in which the leader provides rewards for the group by helping members to achieve their goals and the group provides rewards for the leader in the form of status and increased influence. However, this is only one way of conceptualizing leadership and the topic of leadership has been of interest to both psychologists and sociologists. It may usefully be thought of as a bridge topic between these two disciplines. It is neither a phenomenon which can be totally explained in terms of individual characteristics nor can it be simply reduced to group-centred processes, that is, the leader does more than epitomize the norms of the group. Furthermore, to answer the question of who becomes a leader and who maintains himself in that position involves an analysis also of societal goals, expectations and ideology.

Early work on leadership attempted to identify the *personality characteristics* which successful leaders have in common. This proved an unrewarding exercise since successful leaders could be shown to exhibit a wide range of rather different traits and attributes.

Due in part to the success of new group-based methods for selecting soldiers for training as officers during the Second World War, research on leadership in the 1950s focused on *situational determinants*. The main thrust of this approach was to highlight the dependence of the leader upon situational demands. This is the opposite of the trait approach which locates the leader's power within his personality. The situational approach reduces the leader's status to his ability to command liking from his group. This approach appealed more to sociologists than psychologists and Gouldner's (1954) description of wildcat strikes is an example. Dissatisfaction with the limitations of the

CHAPTER 9

David R. Weeks

Organizations and decision-making

Decision-making: an overview

Making decisions is something all of us do several times each day on a variety of issues which may have more or less important consequences for our lives. But what is 'a decision', what are its characteristic features? We can start this chapter by considering two fairly abstract and widely applicable definitions of a decision offered by social scientists. Firstly, Rose has suggested: 'Decisions are acts of choice between alternative courses of action designed to produce a specified result, and one made on a review of relevant information guided by explicit criteria' (Rose 1969 p 92). As an alternative formulation Shull *et al* offer the following definition of decision-making: 'a conscious and human process, involving both individual and social phenomena, based upon factual and value premises, which conclude with a choice of one behavioural activity from among one or more alternatives with the intention of moving toward some desired state of affairs' (Shull *et al* 1970 p 31). Thus to make a decision involves choosing a course of action, in a conscious way, in order to achieve some goal, taking into consideration such information as is considered relevant and is available; the outcome of such activity is a decision.

Before going into the general sociological approach to decision-making in organizations a little further it is important to make clear what such an approach excludes. For example, we shall not deal with the psychological problems of how individuals come to perceive the various alternatives open to them or the thought process that manipulate the available data prior to the making of a decision.[1] Nor shall we be

---

[1] A good summary of such psychological research may be found in Shull *et al* (1970) pp 37–168.

concerned with theories of decision-making derived from statistical analyses of decision situations. Such analysis is designed to determine the most 'rational' choice given a set of explicitly stated preconditions. This latter form of analysis is usually referred to as a 'normative' approach to decision making, i.e. it is concerned with stipulating what *should* or *ought* to be done in a situation given a certain goal (or goals) and a set of conditions.[2] The focus in this chapter will be on a 'descriptive' approach to decision-making, i.e. theory built up on the basis of empirical research into how actual decisions are made in their normal social context.

Describing the decision-making process in organizations is a fairly complicated task and our initial definition of the process would cover everything from deciding how many spoonfuls of sugar to have in our tea to decisions which might materially affect, in a major way, the lives of many other people, e.g. the decision to start a war, implement government policy, or declare workers redundant. All these decisions involve different goals, different time perspectives, different strategies of implementation and are based on a variety of information and other data.

Initially we can consider some rather more straightforward features of decision-making as it concerns organizational functioning. Firstly, decision-making is a continuing process; one decision usually calls for several other subsidiary decisions in order to achieve the original aim. There tends to develop a pyramid of decisions with the most general decision at the top, perhaps advocating a major change in organizational policy, followed by an expanding base of more particular decisions each concerned with a smaller area of activity.

This pyramidal structure of decisions within decisions is not limited to long-term decisions. Sometimes one of the decision-makers' goals is to achieve a decision within a specific time period, but even here where the process is fairly short term, a hierarchical structure of decision and sub-decisions still tends to develop. This was the finding of Dufty and Taylor (1970) in their study of a decision to relocate bus personnel in a public transport system in Perth, Australia.

One reason for the need to make further decisions is that the implementation of the initial decision may involve unintended consequences requiring revision of the original aim or the establishment of new organizational procedures. One scheme for overcoming surprise events emanating from within the organization is to involve as many organizational members as possible in the original decision. This

[2] A good introduction to the normative decision-making approach is provided by Kassouf (1970).

technique of 'participation' is considered in more detail later in the chapter.

An important point which must never be forgotten when we attempt to account for decision-making is that it is a *social* process. This is obvious in the simple sense that all decisions are likely to affect human beings in one way or another, both within and outside the organization, but the social influences will also impinge on the decision-making process itself. The goals of decision-making will be socially defined and and procedures through which they are implemented will be socially regulated, the information available will be socially selected and the calculation of possible outcomes will need to take account of the social environment in which the decision is to operate. Thus a whole range of social structures will need to be considered in any sociological explanation.

Initially we can note that the possibility of decision-making is not spread equally throughout an organization. Not all decisions carry equivalent weight and in an organization many decisions which would be covered by our initial definition are not considered to be decisions at all in the working context. Social scientists also tend only to focus their attention on a fairly narrow range of decisions, namely those that are made by members of an organization who hold positions of relatively high authority and power.

The question then arises of how we are to identify these positions of decision-making significance. This has posed no particular problem for organizational theorists and most have followed Simon when he views decision-making as synonymous with managing and managing is done by a relatively small proportion of the organization's personnel, called managers. In fact, decision-making is often considered to be exclusively a management prerogative and the most important aspect of management activity. This general view has been clearly described by Child:

> The term 'decision-makers' has been employed to refer to the power holding group on the basis that it is normally possible within work organizations to identify inequalities of power which are reflected in a differential access to decision-making on structural design, and even in a differential ability to raise questions on the subject in the first place. (Child 1973b p 101).

We must not assume, however, that such significant power to alter the shape of an organization goes unchallenged by other, less powerful, organization members. Organizations do, of course, exhibit co-operative activity; if they did not it is difficult to imagine them existing at all, but we should not be blinded to the other side of the coin where conflicts about goals exist (e.g. more profit as against more wages), and where the role of management as decision-maker is not one of protector of common aims or mutual referee in the interests of all concerned (e.g. all employees, consumers, or society in general), but rather management is the representative of a particular ideology or set of values. To quote from Child again: '. . . decision-making about organizations is not simply a matter of accommodating to operational contingencies. It is equally a political process into which other considerations, particularly the expression of power holders' values, also enter' (Child 1973a p 240).

Even if we can identify the decision-making group with a fair degree of precision the decision-makers themselves are unclear on exactly what constitutes a 'decision' rather than normal 'routine'. According to Child (1967 p 94) managers only describe decision-making as occupying about fifteen per cent of their work time. Thus some decisions which would fall within our original definitions are not regarded as 'proper' decisions by managers. There are a number of reasons why this may be the case. Firstly, decisions which involve implementing the decision of a superior in the organization may not be included as a 'real' or 'proper' decision. It may be only those decisions which place the individual concerned at the top of the pyramid of decisions that are counted. Following orders is not making decisions. Secondly, only decisions that make a positive difference may be counted. Thus to avoid making a decision, by ignoring the problem or deferring it, is in its way making a decision 'not to make a decision'. This can in fact be a very successful tactic in securing a long term objective. Later in the chapter we shall see how avoiding making a decision can help to sustain the status quo in an organization and, therefore, maintain the decision-makers' position of power. Thirdly, only decisions which visibly change the workings of an organization may be considered as proper decisions. Only if decisions change the routine of the organization and are, therefore, not simply concerned with maintaining that routine, will they be included. In fact this last point focuses on a widely used distinction in classifying types of decision, a distinction which is also closely linked to the distribution of decision-making power in the organization's hierarchy of authority positions.

In this respect we shall follow Weber's contention that within a bureaucratic structure it is the position in the organization which bestows authority on the occupant and not the occupant who moulds the position through his personal power and influence.

To return to the question of the different types of decision and how this is related to positions in the organizational hierarchy, we can distinguish between 'programmed' or 'routinized' decisions and 'non-programmed' or 'unroutinized' decisions. Some decisions are almost self-instigating in that they are simply part of a broader work programme or production schedule. March and Simon call this form of decision activity 'routinized':

> We will regard a set of activities as routinized, then, to the degree that choice has been simplified by the development of a fixed response to defined stimuli. If search has been eliminated, but a choice remains in the form of a clearly defined and systematic computing routine, we will say that the activities are routinized. (March and Simon 1970 p 96)

Examples would include many items covered by operational or clerical routines such as pricing normal orders or reordering supplies when stocks fall to a certain level.

The other major variety of decision March and Simon term 'unroutinized' is as follows: 'We will regard activities as unroutinized to the extent that they have to be preceded by program-developing activities of a problem-solving kind' (March and Simon 1970 p 96).

All 'routinized' decisions originally arise from an 'unroutinized' decision which establishes the 'routinized' procedure, e.g. deciding at what level reordering of supplies should occur. Simon uses the term 'non-programmed' to describe this variety of decisions and he stresses that they involve finding solutions to problems which are novel or unstructured. Examples here might include decisions concerned with what new product to manufacture or whether to make other forms of investment in terms of finance, material resources or personnel. In such a situation various forms of uncertainty may exist and in turn lead on to different decision strategies.

This distinction between 'routinized' or 'programmed' and 'unroutinized' or 'non-programmed' is not a precise one, rather the two types represent opposite ends along a continuum. In terms of the organizational hierarchy the tendency seems to be that the higher up the hierarchy one looks the more likely are decisions to be of an unroutinized or non-programmed type.

One other distinction we should bear in mind is that between *what* is decided (i.e. the actual decision) and *how* things are decided (i.e. the decision-making procedures). The major research effort has focused on *how* decisions come about without attempting to explain the origin of the decision-makers' goals. In other words the goals which the decisions are attempting to achieve are taken as given and it is the process of how one particular strategy emerges that is studied. To use Fox's terms, it is the 'procedural' rather than the 'substantive' norms which are scrutinized (Fox 1973b).

The reason for concentrating on procedures is often presented in terms of the social scientist's attempt to avoid bias and stick to those areas where 'objective' and 'scientific' study are possible. A representative statement on this issue is given by Taylor:

> The question of what values should be employed in decision-making is not only outside the province of the builder of normative models. It is also outside the province of psychology or the other empirical sciences, at least in so far as the choice of ultimate values is concerned. The methods of science provide no basis for determining what ultimate values should be. At least, this is the view of the majority of contemporary philosophers of science. (Taylor 1970 p 34)

The main point to be made with regard to this statement is not that social scientists could, or should, attempt to lay down value goals for decision-makers, but that neither should the social scientist ignore the content of the goals chosen by decision-makers. By not attempting to account for such goals the social scientist is guilty of error by omission.

Models of man as decision-maker

Much work has been done on how social scientists can best understand the decision-making problems and capacities of men working in organizations. The approaches to this issue have mirrored to some extent the development of different frames of reference used by social scientists to explain social phenomena. Initially economic arguments prevailed and ideas which described the behaviour of an ideal firm in an idealized economy were incorporated into explanations of decision-making within such firms. This required working with very general and suspect assumptions about human capacities for 'rational' decision-making, and these assumptions were, in many ways, inadequate for dealing with short-term situations:

'Economic Man' as decision-maker

The 'Economic Man' model of decision-making developed, not surprisingly, from a concern with man as decision-maker in economic organizations operating in a free, or relatively free, market situation. In line with the view presented by the 'scientific management' school, man is seen as a relatively passive agent of the organization responding in a fairly predictable way to the problems created by the organization's attempts to attain certain goals. The major goal was of course profit maximization and this was taken as the overriding assumption implicit in all decision-making activity. With this aim clearly in mind the decision-maker was seen as the rational arbiter between the various alternative strategies.

This view of decision-making Cyert and March term 'conventional theory' and suggest it has three main characteristics. Firstly, the decision-maker only deals with a particular and fairly narrow set of decisions, mainly concerned with setting the price of the product and the level of output. These decisions in turn are dependent on only a few variables, in particular, the demand for the product and the costs of producing it. Secondly, the environment in which the decision will operate is viewed in a fairly unambiguous way, the limits of variability being set by the total market demand and supply curves. Thirdly, no attention is given to, or interest shown in, the actual process by which individual firms reach decisions; to uncover the theoretical economic logic of the situation is deemed sufficient.

To summarize we can say that the Economic or Classical model of man involves two major assumptions. Firstly, it assumes that man seeks the optimal solutions (i.e. in economic terms the maximum profit) and secondly, it assumes that man seeks to obtain perfect knowledge of all possible alternatives which, therefore, allow him to select the best course of action. Given these assumptions decision-making does reduce to a simple question of technical expertise.

'Administrative Man' as decision-maker

As a response to the somewhat unreal assumptions involved in the model of Economic Man, several theorists, and particularly H. A. Simon, have sought to generate an alternative model based more firmly on the actual behaviour of decision-makers in organizations. This model we can term Administrative Man.

At a general level Lindblom has pointed out the limitations of any analysis of the Economic Man type when he writes: 'The usefulness of an analytical method cannot be understood in isolation from the social processes through which it is applied' (Lindblom 1958 p 305). In other words if no one can possibly perform according to the criteria of Economic Man then that model is not likely to be a very good guide to understanding actual behaviour.

More specifically we can consider each of the assumptions underlying Economic Man in turn. Firstly, there is the assumption of seeking the optimal or maximizing solution. This implies a definite choice from clear alternatives in pursuit of an unambiguous goal(s). But choices are not always clear cut and much subsidiary information has to be sought out involving the selection and rejection of ideas and often resulting in the search for 'satisfactory' alternatives rather than the 'optimal' one.

Simon has shown how this process works if we consider the aim of maximizing profit. A whole range of qualifications needs to be taken into account: is it long or short term profit; what about other satisfactions which may be important, such as stability; can we assume with the divorce of ownership from control in firms that professional managers will hold the same values and, therefore, seek the same goals as owner-managers? If the goal one is seeking is not clear then it is impossible to formulate distinct strategies as the boundaries of relevance are not known. As Scott has put it, the 'selection of strategies under uncertainty conditions requires the application of judgement, opinion, belief, subjective estimates of the situation, plus whatever objective data is available' (Scott 1971 p 24).

In a situation where incomplete knowledge is used to arrive at a satisfactory solution, a very important part is played by the social criteria according to which a solution is defined as satisfactory. In other words 'satisfactory' may not refer to the technical adequacy of an adopted decision to attain a goal, but rather it may reflect the most acceptable strategy in terms of maintaining the consensus of the decision-making group. March and Simon sum up the situation when they write: 'Most human decision-making, whether individual or organizational is concerned with the discovery and selection of satisfactory alternatives; only in exceptional cases is it concerned with the discovery and selection of optimal alternatives' (March and Simon 1970 p 95). In shorthand terms Economic Man 'maximizes' and is 'comprehensive', Administrative Man 'satisfices' and 'simplifies'.

Rationality in decision-making

The differences in approach that we have noted above between the models of Economic Man and Administrative Man can also be seen in terms of different assumptions about the kind of rationality which decision-making in organizations involves. Economic Man employs the assumption of 'objective rationality' in Simon's terms and this he defines in the following way. A decision is ' "objectively rational" if in fact it is the correct behaviour for maximizing given values in a given situation' (Simon 1965 p 76). As we have seen this is an unrealistic assumption about how human beings actually arrive at decisions, for to make decisions according to these criteria we would need encyclopaedic knowledge of all alternatives and their actual consequences, as well as a clear measure of which alternative best meets our aims.

If objective rationality is beyond our capabilities how do decision-makers come to grips with the problems they face? The quick answer is that they select and edit from their experience those features which they believe to be relevant; in other words, they simplify. This involves, as March and Simon point out in their article, that optimal solutions are replaced by satisfactory ones, that the possible courses of action are discovered as the decision-making process evolves, that former decisions are re-utilized in what are believed to be similar circumstances, that each decision has only a limited aim and application and decisions are seen to be somewhat independent of each other.

This simplifying process involving a limited search for alternatives and a high degree of selection is the basis of what Simon terms 'subjective rationality'. A decision is ' "subjectively" rational if it maximizes attainment relative to the actual knowledge of the subject' (Simon 1965 p 76). In these circumstances rational behaviour means substituting for the complex reality that exists a model of reality that is sufficiently simple to be handled by a human problem-solving process. In this way we can speak of the operation of a 'bounded rationality', that is, the limits to our objectively rational decision-making capabilities are bounded by our limited ability to perceive, understand and manipulate our social world.

One very important element in this kind of decision-making situation is the sort of limit which may be set to the definition of 'subjective rationality' itself. As we shall see later when we consider the role of 'intelligence' in providing information on which to base decisions, the 'facts' presented often appear to be selected and edited according to criteria which the informant believes the decision-maker himself believes to be 'subjectively rational'. Thus the background assumptions underlying the decision-making process in an organization play an important part in determining the decision outcome and in this sense there are no criteria of rationality apart from the decision rules themselves. This point is well put by Child when considering the role of decision-making as analysed by 'contingency theory'.[3] He writes,

[3] The term 'contingency theory' is a general one covering approaches to organizational analysis which suggest that different forms of organizational structure may be 'effective' under differing environmental conditions. For a more detailed discussion of this area see Child (1973a and 1973b).

Not only may the response of organizational decision-makers to
situational factors depend upon their own set of preferences (and
to some extent upon those of other groups whose support is needed)
concerning the mode of organization to be utilized, but additionally
the notion of effectiveness upon which contingency theory relies is
meaningful to decision-makers only in relation to their own criteria
of performance. (Child 1973a p 242)

Muddling through

From what has been said above we can see that two major strands in
the approach to decision-making suggested by the model of
Administrative Man are: (1) decision-making involves selection of goals
and information, and (2) this takes place within a developmental
process. These two points form the central argument of an approach to
understanding what happens in actual decision-making spelt out by
C. E. Lindblom in his article, 'The science of "muddling through" '.
Lindblom contrasts two attempts at describing and explaining decision-
making in organizations. The first approach he terms the Rational
Comprehensive Method, which corresponds closely to the Economic
Man model, and the second approach he labels Successive Limited
Comparisons, which includes and expands what we have said about
Administrative Man.

In particular Lindblom considers five specific differences between
the two approaches he outlines. According to his method of Successive
Limited Comparisons it is a mistake to consider the selection of goals
and values and the empirical investigation of particular problems as
independent; they are often closely intertwined. Consequently, given
that the distinction between policy ends and policy means is not a clear
one, any analysis which assumes such an ambiguous distinction will
only be of a limited utility. Thirdly, as a result of such a general
ambiguity a 'good' policy tends to represent a consensus amongst the
decision-makers and not a policy which is an optimal one in terms of
well-defined goals. One result of this necessarily partial analysis is that
the policy outcomes which emerge tend to deal with very limited areas
and this means that many potential policies and possible consequences
are neglected. Lastly the gradual evolution of decisions suggested by
this analysis, where policies emerge in fits and starts in response to
particular stimuli, means that the influence of any overarching theory
about the effectiveness of the decision tends to be passed by. What
emerges instead is what Lindblom calls policy formulation by 'incre-
mental comparison' where small changes (marginal variations) are
compared in order to arrive at the most appropriate decisions.

Decision-making goals

We can now turn to consider the nature of the goals which decision-makers may pursue and investigate how these relate to general problems faced by a wide variety of organizations. There is an inherent difficulty in attempting to analyse the aims and values of decision-makers in this way, in that it involves making general assertions about decision-making goals which will not necessarily coincide with the views that the decision-makers themselves hold about those goals. This problem is more or less unavoidable, however, if any attempt is to be made to generalize.

Conflict often occurs between the various goals as the pursuit of an optimal course of action to attain one goal may involve unwelcome costs in terms of the pursuit of one of the other goals. Cyert and March suggest that this form of conflict is never fully resolved, but rather that by decentralizing the decision-making process, direct clashes between goals are avoided and what results is a sequential attention to the various goals. Another important element in maintaining fairly smooth organizational functioning is the existence of 'organizational slack'. This is defined as follows: 'Slack consists in payments to members of the coalition in excess of what is required to maintain the organization' (Cyert and March 1963 p 36). In other words organizational slack is surplus capacity in one form or another. Slack operates to stabilize organizational functioning in two main ways: '1 by absorbing excess resources it retards upward adjustment of aspirations during relatively good times; 2 by providing a pool of emergency resources, it permits aspirations to be maintained (and achieved) during relatively bad times' (Cyert and March 1963 p 38). In this way crises associated with the failure to attain goals may be overcome, although this system can only operate within certain limits. If the degree of slack cannot provide sufficient resources to meet a particular situation, then an organization may fail to meet its goals to such an extent that its entire existence is threatened. The manner in which awareness of a crisis develops and draws on the organization's slack has been suggested by Downs. He contends that the search for new forms of activity will be triggered off when the level of utility yielded by current activities falls so far below aspirations that an unacceptable performance gap develops. Who actually sets the level of unacceptability and in what terms is a question that can only be answered by empirical research (Downs 1971).

In more general terms Cyert and March suggest that there are four main ways in which organizations attempt to secure internal stability in order that external goals may be pursued and attained. In a sense these attempts to maintain stability represent the internal goals of the organization. In considering Cyert and March's analysis we must bear in mind that they are speaking of the situation as it mainly applies to commercial firms.

The first internal goal which organizations seek is one we have already mentioned, that of the reduction of conflict between organizational goals. This is termed the 'quasi-resolution of conflict' by Cyert and March since, they suggest, for the reasons mentioned above, that conflict is endemic in organizations, and, therefore, impossible to eradicate completely. Means for keeping the conflict within manageable proportions include only requiring decisions to conform to a 'local rationality' within the firm, i.e. the total consequences of a particular decision are not known or required to be known. Also 'acceptable-level decision rules' develop which delegate decision-making authority to particular units, departments or positions within the organization. This policy clearly has important drawbacks and considerable risks attached to it. If the various autonomous decision-making units become too inconsistent one with another then the overall stability of the organization is put in danger. Another means for resolving conflict is by only giving sequential attention of the organization's various goals and thereby avoiding direct confrontation.

A second problem facing organizations is how to keep the relative ignorance with which they operate within reasonable bounds. This Cyert and March refer to as 'uncertainty avoidance', which is sometimes also called 'uncertainty absorption'. In order to reduce the strain of living with ignorance organizations tend to limit their decision-making to those areas where the degree of certainty is greater, or rather to those areas where the degree of uncertainty is relatively less. Thus they adopt short-run decisions, and rules which require frequent reviews of the situation. They avoid as much as possible planning for uncertain futures and emphasize 'planning where the plans can be made self-confirming through some control procedure' (Cyert and March 1963 p 119). One example of this last procedure is profit-making through a price mark-up on costs rather than attempting to calculate what the actual market demand will bear. The various channels by which decision relevant information becomes available also contribute to reducing many forms of uncertainty encountered in organizations.

A third mechanism contributing to internal stability is the institution of 'problemistic search', i.e. search which is motivated and guided by the need to find a solution to a particular problem. Thus when the organization is believed to be functioning 'adequately', regular, planned search is relatively unimportant in inducing changes in the organization as the 'need' for change is not highly visible. When a problem does arise and causes sufficient concern, however, then a specific solution will be sought, but even this is likely to occur within the general set of implicit organizational rules requiring 'uncertainty avoidance' and the 'resolution of conflict'. In these circumstances the most simple satisfactory solution will usually be adopted and is likely to reflect the particular training and experience, hopes and expectations, of the personnel involved.

Finally, the organization does not need to tackle each new threat to its stability afresh, as Cyert and March suggest there is a continuous process of 'organizational learning' in operation. In this way, by feeding back relevant experience into its own system the organization may seek to avoid future problems by adapting its goals or its 'attention rules' (i.e. procedures designed to detect problems), or by changing its 'search rules' (i.e. the way in which it attempts to locate solutions).

Influential and stimulating as the work of Cyert and March has been it shares many difficulties with other 'systems' approaches to organizations. In particular it is all too easy to talk about organizations as if they were individual decision-makers. The general point has been well made by Silverman: 'By concentrating on organizations as decision-making systems, one may too easily conclude that all that happens within them can be understood purely in terms of this system, and that meanings which derive from outside it are residual or random' (Silverman 1970 p 205). In this way the external environment that makes, for example, the search for profit a necessary and desirable goal (to which the various internal goals we have considered above are subservient) tends to be overlooked.

Organizational decisions and organizational structures

Although the concept of organizational structure is by no means an unambiguous or uncontroversial one, sufficient has been said in earlier chapters to justify speaking of structure as patterns of regularity of social behaviour which persist and typify an organization. On this basis Gore and Dyson make the following comment on the relationship between decision-making and organizational structure. They write:

> . . . it is doubtful that decisions account for much of what happens within organizations except as they lead to or provide linkages between other elements of organization. Vastly more important is structure, formal and informal. It is the structure of organization

which embodies the authoritative allocation of values, defines communication patterns, and specifies the division of labour. (Gore and Dyson 1964 pp 1—2).

Thus Gore and Dyson are suggesting that the external constraints faced by the organization and the internal routines embedded in the organization, are more important in determining decision outcomes) than is often supposed. It is the premises on which decision-making behaviour is based that are of particular interest. In what follows we shall consider in turn a number of the influences hinted at in Gore and Dyson's general statement, namely, the factors of environment, technology, intelligence, communication and chance. Firstly, however, we shall review a piece of empirical research which considers the general nature of structural influences on decision-making in organizations.

'Organizational structure and managerial decision behaviour' — an empirical investigation

In a study of the way in which various aspects of organizational structure were interrelated with associated managerial decision behaviour, L. Vaughn Blankenship and R. E. Miles collected evidence on decision-making from 190 managers at all levels, working in eight organizations in the light manufacturing and electronics field. The data they collected on decision-making was provided in the form of self-reporting by the managers concerned. The aim of the study was to redress the balance in research on decision-making which had mainly concentrated on attitudinal, demographic and personality variables to the exclusion of structural variables.

The authors divided the managers' involvement in the decision-making process into three categories. Managers could *initiate* the process or be involved in *consultation* during the process or be responsible for approving the *final choice* at the end of the process. These aspects of involvement were considered in relation to three structural variables which defined the managers' position. These structural variables were: the size of the organization in which they worked, in terms of the number of employees; their position in the authority hierarchy of the organization; and the span of control of each manager, measured in terms of the number of subordinates he directly controlled. They were questioned with regard to decision-making in five areas: personnel expansion, personnel selection, personnel promotion, equipment purchases involving expenditure in excess of a certain figure ($500) and decisions involving other purchases.

According to their data the authors found that by far the most important structural factor was the position which the individual held in the authority hierarchy. For those at the top end of the hierarchy the typical pattern was that they enjoyed considerable autonomy from their superiors, they often made final choices and their opinions carried considerable weight when consulted by their superiors. To a much lesser extent did they initiate the decision-making process, but rather they depended on their subordinates to raise the problems. At the lower end of the hierarchy the pattern is more or less reversed. Managers there did not consider their opinions carried much weight with their superiors when they were consulted, they did not rely on subordinates to raise issues, but rather received instructions from above although a surprisingly high proportion of them claimed the right to make final choices. The structural variable of organizational size seemed much less significant than hierarchical position; span of control was found to be the least important influence on decision-making behaviour. From this study, which stresses the importance of hierarchical position we can turn to some other factors, both external and internal, which are likely to influence decison-making processes.

Organizational decision-making and environment

The environment, in interrelationship with which an organization operates, is clearly a massive and complex influence on its functioning and to detail all such possible influences stemming from this source would be impossible. Moreover the environment is changing all the time adding a dynamic element to the analysis. In face of such overpowering complexity it is still perhaps worth noting two aspects of the environment which are of particular importance.

Firstly, as Thompson and McEwen point out, if an organization has a discrete product with a stable market for that product the problem of goal-setting is likely to be a much less difficult one for the decision-maker than if those conditions did not exist. In Cyert and March's terms intergoal conflict is likely to be much reduced in that the degree of uncertainty avoided will be higher, requiring less problemistic search and resulting in a positive and consistent body of organizational learning.

Secondly, the manner in which decision-making is distributed throughout an organization may be dependent on these same factors. We will consider this more fully later but it is clear that Marks and Spencer can afford to extend participation in decision-making to their lower-grade workers because the firm enjoys a profitable and secure market position. This may not be the only reason for the introduction of participative management, of course, and one other factor may be a legal requirement to establish a works council or similar body, i.e. government intervention may be a very important environmental influence in any number of ways.

Technology

We can consider the influence of technology on decision-making in two main ways. Firstly we can investigate the relationship between the production technology of an organization and the kind of control mechanisms, i.e. the decision-making machinery which may be associated with this technology. Secondly, we can consider the effects of advanced technology, namely computers and the like, on the traditional prerogatives of the human decision-maker.

The relationship between production technology and managerial control mechanisms has been investigated by Kynaston Reeves and Woodward (1970).[4] They found a definite relationship between the type of production technology and the forms of decision-making authority that accompanied them. Where firms were involved in unit or small batch production then managerial control normally had a unitary character administered by personal directives. After organizations had grown in size and begun to utilize large batch and mass production techniques involving a considerable degree of specialization, managerial control tended itself to become specialized or fragmented although personal administrative direction still persisted. Further growth or specialization, but retaining the same technology, tended to be associated with fragmented control co-ordinated and implemented by impersonal or mechanical administration techniques. This change typically occurred after a firm's operation has been analysed by Operational Research techniques and the organization had introduced computerized elements into its administration. The final phase in this developmental sequence occurred if firms adopted process production technology when control tended to revert back to a unitary form, but was administered by mainly impersonal or mechanical techniques.

The exact relationship between the technology and the forms of managerial control remains a complex one and certainly it would be rash on the basis of this evidence alone to speculate as to the causal relationships involved. One interesting sidelight is thrown on this issue by Burns (1964) in terms of the effect on managers' behaviour. He

---

[4] This is not to suggest that Kynaston Reeves and Woodward are the only workers in this area and for a stimulating alternative analysis see Pugh *et al* (1969).

noted a definite positive relationship between the rate of technical and other changes occurring in an organization, and the percentage of their work time that managers spent talking to other organizational members and outsiders. One possible explanation of this phenomenon is that if change is occurring at a fast enough rate, more formalized means of communication and control simply do not have time to develop adequately to meet the demands. On this basis an organization where managers spend much of their time on the telephone or out of their offices may be displaying a sign of health rather than one of degeneration.

The other important issue involving technology is how traditional human decision-making skills have been affected by the development of electronic data processing and problem-solving machines. Firstly, it has led to a greater rationalization of decision-making processes. In particular, relevant information tends to become much more readily available in a precise form, sooner. Secondly, as a result of this greater knowledge, decisions of a wider scope, involving greater repercussions, can be contemplated and this tends to push the decision-making process higher up the authority hierarchy of an organization. Thirdly, the whole rhythm of work may be altered in order to ensure the continuous supply of information to the data processing machinery and this leads to the fourth effect, the need for a new understanding of the man/machine relationship, particularly where machine expertise may mean redundancy for personnel in middle management. At the end of all the technical manipulation, however, it must always be remembered that it is ultimately human beings who programme the computer, set the goals and make the final decision as to which alternative to adopt.

Intelligence

Organizational intelligence can be defined as the gathering, processing, interpreting and communicating of the technical and political information needed in the decision-making process. The nature and degree of intelligence utilized by an organization will vary according to the external and internal problems it encounters in its decision-making procedures. Wilensky (1967) suggests that the more an organization is in conflict with its social environment or the more an organization is dependent on it for achieving major goals, then the more resources will be allocated to the intelligence function especially in the employment of 'contact men'. The contact man supplies political and ideological intelligence the leader needs in order to find his way around modern society.

If an organization is especially dependent upon the unity or support of its personnel it will again devote considerable resources to the intelligence function, in particular by employing 'internal communications experts'. The internal communications specialist supplies political and ideological intelligence the leader needs in order to maintain his authority.

If, however, both external and internal environments are believed to be stable and rationalized, then the main intelligence thrust will involve expenditure on what Wilensky calls 'facts-and-figures' men. The facts and figures man supplies technical, economic, legal or scientific intelligence that helps the leader build his case in dealing with outsiders and members, fend off attacks, and compete with rival organizations for markets, power and prestige. Thus intelligence is not a uniform commodity, but rather it is a many faceted resource which decision-makers use in whatever way they believe to be necessary to enable them to minimize that area of organizational functioning about which they feel most uncertain.

Uncertainty may take several forms, but two kinds of intelligence information are particularly important in determining the decision-making procedure considered appropriate. Firstly, decision-makers may be certain or uncertain about their preferences regarding possible outcomes, and secondly, they may have certain or uncertain beliefs about the cause and effects relation underlying courses of action. Deciding between outcomes involves employing value assumptions which intelligence information alone cannot determine, but the interaction of this form of uncertainty with the other more technical variety does produce an interesting analysis of decision-making strategies.

If outcome preferences and beliefs about cause and effect are certain, then decision-making is a simple computational procedure. If preferences are uncertain, but beliefs about cause and effects are certain, then a compromise strategy may apply. If preferences are certain, but cause and effect beliefs uncertain, then a judgemental procedure will be required, but if uncertainty exists on both counts, then only inspiration can provide an answer (Hall 1972 pp 263–5). This analysis, taken from Thompson (1967), can be represented in diagrammatic form (see fig. 1).

Wilensky also points out that decisions do not necessarily improve because there is more time or intelligence available, in fact this may be a disadvantageous situation in more ways than one. He writes:

Decisions involving many people, much money, great uncertainty or vast risks, and major innovations evoke action and advice from every

Figure 1 Decision strategies

		Preferences regarding possible outcomes	
		Certainty	*Uncertainty*
Beliefs about cause/effect relations	Certain	Computation	Compromise
	Uncertain	Judgement	Inspiration

Source: Thompson, J.D. (1967) *Organizations in Action*
McGraw-Hill Book Company

> specialized unit at every level of the hierarchy, thereby increasing the dangers of overload, distortion, or blockage of communication and of paralyzing delays. At the extreme, a costly decision that fails can activate an energetic search for evidence to confirm the mistaken policy. (Wilensky 1967 p78)

In the light of this judgement he concludes that

> Only the big (costly, risky, innovative) policy decisions that are also urgent are likely to activate high-quality intelligence, because deliberation then moves out of channels toward men of generalized wisdom, executives and experts alike, communicating informally and effectively at the top. (Wilensky 1967 p 81)

Communication

Much work has been done studying different patterns of communication in order to discover their relative effectiveness in decision-making situations. A good deal of this research has been based on laboratory controlled experiments and such findings as have been derived may, therefore, not be directly relevant to communication within a functioning organization.

The general problem facing any communication system has been well stated by Rose: 'The communication and control system . . .is paired with a dynamic social system in which struggles for power and status often intrude on harmonious technical functioning' (Rose 1969 p 193). A specific piece of research that investigates this situation has been conducted by Webber (1970). His interest in this area was stimulated by the work of Burns (1964). In particular, Burns had noted how the perceptions of superiors and subordinates in management positions contrasted when, say, a superior's description of his own job was compared with the description given by one of his subordinates, or vice versa. In order to clarify this finding Webber tested thirty-four pairs of managers, each pair being composed of a superior and his immediate subordinate.

When the findings were analysed Webber found that consistent distortions in the perceptions of verbal interactions had occurred. Specifically, initiating personnel in an interaction tended to exaggerate and receivers to underestimate the volume of the interaction. Superiors tended to exaggerate their initiation downwards while subordinates underestimated this form of interaction. In general perceptual distortion of downward communication was greater than the distortion of subordinates' initiations up to their superiors. Thus superiors perceive more total time interacting with subordinates than the latter perceive occurring. Webber also found that systematic distortions occurred according to whether an individual typically received many or only a few communications. The fewer received, the more likely was their volume to be exaggerated; a similar exaggeration occurred amongst people whom Webber defined as having passive personalities.

The findings reported do not, of course, provide reliable evidence about the kind and degree of distortion likely to be found elsewhere, but, as Webber points out, the considerable emphasis which is nowadays placed on democratic and supportive management style, may be largely wasted effort if the message gets lost in the distortion of its communication to those it is intended for.

At a broader level Pettigrew (1972) has noted how control of communication channels can be a powerful tool in influencing decision outcomes. He reports how the decision to install a computer and associated facilities was influenced by the ability of the Head of Management Services to control the flow of information and opinion stemming from alternative sources within the firm, namely from the Systems Department Manager and the Programming Department Manager. By acting as a 'gatekeeper' for technical information, the Head of Management Services was able to prevent what he considered undesirable information from reaching the ultimate decision-making body, the Board of Directors. In this way he was able to persuade the Board of the superiority of his own preferences and thus circumvent the established procedures for rational search and intelligence activities.

Chance

This is a factor which Deutsch and Madow (1961) suggest may influence which individuals rise to powerful decision-making positions in an organization. If we assume that promotion to such positions is dependent on a history of successful decision-making, then Deutsch and Madow assume that some individuals will make what turn out to be 'correct' decisions purely as a matter of chance, they will then display what the authors call 'pseudo wisdom'. On this basis they may well be promoted, although for the wrong reasons, but they are unlikely to make further correct decisions any more often than their less successful former peers.

The effect that this kind of chance occurrence will have on the decision-making structure of the organization will depend on a number of factors. Firstly, the number of decision-makers gaining promotion through demonstrating 'pseudo wisdom' will depend on the difficulty of making a 'correct' decision by chance and the number of such decisions necessary to be considered for promotion. Secondly, the degree of influence which a promotion is likely to bestow on an individual will be determined by the kind of decision-making freedom to which it introduces him; if the structural constraints are as great as some theorists suggest, then any particular individual's influence may be fairly slight.

The legitimation of decision-making

As we noted earlier the possibility of conflict is endemic in organizations, not only in terms of the conflicts managerial decision-makers face between different decision-making goals, but also with regard to the conflicts which may arise over the implementation of decisions and the nature of the decison-making processes. In other words decision-makers face not only a technical problem, but also a legitimatory problem arising out of the unequal distribution of power within the organization.

We can consider this problem of legitimation in relation to two broad strategies of decision-making common within formal organizations.

The first strategy designed to achieve effective control over the organization and ensure the implementation of policy decision is that of centralization. Centralization of decision-making (i.e. concentrating decision-making power in the hands of a few decision-makers at the top of the organization) has three main purposes according to Simon (1965). These are that centralization secures co-ordination, maximizes the use of expertise and locates responsibility. Whether these aims are achieved, however, will depend on the degree of acceptance that such centralization receives from other members of the organization. Centralization may be effected in two main ways, either by introducing general rules to limit the discretion of subordinates, or by relieving subordinates directly of their decision-making functions. An example of the first method is given by Sampson (1973) in his study of the giant multinational company ITT (International Telephone and Telegraph). Sampson relates how detailed sets of objectives are laid down for each section of the company and the consequent performance closely and frequently monitored. In this way the decision-making discretion available to even quite senior members in the management hierarchy is strictly limited. Repeated failure to achieve the set objectives leads to reallocation, demotion or dismissal.

Centralization as a strategy of organizational control may not always be available or appropriate. Some decisions may need to be taken quickly to be effective, for example, where technical innovation and flexibility are important organizational, and, therefore, decision-making, goals. Also where decisions involve mainly technical expertise related to the complexity of the manufacturing process, a centralized decision-making procedure may be unworkable if local problems are to be solved quickly and easily and not disrupt the pursuit of more general, long-term policy goals.

If we focus on the area of decision-making which is concerned with general policy in an organization then one alternative strategy to centralization is decentralization, and this mode of maintaining control has enjoyed a certain vogue in the recent management literature designed to help the manager cope with practical everyday problems of control. By policy decisions in this context we mean general decisions which affect the operation of an organization in a major way. Such decisions would focus upon issues like the nature and level of production, and the consequences for the kind and number of employees, the general terms and conditions of employment, the introduction of major changes affecting production and/or employment.

Simon (1960) suggests that in business firms decentralization may be effective for two major reasons. Firstly, it may bring the profit motive to bear on a larger group of executives, thereby allowing profit goals to be established for individual subdivisions of a company, and secondly, it may allow decisions to be taken at a local level which co-ordinates related activities without the constant need to refer decisions upward.

This procedure is quite safe for higher decision-makers if they are certain that the degree of socialization of organizational members is so great due to training, knowledge and commitment, that each individual member is self-policing. One example of this degree of socialization where decentralization poses no threat to higher authority is given by Wilensky when discussing the United States Forest Service. He writes:

> The classic intelligence problem of branch, plant or field unit 'covering up' (i.e. rigging performance figures or hiding local problems) is minimized. Infused with professionalism, imbued with *esprit de corps*, the Forest Service is able to centralize intelligence sources, yet do without close supervision and elaborate inspection machinery. (Wilensky 1967 p 60)

In other words the organization members are adequately 'programmed' to 'make' decisions in a highly predictable fashion.

This degree of control and acceptance of authority as legitimate is probably limited to relatively few organizations although Daniel and McIntosh stress that careful recruitment and training is an important element in the participative management system of Marks and Spencer, for example. In most other, particularly commercial, organizations the incidence of strikes and other work disputes is sufficient evidence to suggest that the degree of legitimacy accorded to managerial decision-makers is quite often not very high. One tactic adopted by management to cope with this problem is to attempt to convey the impression of organizational unity by inviting workers to participate in decision-making processes in some form or other.

Lammers (1967) has suggested that participation may take two main forms: direct participation and indirect participation. Direct participation means a personal involvement by each individual worker in the decisions that directly affect his day-to-day work routine. The scope of such decision participation is fairly narrow and the evidence seems to suggest that involving workers in this way does increase their job satisfaction and, to a lesser extent, their commitment to the organization. Indirect participation involves decision-making at a higher level of control and, therefore, poses a much greater threat to traditional management prerogatives. A common method of indirect participation involves representatives of the workers contributing to decision-making through such bodies as Works Councils. In many European countries the establishment of Works Councils is a statutory requirement, but their actual effectiveness is a question for debate and research.

In summarizing many research studies on the workings of such bodies Lammers notes how a whole battery of defence tactics have been developed by management to make such decision-making bodies impotent. Among the more common tactics are: not convening meetings; using meetings solely for the downward transmission of information; and attempting to transform indirect participation into direct participation. This last tactic may be implemented in several ways: by treating members of committees as individuals and not representatives; by ensuring that the management representative is of a low authority with insufficient power to deal with important issues; by restricting discussion to trivial items; by limiting the extent to which Trade Union representatives are able to consult with their full time Trade Union officials; by not co-operating in the drafting of necessary bylaws to implement decisions made; or refusing to keep official and detailed minutes of meetings.

Given the complexity of the situation any general conclusions about the effects of participation are hard to draw, but we can review the results of particular cases. One fairly successful attempt at introducing participation by ICI at Gloucester is reported by Daniel and McIntosh (1972). In this case an early attempt was made to involve all workers, including those at the lowest level, and their proposals and preferences were conveyed upwards through a joint management and union working party who further refined the suggestions before a final decision was made by a joint union/management negotiating body.

The results of this process appeared to be: a higher commitment to the firm by workers; an increase in the transmission of relevant information from the shopfloor; an improvement in negotiation machinery and greater speed and smoothness in introducing the agreed changes. The question of whose success this ultimately represented we shall return to shortly. (At ICI the agreement reached entailed cutting the number of employees by twenty-five per cent.)

In another setting Alutto and Belasco (1972) investigated the degree of participation in decision-making enjoyed by school teachers in Western New York State. Although the authors took into account a wide range of variables their main argument sought to show that it is not the absolute level of participation that determines commitment to an organization, rather it is the difference between the degree of participation an individual desires and the amount he actually enjoys that is significant. On this basis organizational members could be in a situation of 'decisional deprivation' (i.e. they desired a greater opportunity to participate) or experience 'decisional equilibrium', or even 'decisional saturation' (i.e. actually be more involved in decision-making than they desired). Using these categories they concluded that a situation of decisional deprivation does not necessarily imply a lower commitment to the organization. Indeed, for those experiencing decisional saturation, increased decision-making obligations actually became counter productive to their commitment. One major effect of decisional deprivation, however, was to increase the militancy of claims for organizational change.[5]

We can now turn to the question of the likely outcomes if workers are involved in the policy decision-making process to a greater degree. As we have seen, on the level of individual work tasks direct participation does seem to increase job satisfaction, at least in the short term. Whether this is likely to persist is another question, for as Daniel and McIntosh point out, the extension of participation tends to increase demands for further change in the same direction (1972).

Even where indirect participation of workers at a higher level has been instituted, as for example, in Yugoslavia and Holland, it is doubtful whether it is the workers who benefit most. In an extensive review of the literature on this issue Mulder (1971) has pointed out that simply allowing workers to participate in decision-making does not overcome the knowledge differentials which exist within an organization, and 'knowledge' may be a key factor in the decision-making process. In fact Mulder suggests that participation may decrease the power of the workers and not increase it as might be assumed.[6] He summarizes this proposition in the following hypothesis: "When there are relatively large differences in the expert power of members of a system, an increase in participation will increase the power differences between members' (Mulder 1971 p 34). Several studies of participatory decision-making in organizations, as well as laboratory experiments, tend to confirm this view.

The benefits of participation must, therefore, be seen within a framework of consensus or common interests which all participants in the decision-making process share. If all are agreed upon the organization's goals (and their relative priority), then participation may have beneficial results for an organization's efficiency and productivity

[5] Some research on the personality determinants of the effects of participation can be found in Vroom (1959). In brief his findings were that authoritarians and persons with weak independence needs are apparently unaffected by the opportunity to participate in making decisions. But egalitarians and those with strong independence needs develop more positive attitudes towards their jobs and increase in job performance through participation.

[6] This argument assumes a 'zero-sum' model of power, i.e. a gain in power by one group necessarily entails a loss of power by another group. An alternative analysis of power which seeks to demonstrate parallels between economic growth and general benefit, and the extension of power through participation and all round benefits, is offered by Lammers (1967).

within those terms. The major problem, of course, is securing agreement on those common goals and in this respect an expanding economy with visible social change may provide a particularly conducive environment for the discovery of shared aims. But this takes the question of how to achieve 'organizational effectiveness' out of the realm of simply the organization itself and places it firmly in the arena of political issues which are significant in the wider society. As Fox (1973a) points out, if workers start challenging the *status quo* on, say, income distribution, then their demands tend to be labelled 'unreasonable', 'irresponsible' and 'unpatriotic'. In this way we can see that the attempt to separate out 'industrial' or 'organizational' issues and decisions from 'political' issues and decisions in any absolute sense is unrealistic. The desire to propagate a belief in such a distinction may be seen as one element in a managerial ideology which is striving to maintain or increase the decision-making powers of the managerial group.

Another form of the legitimation problem which managerial decision-makers face may be in terms of justifying their continued existence as part of a decision-making group. Cohen *et al* (1972) raise this aspect of organizational functioning when they write:

> . . . an organization is a collection of choices looking for problems, issues and feelings looking for decision situations in which they might be aired, solutions looking for issues to which they might be the answer, and the decision-makers looking for work. (Cohen *et al* 1972 p 2)

If this is the case, then we should bear in mind Garfinkel's suggestion that instead of viewing decisions as responses to problems we should also consider the possibility of past activities being retrospectively defined as decisions. He writes:

> Decision-making in daily life would thereby have, as a critical feature, the *decision maker's task of justifying a course of action.* The rules of decision-making in daily life, i.e. rules of decision-making for more or less socially routinized and respected situations, may be much more preoccupied with the problem of assigning outcomes their legitimate history than with the question of deciding before the actual occasion of choice the conditions under which one, among a set of alternative possible courses of action, will be elected. (Garfinkel 1967 p 114)

Finally, we can pose the question of whether the various forms of participation experiments considered above disclose any real promise for radically changing organizational decision-making processes and consequently organizational structure. It is of course difficult to generalize, but the outlook for the immediate future can only be described as 'not bright'. As Perrow (1973) points out, organizations make enormous investments of all kinds in order to continue operating in a stable and predictable fashion. They develop vocabularies of communication and procedures of operation which insulate them against the threat of change.

One way in which the premises which underlie decision-making are maintained is by careful selection and recruitment of personnel. For example, take the following recommendation of Simon: 'We haven't known very much about how to improve human decision-making skills, but we observe that some people have these skills much better developed that others. Hence, we rely on selection as our principal technique for improving complex decision-making skills in organizations' (Simon 1960 p 12). If we reasonably assume that the criteria for selection are the same as the criteria the selector applies to his own decision-making, then it is hardly surprising that the continuity of decision-making procedures remains unthreatened.

An empirical example of how this process of self-maintenance operates is provided by Cyert and March. They recount the series of events that led up to selection of one particular firm of consultants to advise on the desirability of installing electronic data processing equipment. The choice of possible consultant had been whittled down to two firms. Firm Alpha was originally selected, but then further search was instigated (on quite what grounds remain unclear) and a second firm, Beta (and only Beta) came into the running. On almost every count both firms were equally well qualified and this added further difficulties to the decision-making process, as Cyert and March note:

> The ambiguity in expectations that arose from the difficulty of making objective rankings of Alpha and Beta resulted in a decision process that seemed to be dominated in large part by unexpectational factors. The final staff memorandum on the decision clearly recommended Beta. This recommendation was accepted by the controller. As he put it, 'I asked the boys to set down the pros and cons. The decision was Beta. It was their decision'.
>
> The staff members involved, on the other hand, seemed to have felt that the decision to search further rather than hire Alpha immediately reflected some bias in favour of Beta on the part of top management, and this was probably reinforced by the fact that the controller specified that Beta and only Beta would be asked to make

a proposal. Since the differences between the two firms were not particularly striking, it is not surprising that these plausible assumptions about the attitudes of others were consistent with subsequent perceptions of the alternatives and the final recommendation. (Cyert and March 1963 p 64)

A second incident revealing the same kind of influence of established procedure or preferences occurred later in the same organization. Once the consultants had assessed the conditions and requirements of the firm they offered two alternative plans to management, each equally cost efficient systems. They were then asked to make a concrete recommendation and eventually they came down in favour of a computer installation. Cyert and March make clear that they did not arrive at this choice by falsifying any of their research data, but because '... they had to make a judgment as to which uncertain costs and savings should be counted, and this judgment was almost certainly affected as had been earlier judgments of staff members within the organization, by their perception of management's attitudes and predilections' (Cyert and March 1963 p 66). Thus in this instance we can see that even individuals external to the organization had been drawn into the prevailing organizational climate, thus adding further evidence to the view which stresses the strength and pervasiveness of established decision-making procedures.

Concluding comments

As has hopefully become clear during the course of this chapter, decision-making in organizations can be studied from many angles. We have offered a sociological interpretation of that process, an interpretation which in many ways ties together some of the aspects of other forms of analysis. With regard to psychological variables for example, whilst a sociological perspective does not deny the importance of personality factors and the perceptual capacities of individual decision-makers, it places them within a structure of social organization, i.e. it locates them in the context of their operation. Similarly, with economic or statistical analyses, a sociological perspective adds a depth of background factors which help to explain why organizations often fail to operate according to the mathematical predications derived from statistical models of their functioning. In these ways a sociological analysis provides a central key to understanding how and why decision-making processes in organizations are the way they are. Sociological analysis itself, however, is not without its own problems. We have seen that a wide range of behaviour could fall under the general heading of decision-making, but we do not possess one form of sociological analysis which would cover them all.

One final point needs to be added about the general form of socio-logical reasoning underlying the arguments of this chapter. Throughout we have adopted in many ways an uncritical approach to the kinds of 'data' and 'facts' which form the basis for any analysis of 'decision-making' behaviour. The existence and importance of social structures, as defined in the various pieces of research referred to, has been assumed without very much question. This type of approach accurately reflects the majority of sociological research on decision-making in organizations, and such assumptions are often taken as a prerequisite for generating useful sociological generalizations. Other varieties of sociological approach, however, regard such assumptions as problematic and question, for example, the basis on which any analysis of 'normal' decision-making is built. This theme is continued and expanded in the following two chapters, which in many ways provide a stimulating and critical alternative sociological approach to that presented here, but still within the substantive area of knowledge and information as aspects of organizational control.

CHAPTER 10

Kenneth Thompson

Organizations as constructors of social reality (I)

Introduction

The primary intention of this chapter is to explore some ways in which the 'reality' of organizations is constructed by participants employing various shared rationalities and logics. In particular, it will explore the ways in which some rationalities perform ideological functions, taking as examples managerial or business ideologies.

1 System and action approaches

Despite some of the exceptions discussed in the previous chapter, decision-making theories have tended to adopt a systems approach to organizational analysis. They have viewed organizations as co-operative systems oriented to the pursuit of a systems goal which coincides with the production task.[1] The central criticism of such system theories is that by framing their analyses in terms of organizational tasks or functions, they reify the organization as an entity, with characteristics independent of the social processes through which organizational members construct and construe social reality. In so doing they miss some of the most interesting questions as far as sociology is concerned.

It can be argued that, by concentrating on organizations as decision-

[1] The cybernetic models of organizations as systems do not altogether escape this criticism, even though they may claim to dispense with the 'short-cut' explanation of organization as simply the epitome of the purposes of its designers, its leaders, or its key members (cf Katz and Kahn 1970 pp 149–58). They still tend to assume that the sensing and feedback mechanisms so crucial to the cybernetic system are oriented to organizational purposes.

making systems, we are too easily led to conclude that all that happens within them can be understood purely in terms of this system, and that meanings which derive from outside it are of little account. This is to examine the organization only through the minds of the top level decision-makers. But systems in themselves only have problems from the perspective of the participants, and there are as many different problems as there are definitions of the situation and ends (Silverman 1970 p 206). Thus a study of conflict in the British coal industry showed how specialization favoured the development of separate outlooks and perceived interests among different occupational categories such as managers, clerks and manual workers. And within each of these categories there existed separate definitions of the situation deriving from experiences at work and in the local community. These different definitions were reinforced by the cultures which developed in the face-to-face work groups (Scott 1963; Silverman 1970 pp 206–8).

It should be evident from the discussion in Chapter 6 that an action approach to organizations treats members' ('actors'') involvements and interests as having a problematic relationship to such goals and procedures as exist in the organization. The assumption of organization-wide consensus on goals and values is sacrificed in favour of examining the ways in which actors actively interpret and seek to control relevant aspects of the organization. It emphasizes that the impact of 'organizational goals' on 'organizational action' is mediated by processes of interpretation and negotiation in which groups attempt to protect and advance their specific interests. It cannot be stressed too strongly that what is at issue in this type of analysis is not simply different viewpoints and interests regarding rewards and effort (inducements and contributions), but also different contributions to the *social construction of reality* – the reality in the case of organizations being such notional entities as goals, rules, roles and other elements that are believed to consitute the organization's structure (Cf. Elger 1975). The same basic issues arise whatever the type of organization – whether it is a powerful industrial enterprise like the National Coal Board, or more precarious enterprises such as religious sects.

2 The social construction of reality in organizations

In their seminal book, *The Social Construction of Reality*, Berger and Luckmann discuss the paradoxical process by which people construct social order and yet regard it as a reality that exists independently of themselves. Berger emphasizes that the relationship between man, the producer, and the social world, his product, is a dialectical one, in that the product continuously acts back upon its producer:

> The fundamental dialectic process of society consists of three moments, or steps. These are externalization, objectivation, and internalization. Only if these three moments are understood together can an empirically adequate view of society be maintained. Externalization is the ongoing outpouring of human beings into the world, both in the physical and the mental activity of men. Objectivation is the attainment by the products of this activity (again both physical and mental) of a reality that confronts its original producers as a facticity external to and other than themselves. Internalization is the reappropriation by men of this same reality, transforming it once again from structures of the objective world into structures of the subjective consciousness. It is through externalization that society is a human project. It is through objectivation that society becomes *sui generis*. It is through internalization that man is a product of society. (Berger 1969 pp 3–4)

Internalization occurs in the process of socialization. Initiation into institutions, both in childhood and adult life, involves learning the various patterns of meanings and values which have become dominant in that institution. The more socialization into institutions is effective, the more predictable and controlled conduct will be. But to what extent this occurs is dependent on a variety of factors — and it is in analysing such factors that one of the main tasks of sociology lies so far as the problems of order and control are concerned. We will discuss two sets of factors:

1 the relative dominance of different types of rationality or logics-in-use in organizational settings;
2 the mechanisms by which definitions of social reality are validated and maintained, as illustrated by the operation of ideologies, especially business ideologies.

2.1 Different types of rationality or logics-in-use

Max Weber's discussion of bureaucracy as the dominant form of organization in industrial societies was set in the context of a discussion of a wider process, that of rationalization. He was particularly concerned about the spread of *formal rationality* as distinct from *substantive rationality,* in this process of rationalization. Formal rationality involves the translation of all situations and decisions into numerical calculable terms or their subsumption under technical rules. Substantive analyses, in contrast, differ from formal rationality in that:

> they do not restrict themselves to note the purely formal and (relatively) unambiguous fact that action is based on 'goal-oriented' methods, but apply certain criteria of ultimate ends, whether they be ethical, political, utilitarian, hedonistic, feudal, egalitarian, or whatever, and measure the results of the economic action, however formally 'rational' in the sense of correct calculation they may be, against these scales of 'value rationality' or *'substantive* goal rationality'. There is an infinite number of possible value scales for this type of rationality, of which the socialist and communist standard constitute only one group. The latter, although by no means unambiguous in themselves, always involve elements of social justice and equality. Others are criteria of status distinctions, or of the capacity for power, especially of the war capacity of a political unit; all of these and many others are of potential 'substantive' significance. These points of view are, however, significant only as bases from which to judge the *outcome* of economic action. In addition and quite independently, it is possible to judge from an ethical, ascetic, or esthetic point of view the spirit of economic activity as well as the *instruments* of economic activity. All of these approaches may consider the 'purely formal' rationality of calculation in monetary terms as of quite secondary importance or even as fundamentally inimical to their respective ultimate ends, even before anything has been said about the consequences of the specifically modern calculating attitude. (Weber 1968 pp 85–6)

Social order and control within organizations can more easily be maintained if issues can be reduced to purely formal rationality terms. It is formal rationality that is epitomized in the specialized roles and technical rules that constitute a bureaucratic structure of organization. Differences over what Weber terms the outcome (product) and the spirit of the organization are minimized. The processes which bring this about can be discovered in the model of organizations presented by March and Simon (1970). This model of organization decision-making is concerned with the individual only as a tool of the organization. There is specialization of activities and roles so that attention is directed to 'a particular restricted set of values'; 'attention-directors that channelize behaviour'; rules, programmes and repertories of action that limit choice in recurring situations and prevent an agonizing process of optimal decision-making at each turn; a restricted range of stimuli and situations that narrow perception; training and indoctrination enabling the individual to 'make decisions, by himself, as the organization would like him to decide'; and the factoring of goals and tasks into programmes that are semi-independent of each other so as to reduce interdependencies (summarized in Perrow 1972 p 151). The organizational control need not be exercised anew with regard to each situation and decision, it is pre-established in the premises of the decision-making. 'These premises are to be found in the "vocabulary" of the organization, the structure of communication, rules and regulations and standard programmes, selection criteria for personnel, and so on — in short, in the structural aspects' (Perrow 1972 pp 155–6).

Not only do decision-making theories of organizations tend to focus on formal rationality to the exclusion of consideration of differences over the purposes or outcome of organizational activity, but they also ignore those aspects of substantive rationality concerned with the 'spirit' of organizational activity. If we substitute for 'spirit' the term 'culture', it becomes easier to see why Weber thought this aspect of substantive rationality to be important. It includes the whole symbolic sphere of organization — issues to do with what the organization's structure and activities symbolize and mean to people. An extreme example of the importance of substantive rationality is to be found in the priority given to the logic of symbolic-appropriateness (a standard of the order of the relation of symbol and meaning, not of cause and effect) as used by members of a religious organization in judging its structure and activities (Cf. Thompson 1973).

Political parties and trades unions are also, to some extent, ideological in character. An extremely influential study of socialist parties and trades unions by Robert Michels made the point that it was a constant problem for these organizations, devoted though they were to promulgating notions of democratic participation, to avoid becoming oligarchic in their own organizational structures (cf. Michels 1970). But even business firms, which are not (supposedly) ideological agencies, nevertheless pay some attention to criteria of symbolic-appropriateness in evaluating and selecting their structures and procedures. They engage in a certain amount of 'appearance-management' or 'window-dressing'. The implication of both these terms is machiavellian — that such considerations are really instrumental, aimed at disarming possible critics or opponents, or even attaining more legitimate ends such as efficiency and greater productivity. Certainly these are among the considerations that have prompted the adoption of schemes for worker participation in management, works councils and joint consultation schemes, job enrichment and enlargement. But a concern for the 'appearance' of structures and procedures can also stem in part from ideological concerns relating to symbolic-appropriateness or inappropriateness. For example, industrial organizations which appear to be dictatorial and to treat workers like machines may appear incongruous in a society which subscribes to a democratic ideology. It is not unheard of for a Prime Minister who supports capitalism to express concern about the 'ugly face of capitalism'.

Symbolic-appropriateness is only one example of a logic-in-use in organizations that differs from the logic of formal rationality (or an instrumental logic-in-use). However, the distinction is sufficient to make the point that there is more than one system of meaning in an organization, and also more than one mode of interpretation of such meanings. The social scientist must take account of such differences. To fail to do so, and to elevate just one logic-in-use as the basis for understanding an organization, is to risk falling into an ideology.

It must be emphasized that the social construction of reality in organizations, the process of defining and interpreting what exists, is an ongoing accomplishment. And the rationalities and logics employed are seldom merely technical and neutral; in fact, the very claim to technical neutrality frequently constitutes a value-laden ideology.

2.2 Ideology and organization

Trent Schroyer suggests that sociologists fall into an ideology when they concentrate solely on the instrumental logic-in-use in the organizations they are studying. The main function of such a mode of reasoning is to contribute to a process of decision-making whose rationality is concerned with instrumental effectiveness and efficient control. He believes that for the sociologist to side with that mode of thinking is to contribute to a technocratic ideology. He contrasts this with the possible results of adopting a hermeneutic (interpretative) logic, which is concerned to understand symbol systems and the processes of interpretation that enable everyday actors to understand each other. This latter approach can contribute to a critical social science which tries to reflect upon the 'necessity' for the conditions of law-like patterns of organization; it seeks to disclose what, for the participants, might be unnecessary modes of authority, exploitation, alienation and repression (Schroyer 1970).

The links between an instrumental logic, formal rationality, and technocratic ideology are exposed in a famous book by Jacques Ellul, *The Technological Society*. He begins with a very broad definition of *technique*, maintaining that in our technological society, 'technique is the totality of methods rationally arrived at and having absolute efficiency (for a given stage of development) in every detail of human activity' (Ellul 1964 p xxv). What else but technique, he asks, is organization as it is commonly defined in organization studies? As, for example, in the definition: 'Organization is the process which consists in assigning appropriate tasks to individuals or to groups, so as to attain, in an efficient and economic way, and by the co-ordination and combination of *all* their activities, the objectives agreed upon' (Ellul 1964 p 11).

The way in which this becomes an ideology was discussed in Chapter 1 when we first introduced Habermas's definition of instrumental action as purposeful rational behaviour that proceeds according to technical rules based on empirical knowledge. We noted that Habermas saw instrumental action systems as the result of the development of science and technology (to which we added the concomitant development of bureaucracy) as major forces of production. The problem with such action systems was that they left no choice open to the actor. In contrast with the breaking of social norms, which is punished by sanctions external to the norms themselves, the breaking of technical rules is simply *incompetent* behaviour, which is sanctioned by the immediate failure of the intended strategy. The claim to *rationality* thus becomes a *legitimism in itself* (i.e. an ideology). The loss of choice this entails is emphasized by Ellul:

> It is no longer the best relative means which counts, as compared to other means also in use. The choice is less and less a subjective one among several means which are potentially applicable. It is really a question of finding the best means in the absolute sense, on the basis of numerical calculation.
>
> It is, then, the specialist who chooses the means; he is able to carry out the calculations that demonstrate the superiority of the means chosen over all others. Thus a science of means comes into being — a science of techniques progressively elaborated. (Ellul 1964 p 21)

A great deal of the literature on decision-making in organizations would allow that many decisions follow from prior higher level decisions, and that below the level at which 'strategic' choices are made it is largely technical considerations that are decisive. We will examine this argument further, but it needs to be said at this stage that Ellul, Habermas, Schroyer, and those who think like them, fear that even the area of strategic choice is being rapidly eroded, or pre-empted, by the spread of instrumental action systems and techniques. Ellul terms this the 'automatism of technical choice':

When everything has been measured and calculated mathematically
so that the method which has been decided upon is satisfactory from
the rational point of view, and when, from the practical point of
view, the method is manifestly the most efficient of all those hitherto
employed or those in competition with it, then the technical movement becomes self-directing. I call this process *automatism.*

There is no personal choice, in respect to magnitude, between
say, three and four; four is greater than three; this is a fact which has
no personal reference. No one can change it or assert the contrary or
personally escape it. Similarly there is no choice between two
technical methods. One of them asserts itself inescapably: its results
are calculated, measured, obvious and indisputable ...

The worst reproach modern society can level is the charge that
some person is impeding this technical automatism ... Technical
automatism may not be judged or questioned; immediate use must
be found for the most recent, efficient, and technical process.
(Ellul 1964 pp 79—81)

It is clear that this seemingly 'neutral' instrumental logic, with its formal
rationality, is in fact easily converted into an ideology. It can make
issues that are inherently 'political' — that is, concerned with values,
interests and choice of priorities — seem to be merely technical matters.
As such it effectively reduces awareness of possibilities for choice and
it limits participation in strategic decision-making. It may even reduce
the number and scope of strategic decisions. In other words, if those
decisions that have to be made about organizational goals, structure and
courses of action can be made to appear as subject solely to an
autonomous technical logic, then organizational control need not be
exercised anew with regard to each situation and decision, it is pre-
established.

It is this process of unobtrusive control through the medium of a
seemingly irresistible rationality and an unquestioned everyday logic-in-
use that explains how it is that organizations are protected from a too
precarious dependence on the individual perceptions of their members,
but rather develop what seems to be a facticity external to the
individual members. The seeming facticity, experienced as external and
constraining, derives from the shared rationality and logic-in-use of the
members.

This has fundamental significance for the issue of the relationship
between structure and decision-making in organizations. John Child has
criticized many studies of organizational structure and behaviour for
using an over-simple explanation which implies that both are determined
by 'functional imperatives' or 'system needs' — such as technology,
scale of operation, or environmental conditions. His point is that such

models are inadequate because they neglect the political dimension — the choices made in strategic decisions by those who exercise power in the organization. He refers to those who exercise power as the 'dominant coalition' and explains that the usefulness of this concept is that it draws attention to the question of who is making the choices as to how the organization as an ongoing system will be maintained. The process of strategy formulation is described as a major interface between the 'working organization' and the 'political system' within organizations (Child 1973).

What we have been discussing, however, might in turn be described as the major interface between the political system and the cultural system within organizations. The cultural system or dimension is composed of rationalities, logics and symbols. (An obvious link between the political and cultural systems is provided by ideology, as we will see in the next section on managerial ideologies.) The subject here is not strategy formulation, but the prior determination of what would constitute a strategy and what it is that requires a strategy, i.e. issues concerning the definition of social reality, and so requiring from us an effort to interpret the rationalities and logics employed.

The importance of this focus will be demonstrated in the ensuing discussion of managerial ideologies, but it can also be summarized in terms of what it prevents. Firstly, it prevents us from viewing the decision-making of powerholders simply as the action of highly rational, very knowledgeable games players. Secondly, it prevents us from over-emphasizing the direct effect of interests on the actions of power-holders. In the first case we are compelled to analyse the nature of the rationality being employed. In the second case, we are led to examine the nature of the powerholders' perceptions and interpretations of their position and interests, and the ways in which they articulate these in the form of an ideology. We can examine these issues as they relate to one influential section of modern society — business. There has been a great deal of discussion and research about the part played by managerial or business ideologies in the development and maintenance of modern industrial enterprises, and it is to this subject that we now turn.

2.3 Managerial ideologies

Reinhard Bendix has defined managerial ideologies as 'all ideas which are espoused by or for those who exercise authority in economic enterprises, and which seek to explain and justify that authority' (Bendix 1970 p 529). The function of such ideologies, according to Bendix, is to interpret the facts of authority and obedience so as to neutralize or eliminate the conflict between the few and the many, and so to promote the interest of a more effective exercise of authority. In order to achieve this the exercise of authority may be denied altogether on the ground that the few merely order what the many want; or it may be justified on the basis of supposed qualities of excellence possessed by the few which enable them to realize the interests of the many (Bendix 1970 p 531). As an example of the former appeal Bendix cites the case of Soviet Russia where industrialization was advanced by an ideology of management in which the commands of managers and the obedience of workers received their justification from the subordination of both groups to a higher body – the Communist Party and its governmental organs. An example of the second ideology appeared in British industrialization, when superior qualities were attributed to employers and managers.

It has been argued by some sociologists that the effectiveness of both these ideologies has waned and that they are both in competition with a new technocratic ideology in which authority is no longer primarily vested in position, but in techniques – impersonal forces. The technocratic ideology does not rest on claims about the superior qualities of the office-holder, nor some external source of authority; it rests its claim for obedience on the self-evident and immanent logic of the 'one best way' as enshrined in the technically most effective organization form. Hierarchy is no longer discussed; it is merely a matter of different functions deriving from the various needs of the system.

Implicit in this argument is a 'convergence theory' about societies with different political and cultural systems. It is a variant of economic or technological determinist theories in that it maintains that common economic/technological developments in these societies will cause them to grow to be more fundamentally alike, thus overriding political and cultural differences. This thesis has been extended to include the spread of bureaucratic organization, in which managers and managerial interests come to be dominant to the exclusion of other principles and interests – such as shareholder interests, elected legislatures and party policies, and traditional ruling groups and their values.

A British sociologist, Theo Nichols, has examined some of these theories of 'managerialism' in relation to the business ideology of directors and senior managers (Nichols 1969). One aspect of Nichols' study is of particular interest to us, and that is his examination of the question as to whether the traditional managerial ideology in Britain, based on notions of 'leadership qualities' and the general diffuse superiority of the leader/manager has given way to a new ideology of a 'technocratic' type based on an appeal to technical and professional expertise (which in turn is functionally related to the requirements of mechanical and organizational techniques). Both in terms of the qualifications of British managers and their replies to questions about what makes a good manager, Nichols found little evidence of such a change. When asked their opinion as to what made a good manager, most respondents thought that 'character', 'personality', social skills and personal characteristics in general were more important than technical skills. By far the largest category of response contained reference to 'leadership' or some supposed aspect of this, such as 'commanding respect'. This raises the question of whether these social skills and personality traits thought desirable for management are very different from those inculcated and valued in the upper middle class in general, and in recipients of a public school and/or Oxbridge education, in particular.

Nichols suggests that the management hierarchy itself is stratified in terms of public school education:

> The data suggests that as we move up the corporate hierarchy the proportion of those with public school education increases from approximately two out of ten for managers, to four out of ten senior managers, to about five out of ten directors. The Institute of Directors' 1965 survey even suggests that the proportion of public school educated directors is increasing, for whereas sixty-two per cent of all directors were found to have received such an education the percentage for the youngest age group, those aged twenty-five to thirty-five, was seventy-five per cent. (Nichols 1969 pp 116–17)

Over all, we find that directors in Britain are recruited from the top two social classes and that a substantial proportion of them had fathers who were themselves in business; probably about half of them had been to a public school and where they have been to a university at all, it is likely to have been Oxford or Cambridge (Nichols 1969).

Of course, these figures about managers' backgrounds do not 'prove' anything about their frame of reference, value structure or ideology. However, there is a strong correspondence between the values evidenced in managers' responses to the question 'What makes a good manager?' and those traditionally inculcated by the public schools (see Nichols 1969 chapters X and XI).

In business, as in most other major institutions in British society, there is a marked bias in favour of promoting to leadership positions individuals possessing certain diffuse and intangible qualities inculcated by the elite educational institutions. The higher up the hierarchy of management or leadership, the more likely an office-holder is to have had such an education. Despite efforts to make selection procedures more 'equitable', it is clearly the case that 'like chooses like' and elites tend to be largely self-perpetuating. The particular character of the British elite derives from the historical development of the British class system – with its own distinctive combination of mutually reinforcing economic, political and cultural forces. Technological and organizational developments within Britain have made little impact on the elitist nature of the control system in its various institutions. If multinational corporations with foreign origins become dominant in all sections of industry and commerce, then perhaps the 'convergence thesis' (sometimes referred to as 'Americanization' in popular discussion) might begin to come true. It is certainly the case that the elite is stronger in some sections of business than in others – for example there tends to be a higher proportion of company chairmen with public school backgrounds in banks and breweries than in manufacturing industries. But on the whole, the evidence is that the upper ranks of leadership or control in British business hold to an ideology which has not significantly changed from that which Bendix found dominant in an earlier period. It still seeks to explain and justify authority on the basis of supposedly superior qualities of a diffuse and intangible sort. This comes out in the responses given to Nichols' question about what makes a good manager. And it is further illustrated in the response given by the Director-General of the Institute of Directors who when asked why it was that the majority of directors were still drawn from the public school educated stratum of society, talked about the 'rounded man who's used to giving and carrying out orders, and getting people to work' and 'leadership'.

We need to look further at the possible connections between the role of the businessman, his interests, and ideology. Nichols takes the view that 'business ideologies are about power and that they consist of those patterned and selective self and structural representations put forward by businessmen which pertain to its distribution' (Nichols 1969 p 208). Sutton and his colleagues, who were attempting to explain American business ideology of the 1940s in terms of a predominantly social-psychological analysis of the role strains experienced by businessmen, defined ideology as 'any system of beliefs publicly expressed with the manifest purpose of influencing the sentiments and actions of others' (Sutton *et al* 1956 p 2). Along with the definition given by Bendix, these definitions have one thing in common, the implication that such

ideas may be interpreted as maintaining or furthering the effectiveness
of a given system or the position of those who govern it.

The suggestion that the ideology has the function of serving the
economic interests of businessmen, or perpetuating a given authority
structure, fits in with the traditional 'interest theory' of ideology. This
can be distinguished from the 'strain theory' of ideology favoured by
Sutton *et al*: 'Ideology is a patterned reaction to the patterned strains
of a social role' (Sutton *et al* 1956 pp 307–8). Unlike the interest
theory, which tends to employ a 'battlefield image of society as a clash
of principles' the strain theory of ideology adopts a medical analogy. It
is 'a malady (Sutton *et al* mention nail-chewing, alcoholism, psychosomatic disorders, and 'crotchets' among the alternatives to it) and
demands a diagnosis' (Geertz 1964 p 54). With regard to how the
American business ideology functions, Sutton *et al* seem to adopt what
has been called a 'morale explanation': 'By the "morale explanation" is
meant the ability of an ideology to sustain individuals (or groups) in the
face of chronic strain, either by denying it outright or by legitimizing
it in terms of higher values' (Geertz 1964 p 55). Thus according to
Sutton *et al*, the struggling small businessman rehearsing his boundless
confidence in the inevitable justness of the American system is thereby
enabled to get on with his work.

Nichols rejects what he regards as a tendency to explore the nature
of business ideology solely in terms of its consistency as a symbolic
meaning system because it only forestalls what he regards as the
ultimate question – 'why *this* symbol meaning system?' But in
answering this question he tends to develop a mixture of the 'interest'
and 'strain' theories. On the whole, Nichols did not find that the
interests in conflict which gave rise to British business ideology were
conflicts concerning the legitimacy of the capitalist system as such (or
the place of business in that system). In fact he found that the typical
ideological statements used precluded the type of conflict which in
macro-terms relates to system legitimacy and, in microcosm, takes the
form of what Pugh has termed 'role-legitimation conflict' (cf Pugh 1973
pp 238–49; and Nichols 1969 p 220). Rather, the conflicts experienced
by the businessman related to the different expectations held by others
about which aspect of his role he should call into play – 'role-activation
conflict', as Pugh called it when studying the different expectations
pertaining to the role of inspectors in industry.

> The questions at issue are not, for example, *whether* employees
> should be given fair wages, or shareholders a reasonable return,
> or customers or suppliers a fair price. They concern the priorities
> with which these conflicting expectations should be met and are

about what *is* 'fair' and what *is* 'reasonable' at given points in time.
(Nichols 1969 p 222)

The senior managers and directors tended to see the various parties to
industry as having interdependent interests, and this notion of interdependence (an organic view) seems to be central to the ideology of
British businessmen. Furthermore, as Nichols notes, 'they assumed
that their companies were already in a state of "moral equilibrium"
and that the rewards accruing to the various contributors were already
fair' (Nichols 1969 pp 225–6). This ideology fits in with the self-
perception of the senior managers and directors as primarily co-
ordinators, leading a team. It provides an important reason for their
stress on management's need for 'leadership' qualities and social skills.
It also helps to explain why they emphasized a need for a 'common
purpose' when asked what they considered was the greatest need of
industry today. It is significant that in British management writings
there are frequent nostalgic references to the sense of common purpose
in wartime and a recurrent emphasis on the need to recapture such
unity of purpose. Whether in fact this mental adjustment is possible
without prior changes in the British class system is seldom considered.
The elitist nature of the British class system is reflected in its *paternalistic*
ideology. The need for *leadership* is constantly stressed. Business
ideology is not untypical in this respect, although it has been
'modernized' so that leadership is claimed to be a social scientific
concept, having to do with motivational techniques – nothing so crude
as social dominance.
    Child's discussion of the disproportionate influence of a small group
of Quaker employers with regard to the development of British management or business ideology is extremely instructive for our study of the
social construction of reality in organizations. We suggested earlier that
the most problematic element in the construction and maintenance of
a shared perception of the social reality of an institution was the
constant threat of discrepancies arising from individual (or sectional)
perceptions, or from new 'external' developments. An ideology provides
a shield (what Berger calls a 'sacred canopy' in the case of religious
ideologies) against such discrepancies. Unfortunately, neither interest
theories nor strain theories of ideology in themselves provide anything
more than the most rudimentary conception of the actual processes
of symbolic formulation in the development of ideologies. In other
words, they do not tell us how the trick is done. Child's analysis is an
exception. He traces the development of one strand of business
ideology and its interaction and convergence with others. It is

particularly instructive because he distinguishes and relates such important factors as the location and composition of the ideologists, the selective transformation of the content of their doctrines, the appropriateness of its ethical character to the function of providing a legitimation for certain managers, and its convergence with an emerging social science theory (Human Relations Theory).

Child shows how both the Quakers and the Human Relations theorists assumed that personal qualities determined industrial relationships and that a 'psychological' interaction of small numbers of persons comprised their essence, rather than any system of power, class and conflict. 'Most important of all, the whole framework of industrial relations was placed by both in terms not of the sociological "power structure" model, but of a psychological one of "goodwill" or "social skills"' (Child 1964 p 308). Thus the effect of this ideology, or symbolic meaning system, is to portray problems in terms not of conflicts of interests, but of psychological deficiencies, hence management's function is to supply the missing motivation by offering leadership utilizing certain social skills (whether of interpersonal dominance, rhetoric, social manipulation, or whatever will do the trick).

Similarly, Nichols' depiction of British business ideology as being based on an 'organicist' symbol system, shows how a stress on interdependence and common purpose either excludes conflicts or makes them seem minor or transitional. These ideological or selective representations of the situation are not necessarily 'untrue'.

> ... the proposition that workers, customers, shareholders and so on have interests in common is, at a particular level, borne out by fact. At given points in time the interests of all these groups, the local community, and many other 'publics', are intimately related to the prosperity of the company. But so, in the same way, would their short-run economic interests be tied to the existence of any economic unit in the sense that were it to cease functioning, they would receive no wages, no product and so on. In this sense, then, the above propositions and selective representations do not merit being termed 'ideological' rather than scientific because they are 'not true', but because they are not true inevitably — and because those who put them forward imply that they are.
>
> They divert attention from the possibility that other economic arrangements might serve the above and other interests more or less advantageously and by celebrating the economic excellence of the corporation as a wealth producing agency, they divert attention both from the social needs which any given corporation may or may not serve, and the differential distribution of authority which pertains within it. (Nichols 1969 p 232)

Obviously an ideology of this kind can be seen to suit the interests of ~~when theory~~ managers, but the concept of 'interests' does not provide a sufficient explanatory link between ideas (symbols) and social structure. It does not explain why a particular symbolic meaning system was adopted. The same criticism can be made of the 'strain theory'. Managers may be experiencing strains in their role, but that only explains the need for an ideology — not why one particular ideology develops rather than another. Nor does it explain how the ideology itself operates. Nichols suggests that an answer to the first question lies in the convergence of the businessman's work experience, the exigencies imposed upon him by his role within the corporation, and the structurally defined standpoint from which he perceives the corporation itself. He also notes that in recruitment and promotion to senior management positions preference is shown to candidates who have been successfully presocialized (e.g. by elite educational institutions and then within the corporation) into the right values. Child explains the development and convergence of some of the key elements in the ideology by reference to the strategic part played by Quaker businessmen.

In order to consider the second question of how an ideology actually operates we need to look more closely at the relation between ideology and the social construction of reality in organizations.

3 Ideology and the social construction of reality in organizations

A naive, but common view of ideology is that it is mainly a distorted perception of reality in contrast with (social) science. Ideology is regarded as distorted perception because of its supposed bias, as opposed to the 'disinterested' selectivity of science. The interest and strain theories of ideology represent slightly more sophisticated social science attempts to explain that same allegedly biased selectivity. An interest theory, such as that held by Marxists, claims the advantage of rooting cultural idea-systems or symbol-systems in what Marxists believe to be the firm ground of 'social structure' by emphasizing the motivations of those who hold to such systems and also the dependence of those motivations upon social position, especially social class. Strain theory explains the selectivity of ideology by reference to the anxieties of those who exercise it, anxieties stemming from inconsistencies in 'social structure' — such as contradictory role expectations, or discrepancies between various goals and norms. In both theories, therefore, ideology is seen as a way of coping intellectually (and emotionally) with what are taken to be discrepancies in 'social structure' and 'culture'. But they still seem to suggest that somewhere there is, or could be, an unbiased selectivity.

It is here that we can make the connection between ideology and problems concerning the social construction of reality in organizations. We noted earlier that organizational structure and order are not unproblematical realities that exist independently of members' constructive interpretation and constant reformulation. The social construction of reality in organizations involves making shared and binding a 'reality' made up of such notional entities as goals, rules and roles (which we have discussed as problematical entities at great length in this book). Ideology functions as an overarching idea-system or symbol-system that provides a protective shield (Berger's 'sacred canopy') for a version of reality that would minimize the disturbing effects of reinterpretation and reconstruction. It provides a fundamental justification and legitimation for what it would have us believe is an *established order*. It thus provides a rationale for a particular form of selectivity and seeks to exclude others.

It is here that we can see the relevance of our earlier discussion of the need to recognize and decode the different types of rationality that exist in organizations. What we called formal rationality or an instrumental logic-in-use operates most clearly and unambiguously where it is a matter of calculating the most efficient means for attaining an immediate concrete goal, such as increasing productivity. By contrast, substantive rationality and the logic of symbolic-appropriateness apply criteria of ultimate ends and values (ethical, political and esthetic criteria) which may have to do with what is considered right or wrong, fair or unfair, historically-determined or variable.

We stated earlier that social order and control within organizations can more easily be maintained if issues can be reduced to purely formal rationality terms. And it is this formal rationality that is epitomized in the specialized roles and technical rules of bureaucracy. But it must also be clear by now that organizations seldom find it possible to reduce all issues to these terms (although one type of ideology, the technocratic, pretends that they can). In view of this and the differences that are likely to exist between the value scales and symbol preferences of various groups in an organization, it is easy to see how an overarching ideology can be extremely functional for maintaining social order if it can succeed in masking or minimizing such differences.

Unfortunately there has been little analysis of how organizational ideologies actually perform this trick. Both interest and strain theories of ideology pass quickly from the causes of ideology to its consequences without analysing in its own terms the autonomous process of symbolic formulation — the patterning of interacting symbols and meanings, as it becomes a relatively coherent ideology. For example, metaphor often features prominently in such symbol systems, as in the popular organic analogy in British business ideology which views the company as a social organism where all have their fixed functions, appropriate statuses and just rewards (cf examples given in Nichols 1969). The interesting thing about metaphor is that it is often most effective when it is most 'wrong'. As Geertz explains:

> The power of a metaphor derives precisely from the interplay between the discordant meanings it symbolically coerces into a unitary framework and from the degree to which that coercion is successful in overcoming the psychic resistance such semantic tension inevitably generates in anyone in a position to perceive it. (Geertz 1964 p 59)

British business ideology often depicts the company as an organic whole in which all the parts have the same ultimate goal, and in so far as there are separate interests they all converge on this ultimate goal. But this view of reality is not based on simple observation, but rather on a series of value-judgments which define all contrary indications as being 'deviant', 'pathological', or just 'irrational'. In America business ideology often uses the 'rags-to-riches' or 'log-cabin-to-President' metaphor to suggest that, contrary to appearances, the distribution of benefits and of authority is based on merit.

Different cultural traditions can be expected to favour different metaphors in their ideologies. As Bendix points out in contrasting entrepreneurial and managerial ideologies in Britain, America, Russia and East Germany; they

> ... are in part expediential rationalizations for the problems confronting the entrepreneur, and in part the result of historically cumulative response-patterns among social groups. In this way ideologies are formulated through the constant interplay between current contingencies and historical legacies ... ideologies of management can be explained only in part as rationalization of self-interest; they also result from the legacy of institutions and ideas which is 'adopted' by each generation much as a child 'adopts' the grammar of his native language. (Bendix 1963 pp 443–4)

It is for this reason that Bendix criticizes the work of Sutton *et al* for denying that business ideologies change over time. He maintains that emphasis on the impact of cultural tradition on current ideologies is more in line with the facts than the effort to explain current ideologies solely in terms of the problems the businessman encounters in his work. The latter interpretation leads to an elimination of ideological changes and of differences between ideologies, since all ideologies are in this sense responses to the strains endemic in modern society (Bendix 1963 p 444).

And just as there are cultural differences between societies which affect the business ideologies they favour, so there are cultural differences between institutions which produce distinctive institutional ideologies. For example, the Ford Motor Company (UK), the British Broadcasting Corporation, and the British Army, each have distinctive cultures and ideologies. To some extent they also reflect the shared culture of British society, and the relative cultural dominance (or hegemony) of the upper class, although this will be less evident in the case of a multinational company like Ford. The analysis of these various symbol-systems or ideologies and their part in the social construction of reality in organizations requires something akin to the techniques used in literary analysis or linguistic analysis and decoding. This fits in with the view of phenomenological sociologists (e.g. Schutz 1962) and ethnomethodologists (e.g. Garfinkel 1967) that the origins of knowledge held in common by organization members, and its apparently *systematic* nature, is explained by the process of linguistic typification:

> Language is the principal mechanism by which members make their everyday activities 'visibly-rational-and-reportable-for-all-practical-purposes, i.e. "accountable", as organizations of commonplace everyday activities'. It is through the common terms of language that unique or personal experiences are given what ostensibly is taken to be objective experiences in members' accounts of them. These accounts, however, are rational versions of members' experiences partly because of the requirements of linguistic sense, so that shared language is the source of the reflexivity between members' accounts of their experiences and the experiences themselves. And finally, it is in the shared language in which accounts are framed that the context in terms of which the experiences are to be understood and analysed, is implied or explicitly stated. (Filmer 1972 pp 222–3)

This is especially so in the case of organizational ideology, which is aimed at presenting a persuasive justificatory and legitimating definition of 'reality'. This 'systematization' of what passes as knowledge about the organization is most evident in written accounts – such as public relations statements and advertisements.[2] But it is also discoverable in statements made in formal or semi-formal situations where organizational representatives are presenting information, or projecting an image, to interested outsiders – as in selection interviews. The connections between an organizational ideology and that to which it refers (aspects of the organization) are complex and subtle. The complicated interworking of meanings within the ideology, and between the ideology and its referents (aspects of the organization), is itself a social process that deserves the most serious sociological study.

> This interworking is itself a social process, an occurrence not 'in the head' but in that public world where 'people talk together, name things, make assertions, and to a degree understand each other'. The study of symbolic action is no less a sociological discipline than the study of small groups, bureaucracies, or the changing role of the American Woman; it is only a good deal less developed. (Geertz 1964 p 60)

Finally, it must be pointed out that ideology is only one part of the process of social construction of reality in organizations. Its prominence in that process will vary between different groups, different organizations, and different points in time. Certainly, official spokesmen of organizations are more likely to attach importance to ideological formulations than lower level members of the organizations. The attempt of Sutton *et al* to explain American business ideology by reference to the role strains experienced by businessmen has been criticized for taking public statements as evidence of ideology, whilst admitting there may be discrepancies between public statements and private beliefs, and also an unwarranted assumption that professional ideologies express the views of the groups they represent. The latter criticism is especially damaging because spokesmen often do not experience the same role strains as businessmen and, therefore, their ideological statements cannot be explained by their work experience. Rogers and Berg (1961), who first made some of these criticisms after comparing the findings of Sutton *et al* with their own research on American small businessmen, suggest that businessmen accommodate to their situation by a myriad of small attachments that are not covered

---

[2] The ideological function of management is increasingly the activity of specialist departments concerned with public relations. For some examples of their work see B. W. Galvin Wright, 'Projecting the Corporate Image' (1960) and Lee H. Bristol, *Developing the Corporate Image* (1960).

by ideology. This was also the conclusion of Elinor Langer with regard to the perception of their situation by women workers in the New York Telephone Company:

> Working in that job one does not see oneself as a victim of 'Capitalism'. One is simply part of a busy little world which has its own pleasures and satisfactions as well as its own frustrations but, most important, it is a world with a shape and integrity all its own. The pattern of co-operation, in other words, rests on details, hundreds of trivial, but human, details. (Langer 1970 p 21)

The same conclusions are to be found in Roy's account of the integrating effects of the sub-culture of a work group in his 'Banana time: job satisfaction and informal interaction' (1973 pp 205–22). Perhaps where ideology does operate most effectively in the social construction of reality for all these members of organizations is in defining what is possible or impossible as far as changing their situation is concerned. Langer observed that the women of the telephone company could not see even the dimmest possibility of remedial action through collective action, they lacked the magic ingredient – class consciousness (Langer 1970 p 21). So too, Roy found that reintegration of the work group after severe strains was necessary because the operatives could see no escape from their work situation (1973 p 221).

Thus the social construction of reality, and its maintenance in organizations is a process which involves relatively formulated and coherent elements such as ideologies, but also tacit understandings and agreements of a less formal kind. It is to these latter that we turn in the next chapter.

CHAPTER 11

Graeme Salaman

Organizations as constructors of social reality (II)

Introduction

This chapter will consider the importance of, and the ways in which, organizations consist of, create and disseminate (both to their members and outsiders) special knowledge. What we 'know' about the world, and consequently take for granted because of its reality, is '. . . developed, transmitted and maintained in social situations' (Berger and Luckmann 1967 p 15). It is the contention of this chapter that a great deal of what we know, what we take as the-way-things-are, both about the world and about our membership of, or treatment by, organizations, is derived from organizations.

1 Organizations as purveyors of social reality

There are organizations that disseminate world views in society at large, or certain sections of it. Schools, religious organizations and political parties are organizations of this type. Typologies of organizations that are based upon organizational goals contain reference to such organizations. Parsons, for example, calls them 'pattern-maintenance organizations', and he regards them as involving 'cultural, educational, and expressive functions' (Parsons 1970 p 81).

But not only those organizations whose 'formal' or stated goal is some sort of '. . . cultural, educational and expressive function' attempt to construct and impose definitions of the world and the organization. Many organizations that are apparently, in Parsons' terms, economic, political or integrative, also attempt to define their activities and functions, in highly favourable terms, for society at large. Some organizations have the protection and advancement of their members' interests as their prime aim (for example, professional bodies or trades unions), although inevitably such intentions are expressed as, and can only be successful through, an identification of the interests of the members as the interests of all members of society. So, for example, the British Medical Association will justify its demands for fewer working hours for hospital doctors, or higher salaries, or better conditions, not on the grounds that these will make life easier and more pleasant for doctors, but because such things will enable them to safeguard the health of the community more satisfactorily, or enable them to devote more time and attention to patients. Yet it could be argued that the current distribution of resources and expertise within the health service suggests that patients' well-being is by no means a prime value.

There are other ways in which organizations can, as it were, create reality, and define the nature of the world for us, with reference to particular activities or areas. One occurs when organizations create news, information or facts, that is when the information they produce is accorded some sort of authoritative status. Examples of this sort of organization are mass media organizations, research institutes, or what Kitsuse and Cicourel have aptly termed 'rate producing agencies', that is organizations that create and disseminate statistical rates such as government agencies or information departments (Kitsuse and Cicourel 1963). Douglas has noted that, for example, in the field of deviance, official statistics must be viewed with scepticism since not only are they closely related to political priorities and policies, they are also highly morally biased and concerned with practical solutions to official problems. His comments on governmental capacity to decide when, how or if information becomes available has a particular contemporary significance.

> ... control over information and the power it gives officials over society has been accelerating so rapidly in recent years, under the guise of the 'foreign threat', that certain of its extreme forms, especially that of 'official secrecy' and 'classified data', have come to be seen as 'pathologies' of 'intelligence' which require new laws to enforce 'public disclosure' or more official information. (Douglas 1971 p 70)

Douglas argues that official statistics are tenuously related to what people actually do or have done. This argument can be seen to emerge from Douglas's insistence on the situational nature of rule application, which makes the construction of statistics itself a problematic exercise and one worthy of investigation. But Douglas's concern for *official* statistics also derives from his argument that official government bodies have their own political ideologies and priorities, and what's more, that the various official bodies that produce statistics, control resources, administer relevant institutions, control police forces, etc., share assumptions and views of the world.

These points on the nature of official statistics have particular reference to any analysis of organizations for not only are such statistics created by organizations, but our knowledge of organizations has sometimes been excessively influenced by organizationally official statements and descriptions – that is information gathered from interviews with senior personnel, or from official documents and charts and official versions of organizational goals, which, as Cicourel has pointed out, serve as 'fronts' to colleagues and publics. Cicourel suggests that what sociologists have called the formal or official aspect of organizational structure is not simply what senior members expect, imagine or intend should take place, but is a deliberate performance or line which is laid on for the audience concerned, and will vary with it. He writes, 'A given organization may similarly present a front to members and public by way of its physical plant, its produce or service, stationary and other items designed to paint a specific image of itself.' (Cicourel 1958 p 55).

2 Organizational definition of publics

The point about labelling theory is that it draws attention to the consequences of *official* (i.e. organizational) judgments and categorizations. 'When officials define someone as mad or criminal they create a situation in which the person is treated in such a way that the appropriateness of the description is confirmed.'

The consequences of organizational processes of labelling persons as types (and, by implication the sorts of behaviours one can, therefore, typically expect from them) are not restricted to the self-fulfilling nature of others' reactions, who, in their behaviour, confirm the stereotype of the official definition. They also include the person's own self conception: without outside confirmation the labelled person is prone to accept the official stigma, and conform with it. Goffman describes how inmates of 'total institutions' – that is organizations which restrict to an extreme or total degree, through physical means, their inmates' involvement in or interaction with the outside world, and which involve a 'breakdown of the barriers ordinarily separating' sleep, work and play (Goffman 1968 p 17) – have their ordinary social competences destroyed through processes of mortification and assaults upon the self.

But total institutions – such as army camps, prisons, monasteries, etc. – not only '... disrupt or defile precisely those actions that in civil society have the role of attesting to the actor and those in his presence that he has some command over his world' (Goffman 1968 p 47), they also expose their inmates to new definitions of themselves, to new systems of rewards and privileges. And so develops a whole new sub-culture, with new standards, values and priorities (Goffman 1970).

The dramatic severity of total institutional definitions for inmates' selves, attitudes and social competences is a result of the high degree of control exercised by the organization over all aspects of inmates' everyday lives and of their inability to relate to the outside world with its alternative definitions and social realities. But organizations which lack this degree of pervasiveness (as Etzioni calls it – 1961 p 160) also employ definitions of organizationally relevant phenomena and persons. These emerge from the work based problems and priorities of the organizational personnel and refer to the sorts of treatment they should be allocated and the sorts of behaviours (and their causes) they can normally be expected to display. In short organizations include some sort of classification of 'normal', 'typical' clients, patients, students, and so on. This process is particularly evident among those organiza-tions whose raw material is people, and whose members are routinely involved in interactions with clients, customers, patients and applicants whom they are expected to treat, assist, look after, service or restrain on the basis of some analysis and classification.

It has been suggested that it is possible to classify those behaviours that are considered significant by organizational personnel in their work of processing people. Parsons, for example, has actually described what he calls the patient role, which consists of what the doctor wants of his patient: how he would like the patient to behave. Parsons thus usefully points out that organizational practitioners hold such expectations of 'proper', 'normal' or 'good' clients and patients. However, it would be naive to assume that doctor and patient will always agree on the nature of the 'patient role'. There are bound to be occasions when relations between the two are characterized by disagreement and conflict. Friedson has suggested that the priorities, expectations and definitions of members of organizations and their publics may be inherently conflicting: 'It is my thesis that the separate worlds of experience and reference of the layman and the professional worker are always in potential conflict' (Friedson 1971 p 209).

A considerable amount of work on organizational, work-based definitions and priorities, with reference to those who are processed by the organization, lends support to Friedson's argument, and also shows that practical priorities and events may differ considerably from official or 'front' statements of goals and priorities. For example, Blau shows that from the point of view of the interviewers in the employment exchange he studied, the introduction of statistical record keeping resulted in new problems, which in turn meant that the clients were treated in new ways as a result of new interviewer priorities. Presumably the clients' problems remained the same (Blau 1970).

Elsewhere Blau has developed his point that organizational members may 'bend' the organizational rules with reference to his discussion about the 'dysfunctions' of bureaucracy. It is possible to discern two sorts of criticism of bureaucracy: that they involve the blind and inappropriate application of rules, and that the official rules aren't applied properly, that is they are interpreted to suit the interests of those who apply them rather than of those to whom they are applied. But Blau has argued (1970) that organizational members may bend the rules in order to achieve what they consider to be the 'real' goals of the organization. But before considering the nature, origins and consequences of such interpretation and utilization of organizational classifications of clients and patients (that is, what is 'known' within the organization about the nature of the people who are processed, it is relevant to mention briefly the rationale underlying such processes.

It is a characteristic of organizations that both with respect to internal processes and the external organizational environment, attempts will be made to reduce uncertainty, increase predictability and stability, and achieve orderliness. Such concerns lie behind organizational rules and procedures, the organization and integration of work tasks, and a variety of economic activities such as Galbraith describes (1967). Perrow has argued for the significance of uncertainty for organizational structure and has emphasized the '... number of exceptional cases encountered in the work' and the '...nature of the search process that is undertaken by the individual when exceptions occur' (Perrow 1972 pp 49–50). The sort of organizational, work-based definitions of types of organizational clients discussed here are obviously a technique utilized by organizational personnel to minimize the uniqueness of individuals in favour of gross, simplistic classifications that help to impose some degree of orderliness on the variegated reality. Interestingly, Douglas has described this simplifying characteristic of organizational classifications with reference to statistic-producing government bureaucracies. He writes, '... over the centuries these bureaucracies have moved steadily toward fewer and more isolated categories. ... In addition, the categories used by the officials have become increasingly rigid and abstract'. (Douglas 1971 pp 53–4.) The theoretical justification for

organizational classifications, then, is that those whom the organization treats must be classified according to organizationally relevant
characteristics, in order to expedite treatment.

The point is that the 'purposes' of those organizational members
who actually interact with the organization's clients, and classify and
treat them, will be derived as much from their actual everyday work
difficulties as from any overall organizational goal or rhetoric. Actual
behaviour, classification and treatment of those people processed by
the organizational personnel cannot be predicted from knowledge of
organizational rules and procedures: they emerge from the 'knowledge'
and priorities of those who are charged with applying organizational
policies to their publics. Sudnow's article in Salaman and Thompson
(1973), in which he discusses 'normal' crimes, explores the negotiations
that take place to produce 'guilty' pleas (which do not need to go to
trial) in the public defender operation. Sudnow argues that as long as
the public defender considers the case to be a 'normal' one he will be
prepared to reduce the charge to a lesser one in order to obtain a
guilty plea. He writes:

> I shall call *normal crimes* those occurrences whose typical features,
> e.g. the ways they usually occur and the characteristics of persons
> who commit them (as well as the typical victims and typical scenes),
> are known and attended to by the public defender. For any of a
> series of offence types the PD can provide some form of proverbial
> characterization. (Sudnow 1973 p 351)

In order to achieve a guilty plea the public defender is prepared to
reduce the charge to a lesser one of which the offender is not, in fact,
guilty. He then settles for a charge that is reasonable — that is one that
will give the defendant his due, but will still be a more attractive
propostion than holding out for a trial. So, the exercise of defining
categories of crime and criminals — and these negotiated decisions will
result finally in official statistics of crime rates — cannot be understood
a priori, but is performed by the public defender in terms of his
interpretation of cases in the light of his work priorities and his
organizationally based stock of knowledge about the characteristics of
'typical' crimes and those who perpetrate them. The result of this
'knowledge' is not only that offenders get labelled and treated in
certain ways, which is important enough, but that the public defenders
are actually creating, through their negotiated decisions, data about the
criminal rates of the country; they are then creating a further social
reality.

Zimmerman's study of the receptionists in a public assistance bureau shows, he claims, that they seek so to manage their day's work as to 'provide for the defensible claim that it was accomplished in sufficient-for-all-practical-purposes accord with rule and policy' (Zimmerman 1973 p 256). That is, the job is not simply to satisfy most adequately — within the limits of the bureaucractic regulations, etc. — the requirements of those who apply for public assistance, but to preserve a sense of orderly and routine work processing as *essentially* in accord with the rules.

Finally, a fascinating small-scale example of the sorts of processes described above is contained in Emerson's analysis of gynaecological examinations (1973). Her study describes the '. . . complex composition of the definition of reality routinely sustained in gynaecological examinations'. Furthermore, '. . . some of the routine arrangements and interactional manoeuvres which embody and express this definition' are described (Emerson 1973 p 360). Emerson describes gynaecologists' attempts to control patients' reactions and behaviours by overtly defining for, and with them, the meaning of what is happening, in order to relieve their own tensions and anxieties. In this way the miracle can be achieved whereby an activity which would appear, *a priori*, to have considerable sexual implications is defused and transformed into 'a medical situation'.

To summarize this section: organizations involve definitions of those people who are processed by their members. That organizations should contain classifications of types of relevant persons, should convert individuals into cases, is by no means surprising, since this is an inevitable aspect of organizational attempts to create order and standardization. However, as is so often the case, the classifications and practices of organizational members, who are expected to execute organizational policy or apply the classifications and procedures to members of the relevant publics, derive from the actual work-based concerns, priorities and knowledge of these members, rather than the official rhetoric of the organization.

3 Conceptions of organizations and organizational membership: the search for legitimacy

Members of organizations not only have what they take to be knowledge of the characteristics, motives and predispositions of those whom they are called upon to classify and process, they also have such knowledge and evaluations about other members of the organization, and, indeed, the organization as a whole. Organizations are not homogeneous bodies, but are composed of numerous groups, cliques and cabals each with its distinctive view of the other and the organization generally. Since these groups vary in amounts of organizational power they will also vary in their capacity to impose their view of the nature of the organization.

The most significant intra-organizational distinction (and the one that has been most studied) is that between workers and managers. This significance derives from the status attributed to this distinction by those who maintain that a basic, irreconcilable difference of interest characterizes the relations between those who work in organizations and those who own and control them and that these differences may affect attitudes and values. However, the distinction between workers and managers is by no means only a theoretical one: it also has concrete empirical expression in the organization and is considered by *those involved* as having practical significance. The fact that the categories 'workers' and 'managers' have physical manifestation, derive from different locations (and interests) within an economic order, and are differently affected by market processes (not to mention the various cultural and status differences that overlap with class differences) makes these categories significant for those who own and control organizations. This significance derives from senior managers' concern for establishing the legitimacy of their hierarchic and inegalitarian enterprises and from the fact that the commitment and co-operation of *worker* members of the organization is frequently regarded by senior management as problematic and uncertain. And a concern for legitimacy seems to be a feature of all organizations: apart from anything else it has earlier been argued that legitimated power is more efficient than sheer coercion (Blau and Schoenherr 1973).

However, it should not be assumed that it is only the workers' commitments and attitudes that are problematic, merely because they are the ones who, deriving least benefit from the enterprise, are most likely to resist organizational control and consider their interests as being discrepant from the organization's: the commitment and co-operation of all organizational employees cannot simply be assumed. Consequently all organizations will involve efforts to develop and sustain consensus, co-operation and legitimacy from all levels. Such efforts to create legitimacy involve attempts to manipulate or select suitable attitudes, values and knowledge.

Attempts to achieve co-operation and consensus within organizations involve three elements: supplying an adequate level of rewards to ensure performance (which is not at all to suggest that these rewards will be deemed adequate by those concerned, but merely that given the circumstances and the availability of alternative opportunities, they are preferable to not working); presenting a favourable (and legitimate) conception of organizational structure and organizational activities and in numerous ways attempting to disseminate these definitions, and encourage their acceptance; recruiting, and selecting people who are considered to display some enthusiasm for these conceptions and definitions, who are likely to prove reliable and to be amenable to legitimating ideologies. These three processes will be considered in turn.

3.1 Motivation and performance

It is not possible or appropriate to do more than sketch the major features of the vast body of work on work orientations, needs, motivations and attitudes. The major feature of this work is the variety of different, if not contradictory, findings and conclusions it contains. Viewing it cynically it is possible to argue that a number of different theoretical (political, moral) approaches to the question have produced evidence broadly in line with what was expected.

It is, however, possible to discern two major approaches to the study of work meanings in contemporary society: the psychological universalistic view which refers to man's universal and basic work needs which are, or are not, satisfied within his work and the cultural variation view which emphasizes how persons' work expectations and definitions can vary as a result of the nature of work experience (which leads to attitudinal adjustment or modification), or of community or societal influences outside the work situation. These need not necessarily be entirely mutually exclusive, but in order for the former approach to be any more than an indication of the sociologist's personal moral and political position it is necessary to demonstrate that the evidence for the latter approach is either a result of some sort of modification and corruption of basic needs and expectations, or is merely an epiphenomenon resulting from the inadequacies of the research design or the person's unwillingness, or inability, to express his 'real', basic feelings and aspirations.

In fact as Martin and Fryer (1973) remark, the one thing that can be said with certainty is that the search for a single answer to the question: what is the meaning of work?, is fallacious. These authors quote C. Wright Mills' sensible argument:

> Work may be a mere source of livelihood, or the most significant part of one's inner life; it may be experienced as expiation, or as an exuberant expression of self; as a bounded duty, or as the develop-

ment of man's universal nature. Neither love nor hatred of work is inherent in man, or inherent in any given line of work. (Mills 1956 p 215)

This should not be taken to imply that people will put up with anything or that they will adjust their wants and expectations to the particular rewards and conditions they experience. The point is that people want different things of different sorts of work situation, and that these expectations and aspirations may vary over time. Furthermore, their feelings and desire need not be internally 'consistent' and homogenous at any one time. This has serious implications for those who have attempted to study workers' attitudes. Fox remarks:

> Men questioned about their responses to work may respond on either of two levels: in terms of how they have any picture of work as it is, and in terms of how they have any picture of work as it might be. In other words, men can at one and the same time (i) expect work to be largely instrumental in nature, (ii) become 'satisfied with' (i.e. resigned to) this situation, and (iii) wish that it could be otherwise — that intrinsic rewards were also open to them. (Fox 1971 p 22)

Work attitudes (and experiences) cannot then simply be understood in terms of internal, organizational circumstances and processes. Conceptions of 'how work might be' will derive to a considerable extent from wider political and social views and philosophies and the central feature of 'work as it is' will derive from the actions of extra-organizational events and conditions — namely the organization and vicissitudes of a market economy.

Within organizations there are considerable differences in work experiences and work expectations, along the lines of the worker/ manager distinction. On the whole managers are expected to commit themselves to the organization beyond the levels of grudging acquiescence displayed by most workers. Katz argues that because managers are expected to be more committed to the enterprise than workers, they are relatively less subject to tightly defined and prescribed rules and procedures. The commitment of managers to their employing organization is usually seen to involve the manager's search for a career which will offer him jobs of increasing seniority, status and opportunities for interesting (self-actualizing) work. The possibility of an organizational or occupational career '. . . provides for people a stability in life plan, style, and cycle, engendering their motivation to work' (Glaser 1968 p 15). Careers then, for managers, offer the prospect (if not the reality) of long term pay-offs, and as such, it has been suggested,

'. . . give continuity to the personal experience of the most able and skilled segments of the population — men who otherwise would produce a level of rebellion of withdrawal which would threaten the maintenance of the system' (Wilensky 1968 p 50).

It is difficult and dangerous to generalize about the needs, motives, orientations and expectations of those who work in organizations, but a number of points can be made: organizational control systems are backed up by and depend upon sanctions and rewards. As Etzioni has remarked, levels and types of rewards and sanctions vary between organizations, and within the same organization. Within industrial organizations a marked difference in work experience and work expectations is discernible between workers and managers, and also within each group. The relevance of this all too brief discussion of work expectations of members of industrial organizations lies in the fact that in considering conceptions of organizations and organizational attempts to develop legitimacy, it should be noted that an important source of legitimacy is the satisfaction of members' expectations and aspirations. However, there must be few situations where this match between members' expectations and organizational experience and rewards obtains, particularly with respect to 'lower level participants' as Etzioni calls workers. And even where workers do stress (on particular occasions and in particular circumstances) instrumental rewards and benefits, organizations that emphasize such rewards may still experience troubles. Fox writes:

> Insofar as subordinates are — or can be brought to be — strongly committed to the values of a continuously rising material standard of life, managers may hope to strengthen their legitimacy by trying to meet subordinate aspirations in respect of material rewards, welfare, and fringe benefits. Since this is one of the appetites that grow by what they feed upon, it is apt to prove an unstable base for authority. (Fox 1971 p 41)

However, this should not be taken to mean that all industrial organizations are on the verge of revolution: they are not, usually. From the viewpoint of senior members the sort of acquiescence granted by most workers most of the time is adequate, while management level members of the enterprise, from whom more is expected and to whom more is given, are usually regarded as being committed to the 'management view' because of their personal and social characteristics, their exposure to training schemes and their efforts to achieve promotion and career advancement. Nevertheless, as discussed below, organizations also mobilize other resources in the attempt to achieve consensus and co-operation, particularly with reference to senior members.

3.2 Presentations of favourable definitions of organizational structure and activities

The type and level of rewards that a member obtains from his employing organization will be of importance in determining his orientation and commitment to (or alienation from) the organization; but this chapter is concerned with organizational procedures for creating definitions and assumptions, with respect to organizational members, society at large, the organization's clients or patients, or the structure of the organization. One of the objectives of such activities is to control organizational members and to ensure consensus and co-operation: however, such objectives will not be publicly stated, since this would negate the point of the exercise. The 'real' objectives of such attempts are attributed to them by the observing sociologist who considers the pronouncements of those who manage or own organizations in terms of their interests and priorities, that is, as ideological. The *stated* objective, of course, is simply to inform, or to communicate, the 'truth'.

One of the most striking features of current organizational efforts to define the nature of the organization and its personnel, and the relationships between intra-organizational groups and interests, is a marked emphasis on *individual* qualities, strengths, and failings, at the expense of any consideration of social or group factors. Argyris suggests, '. . . management thinks the fault lies in the employees (not in the company, management's leadership, management controls, and human relations programs). It is the *employee* who must be changed' (Argyris 1957 p 143). This psychologistic emphasis involves a treatment of organizational personnel as though they were entirely amenable to the same sort of analysis evaluation and processing as the physical plant and material of the organization, i.e. with a rationality that derives directly from technology, and which consequently ignores the unique qualities of *social* individuals. Such rationalities are treated in the previous chapter.

Such an emphasis on *individual* qualities and abilities, of course, which inspires so many management communications, has the attractive advantage of ignoring the possibility that organizations may consist of individuals whose experience has led them to consider their interests as basically and irreconcilably in conflict with those of management. However, for those who do conceptualize their relationship with their employers in this way, management communications which attempt to define the nature of the enterprise in terms of the community of interest of *all members* will be unsuccessful: indeed may even increase resentment. To quote from Argyris again: '. . . if the employees feel a basic conflict of interest between management and themselves, if they feel, for any reason, that they cannot trust management, then it is possible that the communications programs used by management may serve to increase these feelings rather than decrease them' (Argyris 1957 pp 143–4).

Organizational emphasis on individuals' qualities, strengths, and weaknesses, characterize a great deal of current personnel thinking and practice. Such psychologism is responsible for the extreme emphasis on 'scientific' selection systems and procedures. It also lies behind the management development or appraisal schemes which are increasingly employed by large-scale organizations. These schemes show the ways in which senior and powerful members of organizations act in terms of, and attempt insidiously to impose, their 'knowledge' of organizational processes and organizational personnel, and their assumptions about human nature and motivation.

According to those who design and install development and assessment schemes in organizations, they are intended to achieve two interrelated objectives: to increase employees' *satisfaction and their satisfactoriness*, they are thus intended to improve efficiency, reduce turnover, raise productivity, etc. Implicit in these schemes is the assumption that individuals' interests and organizational interests are coincident. Another assumption is that organizations are co-operative teams which are organized to achieve certain goals. This assumption, which has been severely criticized in earlier chapters, is apparent in the emphasis these schemes place on establishing targets or objectives for organizational members. Drucker has stated this assumption neatly:

> Any business enterprise must build a true team and weld individual efforts into a common effort. Each member of the enterprise contributes something different, but they must all contribute towards the common goal. Their efforts must all pull in the same directions, without friction, without unnecessary duplication of effort. (Drucker 1968 p 150)

In the appraisal interview members of the organization are meant to be told how their annual performance has been assessed: their strengths and weaknesses are listed, illustrated and discussed. This raises a number of difficulties. For one thing work performance is a social phenomenon as much as a psychological one. Sofer has suggested:

Effective performance is affected not only by one's personal attributes, but also by the attributes of one's colleagues and the precise
character of one's relations with them. Most organizational outcomes
are a function of group processes and some of one's attributes
manifest themselves in one set of relations but not another. (Sofer
1970 p 26)

However, an appraisal system which concentrates on individual
performance, and seeks explanations for level of performance in the
personal attributes and psychology of those concerned, will overlook
the social determinants and contexts of members' actions, and will not
only avoid consideration of relevant and salient factors, but will become
a highly contentious and problematic exercise. The assessment of
people's work performances and the communication of this information
to those concerned is also a social activity; for this reason, it is suggested,
people show a very marked reluctance to carry out their development
of appraisal interviews. Kay Rowe summed up her research into
appraisal schemes as follows: '(i) Appraisers were reluctant to appraise.
(ii) Interviewers were even more reluctant to interview' (Rowe 1964
p 2). The reasons for this are not hard to find: members of organizations
are involved in social relationships with each other – they are not free
floating individuals. Appraisal interviews can threaten these social
relationships – upon which members, and the organization, depend –
and, therefore, members are reluctant to execute them, at least in full
conformity with the specifications. Members of organizations are not
merely superiors and subordinates: they are also colleagues, and
colleague relationships involve some degree of mutual assistance, of
trust and solidarity. These qualities could be threatened by the appraisal
interview.

Not surprisingly, therefore, it has recently been reported that the
appraisal interview is not a very effective form of communication.
Even when members of the organizations studied overcame their
scruples and conducted (more or less perfunctorily) their interviews,
the researchers discovered a considerable area of disagreement after
the interview about the topics covered and the conclusions reached.
Such variance they attribute to the fact that the people involved are not
simply individuals to be assessed, processed and manipulated. They are
members of organizations in various positions with various priorities
and preferences. Because of the nature of organizational life the
researchers suggest:

Our argument is that, just as the appraisers are driven from their side to present the interview as an occasion on which they had conscientiously carried out their duties, so the appraisees are prone to present themselves as persons who have not had quite a fair chance. They tend to underplay what is being done for them and the appraisers tend to overplay it. (Sofer and Tuchman 1970 p 386)

Appraisal and development schemes constitute an important illustration of organizational constructions of reality, since these schemes are based upon coherent conceptions (or knowledge) of the nature of organization and organizational personnel, and the character of, and solution to, organizational problems. Simply, this conception involves an extreme emphasis upon the personal, psychological, nature of organizational personnel, their strengths and failings, and methods of changing them — in short, psychologism. Yet it has also been suggested that the obvious social aspects of organizations means that such emphases are not only misplaced: they are unproductive. Why then are such schemes increasingly popular? Sofer and Tuchman supply an appealing answer to this question with reference to the appraisal interview that is probably generalizable to the schemes overall:

> . . . it does occur to us to raise the question of why enthusiasm is so widespread among managements for appraisal interviewing in the face of known difficulties in getting appraisal done, the embarrassments and resentments they cause and so on. Our tentative hypothesis . . , is that these systems are popular because doubts are over-ridden by the anxiety of those responsible for large technological resources to keep under close control the persons who handle them. In other words, a covert or latent purpose may be served by reassuring senior managers, shareholders and government that rationality is being exercised, or at any rate pursued, in the use of human as well as physical capital. (Sofer and Tuchman 1970 pp 389—90)

But why should members of the organization put up with such treatment? How is it that they apparently concede to a view of themselves as 'organizational capital', as clusters of (more or less) organizationally relevant traits and characteristics? Why do they, apparently, subscribe to such 'knowledge'? One answer, according to these authors is that it is '. . . because they have been so "processed" or are so dominated by organizational and personal values connected with ambition and promotion they have become insensitive to the implications of being objectively evaluated' (Sofer and Tuchman 1970 pp 389—90). In other words, despite its unpleasant implications they find it hard to reject entirely the assumptions and organizational knowledge of the senior members of the organization.

A marked concern for the psychological qualities of organizational personnel, and consequent assumptions about the importance of such qualities for organizational activities is displayed in organizational processes of recruitment and selection. Because these processes too reveal a great deal about the way senior members of the organization conceptualize the nature of the organization (and organizations generally) and organizational personnel, they are worth considering in some detail.

3.3 Organizational procedures of recruitment and selection

From the organizational point of view persons with appropriate skills, knowledge, attitudes and motivations, are regularly and urgently required; and expert members of the organization (who because of their training and orientation are seen as sufficiently reliable) attempt to discover suitable recruits. They are frequently assisted in this venture by expertise and techniques from occupational psychology and, to a lesser extent, industrial sociology.

Organizational processes of recruitment and selection are relevant to our purposes in two interrelated ways. For one thing selection is an important method of organizational control, since senior members of organizations will attempt to select those persons who, in their eyes, display evidence that they will be amenable to methods of organizational control and who appear to hold some commitment to organizational 'goals' and the organizational culture. Secondly, the qualities, dimensions and characteristics that selectors are briefed to search for in their scrutiny of candidates can be seen to articulate the assumptions, which are held within the organization, concerning the nature of the organization, its objectives and personnel. In short, the search for suitable organizational candidates reveals a great deal about the relevant organizational knowledge of senior personnel.

What are the characteristics required by organizations? Firstly, organizations usually involve some sort of attempt to break down systematically the features of organizational tasks and to assess candidates in terms of their job demands: the notion of universalistic criteria has, at least, nominal, if not predominant emphasis. Sofer has related the 'rationalization' of organizational selection to the fact that organizations involve a persistent regularity that survives individual members and which must, therefore, depend upon some sort of selection or training of members, and to the emphasis, within organizations, on technical, systematic rationality, especially the breaking down of tasks and activities into their constituent elements and objectives. However, he also notes that the '... pressure towards the rationalization of human resources or objective (universalistic) and systematic procedures for recruiting, selecting, inducting, placing, training and appraising people' (Sofer 1970 p 20) is modified by the demands of the actual workings of the organization in terms of values, attitudes, loyalties of those involved.

Values and culture permeate the selection exercise, particularly for middle and senior jobs. Despite the rigorous and systematic nature of the organizational search for suitable candidates, and the sophistication of the techniques they employ — including psychological tests of various systematically delineated and operationalized dimensions and traits — the salient qualities, or at least some of them, derive not from some objective assessment of the skills and knowledge required by a particular job, but from a concern to pick people who have the 'proper' or appropriate attitudes and orientations and will thus 'fit into' the ongoing organizational culture and be amenable to organizational control (Salaman and Thompson 1978). That conceptions of suitable recruits are heavily affected by the values and priorities of those doing the selecting has been suggested by Nichols on the basis of his research. He asked his respondents what made a good manager.

> ... the answers given did make one thing quite clear, that 'character', 'personality' and social skills and personal characteristics in general, were considered to be more important than technical skills. By far the largest category of responses contained references to 'leadership' or some supposed aspect of this, like 'being firm but fair' or 'commanding respect'. (Nichols 1969 p 127)

Concern for establishing that candidates will 'fit in' to the ongoing organizational culture with its intrinsic priorities, convictions and assumptions, although a dominant feature of selection for important and 'responsible' organizational posts (the incumbents of which *must* themselves be responsible and mature, and must subscribe to the under-lying organizational system of values and priorities), will not be explicit in the selection scheme or the interview. It will appear as an emphasis upon 'social skills', 'motivation', leadership capacity and so on. Leader-ship is a particularly interesting selection criterion since what is involved is that successful candidates display those qualities that the selectors find impressive, that *they* hold to be signs of personal excellence and value. Whether those in lower positions in the organization share these convictions, or whether indeed obedience and conformity require that the subordinates be impressed by the superior's personal qualities is usually not considered. The search for leadership qualities in organizational candidates, then, reveals a great deal about the values and priorities of senior organizational personnel, and their 'knowledge' of the organization and its goals, and its personnel.

Consider the following analysis of 'leadership' and discipline contained in an Army recruiting brochure (aimed at officer applicants):

Your job is to lead.

You have probably heard a lot about this thing called 'leadership'. You may well have wondered what on earth it means. Almost certainly you have wondered whether you've got it. Let us try to give it some meaning.

First of all then, a leader is a man whom other men will obey, *not* because he can punish them if they don't, but because he has their confidence. You earn their confidence, in the first place, by showing that you know what to do. (The Queen's Commission p 14)

Fundamentally, discipline is *not letting your friends down*. You finish the job — repairing a bridge, or opening a radio link, or holding a position — because if you don't someone else will be in a jam. You obey your Colonel's orders because your friends depend on you — perhaps for their lives — to carry them out in full, and not try to 'improve' on them . . .

All this has a lot to do with the feeling of belonging to something with its own corporate identity. And two other aspects of 'Army discipline' are also related to this: drill, which gives birth to it, and smartness, which expresses it. (The Queen's Commission p 17)

Interestingly, the candidates are, increasingly, being prepared for this sort of general, attitudinal assessment. As far as graduate candidates are concerned this preparation stems from the university appointments boards, some of whom go to considerable lengths to prepare their students for their selection interviews. Consider the following extracts from one university appointments board information sheet.

Many undergraduates are reluctant to consider careers in Industry; in 1967 only four per cent of Hull Arts graduates entered Industry, only seven per cent of Social Scientists and only twenty-four per cent of our Scientists. One of the major reasons why Industry is unattractive is because undergraduates know so little about the challenges and opportunities and what they do know — or think they know — is often a series of half-truths — 'the profit motive', 'the rat race', etc. The purpose of this note is to outline some of the opportunities available for the graduate entering this very important field of employment; to indicate methods of training, and to clear some misconceptions.

(a) The 'Management Side'. Many graduates considering Industry talk vaguely of wishing to enter 'management' or obtaining 'something on the management side'. Organizationally, there is no such thing as a 'management side', no company has a 'management' department. Companies do however have certain specific functions or departments, for example, Production, Sales, Finance, etc., and each of these will have managers. Graduates considering Industry should think of the Function that interests them rather than thinking vaguely of 'management'. Clearly a graduate should aspire to a management *level* post but it is important to consider in which Function this may be achieved. Employers are very critical of graduates who approach them and ask for 'something on the management side' without any real idea of which Function they wish to consider.

(b) 'The Profit Motive'. There are some undergraduates who on moral grounds feel that they cannot consider Industry because of its concern for profit-making. Certainly the private sector of industry is concerned with profit and profit-making and anyone entering this field must accept that one of his major tasks is to help the company to maximize its profits. There are however, openings in the public sector of Industry where the emphasis is on Service rather than on Profit and no one really questions the value to our society of efficiently run power facilities or the value of our railways or docks.

(c) 'The Rat Race'. Certainly most fields of employment in Industry are 'competitive' and it is certainly necessary for an individual to want to be a success. But is there anything wrong in this? Most careers have some sort of 'rat race' and there are many who believe that the academic world is a bigger rat race than Industry! (University of Hull Appointments Board Information Sheet 1968 p 1)

Nor is this all; they are also prepared for the actual interview in terms which directly reflect the value premises upon which organizations base their assumptions about people and their attitudes and motivations. That is, not only are they told what they should 'know' about the world of industry and commerce, but they are advised as to how to present themselves to display this knowledge. A quotation from a recent article in *Career Choice* entitled, 'Market yourself as if you are a new product' (published for final year undergraduates) reveals this:

> The techniques for selling people are exactly the same as for marketing any other product. The same rules apply down the board; identify the market as clearly as possible; define the nature of the product which fits it; pay a lot of attention to the packaging and presenta-

tion; and then concentrate on the USP — unique selling point — and the correct approach at the point of sale, which is where the crunch will come. (*Career Choice* 1973 p 26)

Finally, as remarked earlier, organizational processes of recruitment and selection are interesting because of the way in which they reveal underlying assumptions held by senior organizational personnel, concerning the nature of organizational problems, and their resolutions. The very emphasis on these processes of selection and recruitment, regardless of the attitudes and orientations that are considered relevant and salient, reveals a deep-seated conviction of the importance of individual, psychological variables in determining the nature and outcome of organizational processes, a conviction that is also apparent as underlying the increasingly popular appraisal and development schemes. Argyris has beautifully caught the essentials of such thinking in his analysis of top administrators' theorizing about

> . . . waste, errors, absenteeism, sickness, apathy, disinterest in work, and increase in importance of material (financial) aspects of work as evidence that (1) the employees are lazy. (2) The employees are uninterested and apathetic. (3) The employees are money crazy. (4) The employees create errors and waste . . . it follows *logically* for management, that if any changes are to occur the employees must be changed. (Argyris 1957 p 123. Our emphasis.)

It should be noted that, as so often with organizational rationalities, what is seen as logical is based, ultimately, upon value premises.

Section five
Perspectives on organizations

CHAPTER 12

Charles Perrow

'Zoo story' or 'Life in the organizational sandpit'

1 The variety of organizations and theories

At the least we are all blind men. We fumble about that elephant that we call 'the organization' and dutifully report on the warts, trunks, knees and tails, each of us confident that we have found the nature of the beast. But it is worse than that, for we are not even looking at the same beast. The zoological garden of organizational theorists is crowded with a bewildering variety of specimens. Only after I talk with you for some time do you learn that I was talking about a large industrial firm, publicly held, when I kept saying that organizations are this or that, while you were disputing me, thinking about a small privately held one, or a union, or a government agency, or a church, or a voluntary agency, or whatever. Outside the fence of our zoo is another much larger, more effective and possibly more ferocious beast that we cannot even get close to — the multinational corporation.

What are we to say, then, about organizations and theories of organizations? It may have crossed your mind, in reading collections of articles, such as this, that we theorists are more preoccupied with what each other has to say about organizations, than with describing an actual beast that we have caressed ourselves, let alone one that you, as a reader, might know or be curious about. What we have to say about organizations is in some significant part a commentary on what Weber, or Blau, or Gouldner, or Thompson, or whoever, has had to say about them. And only a few theorists have run their hands over their particular beastie for any length of time, and even then they claim the one they know well is a typical one. It isn't; the variety is enormous, the theorists few in number and their acquaintanceship is fleeting. Organizational theory is not a 'contact' sport.

This observation has occurred to those whom David Silverman

(1970) calls the 'action theorists', or the group more generally known as the ethnomethodologists. You all sit back, this group seems to say, and construct theories about these beasts without actually getting in contact with them and asking how they themselves see their different parts and how they function together and move about. Fair enough. The construction of social meanings goes on endlessly and it goes on between people in specific situations, especially organizations. We sometimes call it 'social life'. But can we equate the social construction of meanings with organizations themselves?

Not at all, others would say. Social life goes on in organizations and is a part of them, but the crucial things about organizations are their characteristics as *organizations*. We can stand back at a safe distance and look at output statistics, profitability, rulebooks, employee turnover, organization charts, proportion of clerks, who is entitled to make a certain decision, and then describe an organization. Furthermore, we can describe many organizations in this way and compare them. This is the answer of the 'structuralist' theorist, such as Derek Pugh and the Aston group, Peter Blau and his associates and well reviewed in Richard Hall (1978).

In the soggy ground midway between these two extremes, tread the bulk of organizational analysts with their paper and pencil questionnaires and their structured interviews. Here it is attitudes that count – your morale, your values, your perception of your superior, your understanding of the goals of the organization, your impression of how much authority or discretion you have. These are assumed to be more or less stable meanings of people, and thus represent neither the ongoing construction of lines of action referred to by the ethnomethodologists, nor the distant statistics and records of the structuralists.

But, say the ethnomethodologists, the stability of these meanings is created by the research instrument itself. Since the questions are preconceived the answers are also preconceived and structured. Respondents are not 'giving accounts' but answering unreal questions which they interpret in a variety of different ways. The structuralists tend to share this criticism and argue that only behaviour, such as employee turnover, can really be trusted or, rather inconsistently, that formal rules are adequate surrogates for behaviour and at least as reliable as attitudes derived from a questionnaire.

By now it should become clear to us that the analogy of a blind man describing an elephant is really not so apt after all because it is not really contact with a different part of the beast that creates the difference among these three types of theorists. After all, somebody should have had the time over their career to have felt the whole of a beast and thus be able to report back to the rest of us what it was truly like. The analogy breaks down because these different theorists are feeling for quite different things. We all bring different intentions to the study of organizations; we are like small children in a sandpit, playing at different fantasies, only occasionally acknowledging the other children.

Organizations, for the ethnomethodologists (and for a large part of the psychologists and social psychologists interested in attitudes and behaviour), are mainly convenient settings for studying what interests them. In the case of the ethnomethodologists, what interests them is the way people negotiate the definition of reality. This involves things that interest other organizational theorists, such as control, consensus, and roles, but it is on a microscopic level that generally leaves the non-ethnomethodologists impatient. Teasing the meanings out of an employment interview is not what interests the structuralists. The structuralists take it for granted, take it as obvious that the interviewer will be dominant in the interview situation, will resent attempts by the applicant to interview him, and at times will use his small powers of discretion to find rules to make a negative evaluation of someone he doesn't like. The concerns of the ethnomethodologist are trivial to them.

The structuralists want to know how different industries vary in their personnel requirements, the level of education required, the dominant ethnic characteristics of whoever gets through the screening devices. A rule that only college-educated applicants need apply for this or that job is sufficiently descriptive for them. Knowing about inter-subjective constructions is irrelevant.

But which is 'true' for the organization — the construction or the rule? Both, of course. But should the observed rule be qualified by the outcomes of the interaction between the applicant and the interviewer? No more so than that the interaction should be hugely qualified by the rule that no one with less than a college degree need apply. The construction of reality goes on in all social life; but the rule that one cannot perform a certain job without a college degree is specific to some organizations, and says something specific about them, whereas the construction of reality doesn't.

Perhaps there is some common ground here — both are observing the operation of social power, and thus some common conclusion might be reached. But it would be only the most general one, I am afraid; something to the effect that power is unequally distributed in society, and especially in the most organized part of society, organizations. Social stratification is pervasive. But the two groups will go on — the ethnomethodologists crying that the structuralists are reifying organizations, and the structuralists saying the ethnomethodologists are trivializing them.

Nor will the in-between group, fiddling about with morale, leadership, satisfaction and autonomy, come any closer to the reality of organizations. Their interests are diverse, but we might summarize some of these interests by saying that they are trying to find ways to make organizations work better. For whom? Well, for the employees, for one, since we can hardly deny that if their satisfaction increases that is a good thing. But also for the employers, since if productivity goes up that is a good thing. It is even good for the society as a whole, since who wants men and women to waste effort? What is the organization then, in this view? It is largely the workings of work groups, led by leaders, co-ordinated by still higher leaders. It has no goals to speak of, except increased productivity and perhaps better morale. Its place in the economic hierarchy is not relevant to them. It doesn't pollute, manipulate consumers, affect government policies, try to bring down foreign governments. Leaders can shape meanings, and they should learn how to; but they should shape them for the good of the organization and its members. The overall degree of hierarchy and the division of labour that the structuralists study is important, they would say, as is the use of organizational power in society, but like the social construction of reality, these aspects can be taken for granted. The important questions are what affects productivity.

There are other schools of thought, other ways of cutting the multilayered cake of organizations, but these three positions will serve to make my point: we have 'instant theories' of organizations — theories that reflect the kind of interest and problems that investigators have been trained and schooled in. Out of these no complete picture of either the elephant or the mouse is likely to emerge. The definition of organizations eludes us, and what is likely to be true for all schools is likely to be commonplace.

2 The relation between interests and theories

If you are trying to use organizational theory to understand a dominant aspect of your life better, rather than just reading about it for course requirements or as an intellectual pastime, then an interest theory of theories is essential. 'Why can't they all agree upon the definition of key terms, such as structure, or decision-making, or power, or even technology' you might well ask. Because concepts are tools, and because

we want to make different ¡
technology has little in commo¡
et al. My interest was in find¡
structure of whole organization
Most of these units do not use n
to techniques used by personi
planners, research technicians, et
Aston group,[1] technology mear
limited to production flow. The¡
and work flow rigidity of the do¡
number of clerks, the standardiza
tion? That is quite a different i
concept of technology and of struc

Why such different interests? It is hard to say, but originally I was struck by the wide variations in the way organizations functioned, the degree to which they were *not* alike, and so looked for some explanation that would not be a tautology – that is, not explaining different structures by different structures. (I also had the misguided hope that non-routine technologies would generate more socially responsive organizations and wanted to check this out.) I suspect that the Aston group wanted to see generally what things went together, and in their view of pure science, you collect a lot of data and see what patterns emerge. So they took a direct, commonsense view of technology (shop floor operations), and threw it into the pot. I have my personal preferences for the former method of inquiry (a fairly explicit problem), but the latter (let us see what relates to what) is also a productive enterprise, and, in the case of Aston, has been productive indeed. But, as a result, we have quite incompatible definitions of a key term. Joan Woodward's is still different, as she had still other interests (1965 and 1970).

Or take the question of power in organizations. Roughly speaking, there is a messy middle ground here of people proposing and testing discrete theories about fairly trivial aspects of organizational power and elaborating distinction after distinction. This kind of work is necessary – for the scholar. It serves to work over basic problems so that some consensus can emerge. For the student who is not going to make a career in organizational theory, it is possibly mystifying, confusing, endless and irrelevant. The interest, for the scholar, is picking up

---

[1] People associated with the Industrial Administration Research Unit at the College of Advanced Technology, Birmingham (now the University of Aston). Members included D. S. Pugh, D. J. Hickson, C. R. Hinings, K. M. Macdonald, C. Turner and T. Lupton.

s and litter in the sandpit and trying to organize,
ighlight them. For the student, who has some
to ask about power in organizations, such as 'must
oritarian?', it all seems a waste of time.

he edge of this littered middle ground are some fairly well
eaks of specific 'interest theories'. These concern real life-and-
issues of power.

1 One of these is the elite view — power is largely held by those at
   the top, because they hold the resources, and because organizations are tools. The candy wrappers in the middle of the sandpit
   are fairly irrelevant, because those at the top decide which goodies
   to order, what quantities of them, and can let those lower down
   in the organization exercise 'discretion' about picking one variety
   or another. The dangling last chapter of Blau and Schoenherr
   (1973), the material on multinational corporations stem from this
   perspective (as does my own piece, 1974, and some of the Marxist
   perspectives currently emerging — see Benson, 1978).

2 Another peak of sand concerns the pluralist viewpoint — power is
   bargained over by groups in the organizations; no one has the
   final say; outcomes are the result of negotiations; goals are
   multiple, conflicting and changing. Richard Cyert and James
   March put forth this position in *The Behavioural Theory of the
   Firm*. The strategic contingencies theory of power set forth by
   Hickson *et al* (1973) is consistent with it. We have less to fear
   about organizations than we have from the tool view, if this be
   the correct posture.

3 Another peak, eroded by the former one, but still a viable viewpoint, sees power as emerging from the negotiations of all people
   (not just the leaders of major interest groups or coalitions).
   Chester Barnard, with his view of organizations as co-operative
   systems, fathered this vantage point, and it has been implicit in
   much of the human relations tradition (Barnard 1970). People
   co-operate in organizations; 'lower participants' (Mechanic 1962)
   have a great deal of power. To use the ethnomethodological
   variation, rules do not really matter that much, it is negotiations
   and definitions of reality that do. As Jack Douglas, a leading
   exponent of that school puts it, 'Anyone who starts with the
   abstract rules and hypothesizes what the concrete, situational
   uses will be, or what the social action of those expressing the
   abstract rules will be, is almost certainly going to be wrong'
   (Douglas 1971 p 171). (You might test that out yourself by, say,

coming to work drunk, or late, or not paying your employees, or not working during the day, or spitting at your boss, or stealing company property. There are quite a few rather important rules that predict very well what social action employees are likely to engage in, and they say more about organization existence than do those vague, intermittently used rules Douglas is presumably referring to.)

The ethnomethodologists and the co-operative systems viewpoints have precious little in common in most respects, but both of them take a quite different view of power from either the 'tool' view or the 'pluralist' view. They will define and measure the concept differently (though the ethnomethodologists would abjure normal measurement and concept-formulation), and use it for different ends.

4 Finally, off in one corner of the sandpit is an old, hallowed mound with its own group of children saying that organizations are natural systems, guided by natural (social) forces, and all the presumed power-wielders are really only acting out their parts on the stage. No persons are in control; it is history, or technology, or the class struggle, or social differentiation, or the grand game of human ecology that writes the script. The leaders of our giant multinational firms are captives of forces that lie beyond their control or comprehension. The individual clerk is the product of long and complicated socialization processes, placed in a situation neither he nor others can affect, making his miserable peace with the terms of his existence. The litter in the soggy middle ground is revealed as a grand pattern (of history, technological determinism, class struggle or whatever). This, too, is an honourable thesis, and has its own definition of power and finds its evidence in different places.

These are 'interest' theories of organization power in the sense that their proponents come to the organization with a viewpoint of what power should look like, and they find it. Each defines common terms (influence, authority, resources, discretion, etc.) differently, measures different things, and writes largely for his look-alikes. Do you want to know about power in organization, as if it were one real thing? Forget it. But if you want to see organizations as threats to our existence, even as we need them to sustain our affluent, polluted existence; or want to know how people are manipulated, how unobtrusive controls are used, then climb up the crumbling sands of the first peak. Do you want a detached, inside dopester, knowing, cynical view of internal struggles, and are willing to lay aside any larger implications? Try the second peak. You might even find the sustenance there for a view that all interests will somehow be represented, and a pluralistic, democratic system is after all possible. Are you mostly concerned with reducing distressing interpersonal conflicts, promoting more individual autonomy and self-realization, greasing the paths of human interaction? Try the human relations variant of the third peak. (The ethnomethodological perspective has little to say about power *per se*, except implicitly in that it favours studies of dependent clients in authoritarian service organizations – welfare recipients, citizen-police encounters, petty criminals in the courts – and the homeless, powerless and victimized people labelled as deviants. No multinational firms here, or even conflicts between sales and production.) Do you want to 'put it all together' and get the *answer*? Try one variety of the last view. But don't ask me to define power in organizations. For that you can go to the middle ground, effectively picked over by Hickson and McCullough in their strategic contingencies theory (Hickson *et al* 1973) and take your pick of the candy wrappers.

One could go on through the other key concepts we utilize – structure, goals, efficiency, etc. – and play the same game. Nor should we act like Noah Webster and try to freeze the definitions in the interest of scientific purity and rigour. We shall never get agreement on these terms because the major positions represent struggles to say what our social worlds are like, and that, ultimately, is a political question.

To complicate matters more, fold the sandpit image into the zoo one, and you will see that not only do we have the variety of interests or models existing in what Jean Piaget called the collective monologue of children in a sandpit, but we have to apply them to the variety of the species. The tool view is rather hard to apply to a voluntary organization (though true to my prejudices, I have tried to in chapter 5 of *Complex Organizations: A Critical Essay* (1979) while the human relations view is rarely used in studies of prisons. Self-realization and autonomy for the guard is not often on their agenda).

Fortunately, the scope of this book makes it easier to discuss this aspect of the subject. With a highly disparate group of authors, you can't help but be properly bewildered by the diversity and volume of findings, perspectives, concepts, and disagreements. Even when we have fallen into the card-file style of 'X said, Y noted, Z showed', trundling out the list of papers, you may have noticed the shifting meanings, unnoted contradictions, and diverse types of organizations involved.

One other distinctive nature of this book gives my remarks some relevance; you have been set up for *the* topical dispute of the first three-quarters of this decade – the gathering strength of ethnomethodology. (Whether it will continue gathering in the final quarter of the decade I cannot say; a similar movement in deviance theory, called the 'labelling perspective', has been under attack for some time for a bit of gross oversell.) This radical perspective has the virtue of all radical perspectives: it offers a resounding critique of received wisdom and theories. I think the first half of Silverman's book (1970) is a splendid attack upon the status quo. It also has the vice of most radical theories: it fails to show how its embryonic alternative will do any better by the big issues in organizational theory. What difference would it make if we made an ethnomethodological study of top management at General Motors or British Leyland? That is not really a fair question, since none of the other schools have studied them either. So let us ask how an ethnomethodological approach would inform us about unobtrusive controls, the US military, TVA, organization-environment dynamics, prison reform, innovations in welfare organizations, scientists in industry, and so on.

But never mind; in this book it has played the role of devil's advocate and set the stage for my sandpit analogy. Like systems theory, it promises much, but is hard put to show what difference has been made by using *it* rather than something else. Both theories give, in my hostile-sympathetic view, a name to a large area of common-sense (things are linked together; people are not robots) and tell us to 'take account'. But they do not show us how different conclusions would have been reached if such and such a study had indeed 'taken account'; or how new insights into the original problem would be generated (which is different from insights into what they think the problem should have been). They can't. Their interests dictate different problems to solve. At the worst, the ethnomethodological viewpoint will erode the existing sandpeaks and increase the size of the middle plane. At best, it will allow some of those peaks to be built on firmer foundations.

3 An autobiographical example of changing interests and theories

Interest theories wax and wane in dominance, but not because new theories come along – all interest theories have their ghosts in other centuries – but because of the shifting preoccupations and political values of the individual theorists. Theorists respond (slowly) to the pressures of social events, and the demands for interpretations and meanings of our social existence.

To illustrate this point the editors have suggested that I comment upon the change in my own work, from conventional paradigm exploration in early articles on goals and the impact of technology upon structure, to a 1972 volume designed to give a sympathetic hearing to the New Left attack on business (Perrow 1972), through a mildly dissenting piece on organizations and environments (Perrow 1974) (which appears with a stronger flavour in an offprint to the Open University course, *People and Organizations*, titled 'Technology, organizations and environment') up to my present concern with the origins of the factory system, the 'bureaucratic fix' at the turn of the last century which was important as the technological fix has been, and the quite new reality of disorganized elite control in a higly interdependent society of organizations (a hint of which appears in Perrow 1979). It is a measure of our inflated preoccupations with 'science' and 'professionalism' that such shifts in perspective go unacknowledged and unexplained in public discourse, and that even a short autobiographical statement such as follows are sufficiently rare that one must self-consciously note the breach of practice and, indeed, apologize in this form. But since I have emphasized 'interest theories', it is only fair that I try to retrospectively account for my own interests.

In the 1950s when I drifted into organizational studies (largely because of the intellectual and personal force of a mentor, Philip Selznick), it just seemed like an 'interesting' area, just as my earlier graduate work had been in the 'interesting' area of Freudian theory and primary group studies. Of course, my initial organization work could accommodate political values. I wrote about such things as organizational goals, prestige, correctional institutions, mental hospitals and so on in a liberal context. I published one obscure attack upon pluralism shortly after becoming an assistant professor but my department did not encourage this direction. A couple of years later after some pieces on goals and hospitals and the draft of a co-authored book surveying several juvenile correctional institutions, I was told that tenure would require an additional empirical book (that is, another questionnaire survey). Instead, I left in 1973 for another university where I could pursue more field work and theory construction before attempting empirical confirmation. None of these career issues were political ones (though they had political implications, or course) and indeed, the 1950s and 1960s were quiet for most academics. Some graduate students and new PhDs were off to the South during the civil rights movement. But most of us were securely and thoughtfully liberal — peace vigils, raising funds for the civil rights groups, supporting the radical students on the campuses in their endless confrontations.

After a few years of working in people processing organizations, I moved over into the study of business organizations when I changed universities. The lunches were better, the people lived better and were more forceful and the scent of real power was about. Vaguely, I was dissatisfied with studying 'trivial' organizations; economic organizations had the power in society. There was also a theory to be tested that had emerged from work on hospitals, prisons, etc. — structures adapted to available techniques of getting the work done. I even hoped that goals might be related to technology, and the apparently growing number of 'nonroutine' firms in the areas of advanced technology might signal a liberalization of American business. But looking for conditions that might make business more responsive was hardly the way to publish one's self to high rank in highly rated sociology departments, or to gain the respect of one's peers in the field, so that growing interest remained muted. The study of organizations was still very much a preoccupation with internal variables and a fumbling with concepts, comparative schemes and case studies. It was fashionable to be critical of business, since it appeared to sin so much, but this was an imperfect world, and reforms were in the air. There was little hint, as yet, that objectionable behaviour by business went far deeper than the sins liberals were concerned with and was the outcome of the system itself, rather than occasional abuses. By the time I had published a theoretical scheme on technology and structure and was busily testing it in a dozen industrial organizations, however, the political climate of the campuses and the nation had changed.

I moved to yet another university. I began to read some of the radical tracts turned out by the young students; most of these were dreadful, but some were intriguing and well researched. A group of SDS'ers — Students for a Democratic Society — organized a seminar for some twenty or so faculty members at the University of Wisconsin. They taught the course, and expected us to do the reading (mercifully, they didn't believe in exams). We, faculty, were good liberals all, and supported their right to protest on campus, but they wanted more of us. That reading began to put into a different framework a number of questions that only hovered on the edge of respectable theory. For example, could more control go with an impression of freedom in organizations and society? The left was wont to spout 'manipulation' and 'false consciousness', but managers sometimes said the same thing — for example, to decentralize, one must first centralize. Another: could there be great stability in a system even though the surface showed turbulence? We all knew about intense competition, but somehow it didn't seem important. Another: what was the effect upon business of all those professionals with liberal education – a smoother image for business, or a liberalizing of goals? Most professionals (engineers and scientists) were concentrated in the military-industrial complex, and they clung to the Vietnam war longer than presumably illiberal blue collar workers. How was it that underdeveloped countries got poorer as we got richer, if we were pouring all that aid and capital in? A close look at official statistics disclosed that we took far more out than we put in, and distorted their economies unmercifully in the process. What could we say about organizational goals – were they the product of the interaction of internal group interests; the fulfilment of functional requisites for the society; the natural play of competition and growing efficiency? Or could they primarily reflect the interests of elites with common class backgrounds and interests? Was organizational theory merely co-operating in tidying up the stables by preaching against authoritarian leadership techniques and wagging a finger at the displace-ment of goals, or could it inquire more deeply into the nature of organizations and the society they maintained?

Over the years of disorder, insurgency, and law and order counter-attacks, my preoccupations gradually changed. At one point, a year or two after the seminar, I found myself (1) teaching in a business school (a visiting professor at Berkeley), (2) finishing a book for business students that dealt with none of these questions, (3) but drafting another that did, and (4) watching unarmed students get gassed by a helicopter and killed and wounded by the police during the 'People's Park' disturbance. I remember cancelling my classes in protest against the treatment of students, but going across the bay to San Francisco that evening to lead a seminar for some prominent industrialist in the area on how to make organizations more efficient by manipulating structures rather than trying to change people directly. The year 1968 was like that; I was in the middle of changing paradigms.

The change was gradual, however. My SDS acquaintances went underground the next year and I spent much of my time fighting the Wisconsin administration's crackdown on dissident faculty members, and then left in disgust. But organization theory went on, and I went on writing about it at another school that paid better. But I also started another book, designed to publicize, for business, the attacks the radicals were making – hoping still that the system was *not* all that systematic and changes could be made. (Some radical groups objected to my reprinting their material because it would just allow business to adapt more easily and retain their power – this was still a time when they thought the system might come tumbling down.)

So one moves back and forth, carrying forward the old skills, investments and (weakened) values, while trying to find new ones that never really materialized as clearly. There is no great contradiction in one sense, because to some extent one paradigm, or interest theory, can support another if one does not have certainty. Thus, I could teach businessmen in politically unreconstructed institutions such as the London Business School for a year, but one of the courses could be 'The Radical Attack on Business' — and the students were intrigued. My academic address would ensure that Consolidated Gold Fields would respond to an inquiry about matters raised in the *Anti-Report* put out by the Counter Information Society (a mildly radical group); my convictions about the issues allowed me to pursue the matters vigorously and at length with the top officers of the firm. Perhaps it is the best of both worlds.

Since the hectic, balmy, dangerous, sweet days of the late 1960s and early 1970s, the protest movements in the United States and Canada have fallen upon evil times. Repression worked. New cohorts responded to a worldwide crisis in capitalism in sensible, if hardly ennobling, ways. They kept quiet and sought jobs. But the universities now had a few radicals, some even with tenure, and new journals and texts and radical scholarly groups appeared. The public interest groups held on in the rest of society, and despite a massive move to the right, there were crucial cracks in the system to be exploited (e.g. the Freedom of Information Act, the anti-nuclear power spillover from the energy crisis). My own growing interest in what I saw as some reasonable aspects of leftist critiques could be sustained. With tenure, a reputation of sorts, royalties and the like, it was no problem to decide that I would like to spend a few years finding out how we got where we were in organizational (and class) terms. It will be an interest theory, no more 'true' than any of the others, but consciousness, and thus theories, are ultimately political.

4 Knowledge of what and for what?

Sandpits and zoos . . . has this book been worth the trip? I think so. The state of organizational theory and research is indeed fragmented and disorganized. You have read enough of it now to look back over it and know that you have forgotten most of it already because it lacks a consistent approach, consensus on definitions, and orientation to problems that once had meaning to you. Yet this book has had some benefits, I firmly believe.

Since we live in an organizational society, almost anything we can learn about them will help us survive among and in them, whether it be about banana time or the strategies of multinational corporations. Perhaps the most meaningful way you have learned about organizations has been through descriptions of actual organizations or situations. It enlarges your sense of what is possible in organizations (even if the possible is also discouraging or even frightening), and your awareness of how much variety there is. I would have wished for more descriptive material and fewer candy wrappers and chewing of the sacred texts, but we ourselves are only well-programmed academics, talking to each other and making our way through publishing for our peers.

In addition to providing descriptive material, we have been quietly telling you in this book about a number of quite sensible stereotypes that need to be abandoned if we wish to understand, rule, manipulate or destroy organizations. Some of these sensible stereotypes are true only in limited situations, some never. It is worth reviewing a few.

For example, it does us little good to say that the trouble with organizations is that people are lazy time-servers, getting by with the least amount of trouble, for we are also fond of saying that the trouble is not the people, but the situation they are forced to function in. In fact, the problem is sometimes that people are too aggressive, bend organizational goals to their own limited conceptions of them, are forever changing things, and grumble because the rules limit them. We complain about lazy people, but we can describe the same group as scrambling for power; about uninventive people who can yet be ingenious in protecting their privileges; about people preoccupied with their privileges yet who are defending the distinctive skills, contributions and interests of their unit and rightly so; about organizations that are incompetent when we speak of the public interest, but are very competent in pushing their narrow or politicized view of the public interest; of organizations as resistant to change, but inventive in resisting change. If bureaucracies or individuals make inventive changes to resist change, we have stated the question and sought the answer improperly. At least, this book should have made it clear that such easy explanations of organizational behaviour as 'resistant to change' or 'conservative' are quite inadequate.

Or take the dirty word 'bureaucracy'. It should be clear that many of the things that Weber described in terms of bureaucracy, are essential for most organizations, and protect people against discrimination, unbounded authority, irresponsibility, corruption, uncertainty, and arbitrariness. Or take the idea that the structures of organizations should vary. It took several decades of organizational theory to finally come to the full realization that there is no one best way of doing things for all organizations (or if your tastes run to destroying or enfeebling organizations, no one best way to do that either).

Or take the matter of goals; it doesn't help to assume that profits maximization is the goal of all business organizations, in fact it tells us very little about them. Probably most of the things that liberals fear about large organizations are not the profits they make, once you analyse these closely, but the kind of power they throw around in society such as the power to hire and fire, to pollute, to corrupt governments, to maintain a class sytem and prevent the redistribution of income, and above all to shape men's minds (including those of us, unfortunately, who write about organizations). We can use the concept of goals as a tool of analysing problems such as these, if we have a sense of the variety of goals and the variety of uses to which organizational power can be put. We are just beginning to get it.

We also learn that however powerless people in the lower strata of organizations may be *vis-à-vis* those at the top to some degree they are able to construct a world of their own and to moderate, diffuse, distract, and derail some powerful impulses stemming from the top command centre. Organizational leaders are not all-powerful. The trouble is, we also hear, that for most important purposes they have power enough to shape the behaviour of employees. The problem now is to decide what kind of organizations most exemplify the tool view – the (recalcitrant) tool in the hands of the masters – and what kind most exemplify the co-operative, consensual view. Or, to sharpen it more, for what kind of issues or situation does one or the other view hold? As organizations increase in power and as social issues change, it may well be that our operational definitions of concepts such as power, authority and influence, as diverse as they are now, will change too, to capture new preoccupations.

There are even a few shaky generalizations that appear to hold for all organizations and which are not commonplace. For example, as organizations grow larger it is not the case in all, or even most of them, that the number of staff people increases at a faster rate than the number in direct production. Perhaps you never cared one way or the other, but some people did, because they saw large organizations covered with a mass of non-productive people such as clerks, finance people, personnel men, buyers, work-study men, planners, computer experts and so on. It's one vision of the nightmare of bureaucracy that appears to be a faulty one. We also suspect that the larger and the more bureaucratic the organization, the more *some* kinds of decisions are shoved down to lower levels, though this appears to be more true of economic than non-economic organizations. This also confronts one of the standard fears, that size and bureaucracy means centralized authority. It probably does in some respects, but not in others.

But on the other hand, whether bureaucracy is good or bad (for whatever or whomever you wish), whether all organizations are slow to react, self-defensive, and uncreative, and other such global questions, for those we have no answers except the one that it all varies with the type of organization and what you mean by slow, defensive or whatever. In a sense, organizational theory is in the neanderthal stage of progressively breaking down large questions for which there are no answers, into specific ones where there might be some answer. But it does this in terms of shifting peaks of interest. That is to say, no one is going to be able to 'put it all together' for a long time to come.

5 Some neglected topics

There are some things which you have not learned from this book, however, and it is worth pointing out the selectivity that was exercised here. For example, a great deal of work goes on in organizations that is never dignified with the label of organizational theory, but has had much more impact upon organizations than organizational theory has had. This is the work of the numbers men – the linear programmers, the PERT people, the econometricians, the specialists in flow-charts and systems design. Largely untouched by organizational theory, and having, unfortunately, little impact upon it, they go about streamlining organizations, and allowing them to do far more complicated things with much better control. Sometimes the cost to the workers or members of the organizations can be quite large, as jobs are rationalized and broken down into minute tasks; but sometimes much labour and inanimate energy is saved and people are not utilized to do stupid repetitive things. This is an area which, to the extent that it gets into organizational analysis at all, is called management science. It is scorned by most of the people involved in this book, but I suspect it is eliminating more kinds of stupidities and wasted efforts than the theories of the scorners can. Of course, it also gives more power to the managers of organizations, since efficient organizations with decent planning (and the higher morale that goes with it) generate more power. The critics are right in the long run. The power to shape our mentalities is more frightening than the existence of inefficiencies.

Another part of organizational analysis that is not covered in detail (there is some discussion in chapters 7 and 8) is probably the largest of all in terms of the number of practitioners and even the sheer output of articles. This concerns attempts to improve the functioning of organizations by manipulating people. Some of the advertising labels for this enterprise are OB (organizational behaviour), OD (organizational development), T-groups (training groups), sensitivity groups, management by objectives, matrix organization, the managerial grid, systems four organization, job enlargement, job enrichment, and so on. They focus upon the 'human side of the organization' (but largely from the point of view of top management), and are designed to increase productivity, raise morale, direct efforts towards the proper goals and generally to make human relations more humane. It is held in considerable disrepute by the more abstract theorists, and treated as a velvet glove over the mailed fist of managerial dominance by the more politically oriented theorists, but it has produced a great deal of information about people in groups, much of which has been filtered into this book through indirect means. In some cases it has probably made organizations more humane places to work.

Finally, let me mention another relatively neglected area — a neglect largely perpetrated by practitioners in the field as a whole, rather than in this book. There has been very uneven treatment of public service organizations. The study of hospitals and prisons has been extensive, but the study of the police, dustmen, the Post Office, county councils, local authorities, the Civil Service, and other government bureaucracies has been much neglected.

I suspect we shall find that the gross inefficiencies so often found in public service organizations are inefficiencies only in the sense of providing public services, but when we look at the real goals of these organizations, we will find they do quite well. For example, if I can believe reports I heard while living in England in 1972–73, the dilatory rate at which the telephone system extends service, improves it, and modernizes its facilities is in part due to the reluctance of the Post Office to force the major suppliers of equipment to go electronic. The four major suppliers (including GEC and Plessey) simply have too much vested interest in Strowger and Crossbar equipment and too much influence with the government. If we include quietly serving the interests of major industrialists among the goals of the Post Office, much inefficiency might be explained.

In the US, our health system is about the most ineffective of any industrialized country, but costs more *per capita* than all but one. But it does very well for the many commercial and academic and research interests involved. McKinsey and Company itself — the large consulting firm — could not have done much better in designing a system that would provide large profits and good livings for a mixed bag of equipment suppliers, pharmaceutical firms, doctors, researchers, governmental administrators, etc., while convincing the public that only more money from the public could provide decent care for all.

Some governmental bureaucracies seem to have employment goals – providing jobs for people who might be troublesome if they didn't have them – that take precedence over service goals, and this is an important source of inefficiency. Some simply serve a dependent, downtrodden sector of society that is without political power, and the goal is to avoid trouble, keep the lid on, and prevent the political activation of these groups. In this they are efficient; service is secondary and can only be in these terms.

But we do not hear much about these kinds of organizations and problems from organizational theorists. Our conceptions of efficiency, diverse as they are, are limited. Perhaps we need another sand pile in that pit, one that ignores administrative ratios, constructions of reality in the examining room, technological determinism, inter-personal dynamics and the like. This, indeed, might be a case where systems theory might lead us out of our corner of the sandpit. (For details on the health example, for other examples, and for the politically motivated emergence of a 'systems view' in the New Left in the US – a case where it does make a difference – see Perrow 1972. For a more embracing critique of organizational theory from this persepctive see Perrow (1979).

6 Conclusion

You should also be warned of a gathering storm which may well dominate a fair bit of the organizational theory sandpit in the 1980s (nothing will eliminate the soggy middle ground because that is where corporate interests play at reducing conflict, increasing output, and manipulating consciousness). This is the Marxist approach. It picked up particulate matter in the stormy 1960s and early 1970s in Europe and America, built some small sandpiles out of English and Continental thought in the middle 1970s, and at the same time drifted into the empirical world of US and Canadian organizational theory. In North America the emphasis has been more on empirical studies of contemporary organizations (see the Benson 1978 collection), historical studies (Braverman 1974; Marglin 1976; Clawson forthcoming), and some mildly radical theorizing (McNeil 1978; Brown 1978). A curious convergence is apparent here, but its outcome is uncertain. The radical theorists embrace a fair bit of the ethnomethodological perspective in their emphasis upon people (generally workers) resisting authority and creating their own reality (as much as they can, under the highly enfeebling circumstances). This micro-level approach is combined with a macro-level approach emphasizing the power of large organizations and elites, and society-wide dynamics, in particular, class relations, technology, world capitalism, imperialism and the like. The connection between the micro and macro concerns is not explicated very clearly, but I think it will come. (I am commencing such an effort, in an historical context of evolving organizational forms from the early nineteenth century on, which I hope to finish about 1980 under the title 'A society of organizations'.) But given our small population in the sandpit, our toddler age, and the variety and power of the beasts in the zoo, it would be unrealistic to expect much more than another unstable sandpile to emerge from all this work.

So in the final analysis it is a very large zoo, and perhaps some of the biggest animals are not even in it, and it is a quite small group of blind-men. They have different interests and march to different scholarly, financial, political, cultural, and normative tunes. And besides, you have all wandered through that zoo, and some of you have been close indeed to some of the specimens, living in them and working in them, so you are your own experts to some degree. This makes the hard-won generalization or finding look trivial to you, if you have had the honour of coming to the same conclusion through your own experience. Worse still, your own experience may contradict the patient, expensive, tedious research findings. Worst of all, as scholars we succumb to the occupational hazard of writing for each other in our attempts to describe more of that beast from yet another point of view, and thus become unable to write for the student, who finds only indirect allusions to the questions he wanted to ask and the theories that he thinks he needs to get on in this organizational society.

You have borne with us this long, bear with us for just one more chapter.

CHAPTER 13

Martin Albrow

The dialectic of science and values in the study of organizations

In recent years we have seen the growing acknowledgement of the complexity of the interplay of science and values in the social sciences. The interpretation of social action, the capacity of human beings to follow rules of their own making and the contribution of social science to structuring the very reality it seeks to analyse all raise issues which transcend the limits of traditional views of a science. Such issues have a heightened importance in the study of organizations where the problems of control and authority are central and where, therefore, the question of whom does organizational science service is always pertinent.

In what follows it will be argued that there is ample evidence from its history that organizational study, even where its proponents may have adhered to public claims of value-freedom, has invariably at fundamental levels both implied and contributed to value-commitments and has thereby helped to structure its own subject matter. The argument follows a dialectical route:

Thesis: organizations may be studied as 'objects' in the manner of the natural sciences; *antithesis:* organizations do not possess the qualities of 'objects'; *synthesis:* organizations are human creations, hence in part the creations of theorists of organizations.

1 Utility — organizational science as technology

1.1 The technocratic view of social science

In the two decades before the First World War the allure of forging an applied science extended to the human side of the large organization. The success of engineers on the material side of the production process encouraged an optimism about similar progress in enhancing the efficiency of the human element in production. The American Society of Mechanical Engineers became a forum for the discussion of 'scientific management'. 'Efficiency experts' were commissioned by railroads, steel firms, printers and other organizations to show the best way tasks might be performed and waste eliminated. To some extent in response to the encroachment of the engineers upon the field of human capacities, psychologists turned to the task of applying their concepts and methods to securing fit motormen for the electric railways, or selecting telephone operators, or finding the right psychological type for the ship's bridge.

In his history of the use of social science in American industry, Loren Baritz recounts how it was in this climate that Henry Ford established his 'Sociological Department' at Detroit in 1914. That department reported in 1916 that, for the Ford Motor Company, concern with human behaviour was, 'looked at from the cold blooded point of view of business investment . . . the very best investment it has ever made' (Baritz 1960 p 33).

An early creed for the social scientist serving industry may be found in *Psychology and Industrial Efficiency* (1913) by Hugo Münsterberg, who taught in both Germany and the United States and may be regarded as the founder of industrial psychology:

> Applied psychology is evidently to be classed with the technical sciences. It may be considered as psychotechnics, since we must recognize any science as technical if it teaches us to apply theoretical knowledge for the furtherance of human purposes. Like all technical sciences, applied psychology tells us what we ought to do if we want to reach certain ends; but we ought to realize at the threshold where the limits of such a technical science lie, as they are easily overlooked, with resulting confusion. We must understand that every technical science says only: you must make use of this means, if you wish to reach this or that particular end. But no technical science can decide within its limits whether the end itself is really a desirable one. (Münsterberg 1913 p 17)

This was written in a chapter headed 'Means and ends', which was followed by a section 'The best possible man' in which Münsterberg showed how the new 'psychotechnic method' was to be used for the 'selection of those personalities which by their mental qualities are especially fit for a particular kind of economic work' (Münsterberg 1913 p 27). It can be no accident that the sections 'Means and ends' recalls the classic discussion of the limits of objectivity in the social

sciences by Max Weber, where he argued that the achievement of given
goals is susceptible to scientific analysis, but that the selection of goals
to pursue will always remain subjective (Weber 1949). Münsterberg had
a high opinion of Weber's own work on the psychophysics of industrial
work, describing him as a brilliant political economist, and this research
had been published only four years later than the essay on objectivity
in the same journal, the *Archiv für Sozialwissenschaft und Sozialpolitik*.

Weber was himself well acquainted with 'scientific management',
referring to it as the 'Taylor system', after its prime mover, F. W. Taylor.
He viewed it as part of the general movement of rationalization in
modern industrial society and regarded it as of pioneering importance
in developing rational specialization according to physiological states
and in devising aptitude tests (Weber 1947 p 261).

Such reciprocal influences may surprise us at first. Scientific management is often thought of as a predominantly American phenomenon,
while Weber's work on objectivity and the nature of social science is
seen as a typical product of German thought. There is some truth in
this. But consider what Lenin had to say about scientific management
in 1918:

> The Taylor system, the last word of capitalism in this respect, like all
> capitalist progress, is a combination of subtle brutality of bourgeois
> exploitation and a number of its greatest scientific achievements in
> the field of analyzing mechanical motions during work, the elimina-
> tion of superfluous and awkward motions, the working out of correct
> methods of work, the introduction of the best systems of accounting
> and control, etc. The Soviet Republic must at all costs adopt all that
> is valuable in the achievements of science and technology in this field.
> (Lenin n.d. pp 332–3)

Thinking in terms of means and ends was common to both capitalist
and socialist modes of production and crossed the frontiers of indus-
trializing cultures at the beginning of the twentieth century. We are
bound, therefore, to acknowledge that we are concerned here with a
cross-cultural phenomenon, a theory of applied social science common
to industrial societies. It may be seen as an aspect of the ideology of
technocracy, which Jean Meynaud has characterized as a belief in
managerial competence to the extent that political decision-making is
rendered unnecessary (Meynaud 1968).

1.2 Techniques, consensualism and control

The cross-cultural coincidence of views we have just noticed also appears to be consistent with the belief in the universality of social science. Perhaps the ideology of technocracy is so prevalent precisely because it is well founded, we may suspect. After all, vaccines and gas turbine engines work in any society and testify to the soundness of the principles upon which they are founded. May we not regard aptitude tests and time and motion study as the analogous products of universalizable social sciences? Certainly in the history of modern science there has been a regular inclination to assume that universal utility follows from the universality of theories. The fact that applied science can be put to use anywhere leads to the idea that it is also always for the common good. From Francis Bacon onwards the progress of science and the coming of utopia have been closely associated ideas.

We may exemplify this from a source, contemporary with Weber, Taylor and Lenin, and influenced by pragmatism, the philosophical movement of the time which stressed that the criteria of truth could be found in usefulness, an appropriate philosophy for technocracy. The source is George Herbert Mead and what he has to say is especially impressive evidence of the strength of the idea of natural science in the service of the common good because, as one of the most important founders of modern social science, he is normally thought of, along with Weber, as one of the advocates of a non-natural scientific methodology emphasizing meaning and understanding. Mead wrote, in criticizing a highly influential French philosopher:

> What Bergson failed to realize is that there is nothing so rational, so self-consciously reflective, as the application of scientific method to immediate conditions, and that the use of this method is just the means, under these conditions, that the human race is using for advancing. The anti-intellectualist attitude of Bergson represents a failure to grasp the import of the scientific method, especially that it puts the environment under the control of the individual. (Mead 1936 p 294)

This is a succinct expression of the extreme consensualism which is so often involved in the idea of an applied science. In two sentences Mead slips from talking about the advance of the human race to the control of the environment by the individual. The interests of all are the interests of each. That conflicts of interest may arise in the course of the application of science is something that is all too often forgotten. The universal benefits of telecommunications, plastics or penicillin have appeared so obvious as to preclude such sophistry.

But in organizations the environment of one individual includes other individuals. Advances in the application of the social sciences, therefore, enhance the control that some individuals exercise over others. In consequence the unquestioning equation of applicability with common utility is no longer possible. The applied social scientist, working in an organization, demonstrating that his theoretical knowledge has practical application, achieves this at the expense of having to serve the values of the organization, either unconditionally by accepting them as his own values, or expedientially to earn an income and other advantages.

The dilemma of the social scientist in the organization is this: to show that his knowledge 'works' and can fashion techniques that can master the world in the manner of the natural scientist he looks up to, because they are based on valid, objective knowledge, he has to commit himself to values which emphasize control. In his objectivity there is a commitment, not to humanity's control of the natural world, as the applied natural scientist may affirm, but to man's control of man, to one side or another in a field of conflict.

The pioneering social scientists we have mentioned were aware of this dilemma, but they answered it in different ways. F.W. Taylor was extremely sensitive to the charge that he was working only in the interests of management. He hankered always after the utopian consensualism we have seen exemplified by Mead. Efficiency, he felt, necessarily worked in the interests of all. Science could only serve both management and men. A follower of his explained how this came about in the course of Taylor's work in the Midvale Steel Company. He was appointed gang boss and sought to increase output through pressure. A serious struggle ensued which Taylor won, but the experience hurt him and he set his mind to the elimination of such conflicts: 'He gave the matter thought and decided that the cause of such conflicts is that management, without knowing what is a proper day's work, tries to secure output by pressure. If management knew what is a proper day's work, it could then get output by demonstration' (Taylor 1947 p x, originally printed in 1911).

Taylor expresses the technocrat's dream, that science will show that conflict does not pay. But the unions were unconvinced. The benefits of management's interest in human behaviour did not seem so apparent to them if time and motion study led to men losing their jobs. The beneficence of Ford's 'Sociological Department' was not unambiguously demonstrated by the employment of a hundred investigators, empowered to enter men's homes to check on their drinking habits, leisure time, sex life, and cleanliness in order to ascertain whether they were worth the newly established wage of five dollars a day (Baritz 1960 p 33).

Weber, and later Münsterberg, were much more prepared to adı
that the social scientist must choose which values he was going to serve.
Perhaps in the spirit of German *realpolitik*, Weber made it clear that
this choice involved taking sides in conflict.

1.3 Where technique ends — organization theory and the sociology of organizations

In the 1917 essay on value freedom Weber argued that the social
scientist's concern with values extended to a full examination of their
meaning, presuppositions, implications and practical consequences.
Only the ultimate choice was beyond the scientific competence of the
social scientist (Weber 1949 pp 1—47). As soon as these issues are
raised, the limited scope of the practical problem-solving organizational science of Taylor and Münsterberg is thrown into sharp relief.
For all students of modern organizations are now fully aware that
organizational goals are frequently the subject of conflict, that they are
more often than not vague and that their implications are often not
understood even by those who frame them. These are circumstances
which fall outside the range of vision of scientific management, which
must anchor techniques upon the assumption of clear objectives. The
true successors, therefore, of Taylor and Münsterberg are the linear
programmers, econometricians, systems experts, as well as all those who
refine methods for the manipulation and control of individuals in
organizations through T-groups, job-enlargement, and so on. Frequently
referred to under the umbrella term 'management scientists', they have
enjoyed considerable success in enhancing efficiency and giving more
power to managers. (A concise account of many of these techniques
can be found in Haniks *New Thinking in Management* 1965).

Organization theorists and sociologists of organization tend to begin
their task at the very point where the very quest for improved control is
critically analysed and where it has generated opposition within the organization. Both organization theorists and sociologists take organizational goals and the values on which they are founded to be problematical
and the subject of scrutiny rather than purposes to be realized by the
researcher himself. This, indeed, is the feature that organizational science
possesses along with the social sciences in general, which distinguishes
them from the natural sciences, that human values are central objects of
enquiry. Various modes of undertaking this enquiry may be distinguished, but in the study of organizations we may distinguish two main ones.
Where goals are vague and inexplicit, one intellectual response is to

xplicit. This kind of conceptual enquiry is usually
on theory'.

(1963) suggests that one part of Weber's essay on
be viewed as a sophisticated form of decision theory,
tline the necessary elements in any complex decision-
Such an enterprise may be considered part of social
science, but it is conceptual rather than empirical in nature. The task is
one of aiding clear thought rather than providing appliances for a job
to be done.

The programme of organization theory (or decision theory, or administrative theory, which for some special purposes may be treated as
distinct, but have the same general orientation and are often regarded as
synonymous) was set out in Herbert Simon's *Administrative Behaviour*
in 1946. He aimed there to provide:

> . . . a theory of human choice or decision-making that aims to be
> sufficiently broad and realistic to accommodate both those rational
> aspects of choice that have been the principal concern of the econ-
> omist, and those properties and limitations of the human decision-
> making mechanisms that have attracted the attention of psychologists
> and practical decision-makers. (Simon 1965 p xi).

The style of organization theory is normally neither exhortatory nor
empirically generalizing. It has a more diagnostic, clinical tone, a 'you-
ought-to-realize-what's-happening-before-it's-too-late' slightly intim-
idatory form of address, evidenced in the paper which considers organization theory to be concerned with identifying the real underlying
objectives of any organization and then warns that organizations which
fail to adhere to these are 'headed for trouble' (Lloyd 1962 p 29).

A British example of this genre is to be found in Wilfred Brown's
Exploration in Management. Brown's belief is that his conceptual
framework is generally applicable to organizations he has not personally
encountered and will provide a more objective guide to decision-making
than the participants possess already. The practice of making people see
what is 'really there' has much in common with the psycho-therapeutic
orientation to personal counselling, and it underpins much of the theory
of the counsellors of organizations, the management consultants, who
represent the practical side of organization theory. One consultant,
writing about the nature of his role, stresses his position as an outsider
with its consequent lack of direct responsibility for taking decisions,
but at the same time occupied in seeking 'constantly to reorient the
men we deal with so that they can grasp our point of view and begin

to think about problems along different lines. In fact much of our work can be thought of as educational . . .' (Gardner 1965 p 80).

In my paper, 'The study of organizations – objectivity or bias?' (1968), I distinguished the intellectual orientation of organization theory, with its diagnostic and clinical aspirations, from the second main mode of enquiry into organizational values, the sociology of organizations. The sociologist may have no interest in organizational improvement; where people are unclear about their purposes he records that fact, and he takes it as axiomatic that management's view of the organization is one perspective among many. The major empirical sociological studies of organizations have this in common, that the views of top management are treated as but one contribution to the structuring of the organization. Gouldner's gypsum miners (1955), Blau's employment agency clerks (1970), Lipset's printing union members (1956) and Crozier's factory maintenance workers (1964) all have an active and creative part to play in the making of organizational structure.

The sociologist seeks a position from which he can view the conflict of values, the struggles between different groups which are represented in any organization. To do this he is forced to adopt a terminology which is distinct from the parlance of the participants in the organization. He tries to make their values his object for description and explanation, and thereby claims a kind of objectivity. In 'Public administration and sociological theory' (1971), I sought to show how a sociological interpretation of changes in the place of public administration in contemporary society emerges from a consideration of the different meanings which are attached to the action of public officials through legal definitions, by the public, by the officials, and by professional groups in administration. Each group has a different capacity to impose its definition of the situation on others, and it is changes in those capacities and their sources which capture the socioligist's attention.

But one may well question whether the sociologist is any more successful than the organization theorist in developing this objective language for organizational analysis. Indeed it is evident that having passed beyond viewing a science of organizations as a kind of technology and having recognized that the study of values involves quite distinct approaches from those of applied science, we are faced with a range of problems which bear directly upon the distinctive character of the social sciences. Are objective accounts of the values of others possible at all? Do sociologists also import values into their perspectives? Do accounts merely describe, or do they also help to construct? These are problems of basic methodology, but they underlie organizational studies as they do the social sciences in general. The second phase of our argument will go on to show their salience for the study of organizations.

2 Relativity and reality — fundamental assumptions in the study of organizations

The decline of faith in the provision of technical, experimentally based knowledge and its replacement by descriptive or diagnostic case studies of organizations are described by Donald Schon in *Beyond the Stable State* (1971). (Schon's own career, philosopher turned management consultant, is itself vivid testimony to the growth of heuristic organization theory). He describes how the rational/experimental model of social policy, where action is seen as a way of generating valid propositions for widespread application, must in conditions of rapid social change be replaced by systems analysis, by which Schon simply means models of interconnected factors, or existential knowledge, where attempts are made to capture the nature of changing phenomena through case histories, models of sequences of events, and typologies generalized from the cases and models (Schon 1971 pp 201–37).

Such a distinction emphasizes that, in the face of the conditions of ephemerality of the social and human objects that surround us, the very act of describing, and still more of generalizing, is a hazardous and contentious enterprise. Descriptions are always from a point of view which itself is subject to change. It is always open to question whether the qualities we impute to objects are really there or merely projections of our imaginations. In the natural sciences the idea of objectivity connotes agreement between observers upon descriptions and replication of observations giving the same results. The theory of relativity itself has a limited and defined scope within the whole field of natural science. In the social sciences relativity of perspective seems to pervade every enquiry.

But over and above the problem of perspective arises the question of the very reality of the objects of social scientific investigation. The natural scientist is able to conduct his arguments at various levels of concreteness or abstraction, using terms like particle, field or force without his objectivity being impugned. In organizational studies, on the other hand, the abstractness of terms like 'organization', 'structure' or 'goals' occasions the charge that fictitious entities are being constructed and that the investigator may be importing collectivist values.

We shall now consider specific ways in which the problems of relativity and reality arise in the study of organizations.

2.1 Assumptions about human nature

It is when one takes the basic and unanalysed terms of description and the facts which are taken for granted about the world that one can identify the characteristic viewpoint of a social scientist. These are what Gouldner calls 'background assumptions' (1970 pp 29–36). Finding this taken for granted area is a game social scientists engage in with considerable competitive enthusiasm.

Nowhere is this better exemplified or more contentious than when comments are being made on the nature of human beings. As an obvious example, because its mechanistic orientation was so blatant, we may take the view of human nature found in scientific management. F.W. Taylor asserted that there were some men suitable for management, while others could merely carry out instructions. The handling of pig-iron, for instance, was the kind of task that could be carried out by the 'intelligent gorilla'. But the science underlying the act could not be understood by the kind of person best suited to carry it out – 'the pig-iron handler is not an extraordinary man difficult to find, he is merely a man more or less of the type of the ox, heavy both mentally and physically' (Taylor 1947 pp 41 and 137). Here is a frame of reference which considers human beings to fall into two classes, mentally or physically endowed, which very conveniently mirrors a productive system where some give orders and others do the physical labour.

But can't we consider men to be much more than adjuncts to the productive process? This is the kind of question which springs to mind, and we find that a characteristic way for a new school of thought to emerge in organizational studies is by way of substitution of a different viewpoint on human nature. Thus the human relations movement in industry which supplanted scientific management in the 1930s as the fashionable mode of management emphasized the human being as a member of a group, with more intangible motives than the desire for money, such as needs for esteem, security and self-expression.

Herbert Simon's development of administrative science as the theory of decision-making is founded upon a theory of 'administrative man', who is constrained to make decisions on the basis of very simplified models of what the world is like, rather than on the full knowledge that theories of economic man had tended to assume. Simon argues that his model of man is a 'correct description' (1965 p xxvi) and suggests that an adequate theory of human behaviour based on the 'decision premise' is far more likely to emerge than one based on the sociological conception of role. He continues, 'the construction of a satisfactory vocabulary for the description of human behaviour is probably the most important task now confronting sociology' (Simon 1965 p xxx). Here we find an explicit linkage of the problems of basic vocabulary and the development of theories of human behaviour.

If his model of man is the basis of his theory it is perhaps understandable that he should wish to dignify it with the title 'correct description'. After all, it would be less convincing to begin, 'For the sake of argument I am going to view human beings in this way and erect a major theoretical edifice on foundations which I recognize as arbitrary and subjective'. Yet criticism of this view of man is so readily formulable that it is difficult not to feel that this might be a more judicious claim. Mouzelis, for instance (1967 p 138), holds that Simon neglects the individual as a group member subject to imposed norms. Even Simon's limitedly rational individual acts through taking decisions rather than by way of impulse or in solidarity with others.

Simon makes his model of man explicit, but it is still fair to say that it takes much for granted and the bases of the choice of characteristics for administrative man are largely unjustified. Not that it is not possible to find plenty of evidence for limited rationality in human conduct, but the warrant for singling this feature out to be the 'correct' description does not seem to be there. It appears as just one of many possible descriptions.

Some organization theorists have been conscious of the arbitrariness of starting points. Mason Haire (1962 p 10) points out that organizational principles early in the century assumed man to be short-sighted, lazy and selfish. An example of an explicit reformulation comes from a consultant with GEC who lists a very different set of assumptions on which to base designs of organizational structure. They include:

> Most people want more freedom in their work to decide for themselves . . .
> Most people have both the desire and the capacity to discipline themselves to a greater extent in their own work . . .
> Most people already have the competence to achieve significantly greater results than they are currently achieving . . .
> Most people really want to learn how to do their own work better . . .
> Most people want the door of opportunity to be open equally to all.
> (Estes 1962 p 16).

In this case the values of the consultant are clearly implicated in the view of man he outlines. But in general we may say that a view of human nature reflects as much how the observer prefers to regard others as it does their 'real' nature. And in that way, if the observers are influential enough, it can be that their view has a chance of becoming a real influence on human nature. If men are viewed and treated as machines, they become machine-like; if they are considered to be free, they can become free. Such persuasive definitions are, by definition, factors in change, and never mere reflections of the world.

2.2 Assumptions about organizational nature

Such selectivity of perspective is not confined to the assumptions we make about human beings in organizations. It applies to every aspect of the vocabulary we use to describe organizations. Whether organizations are described as social, socio-technical, open or open-adaptive systems, or are defined with special reference to formality, goals, tasks, or complexity, from whatever standpoint the same problems arise as with the conceptions of human nature we have been discussing and which underlie such conceptual schemes.

Each scheme is a way of looking which concentrates the attention on some phenomena rather than others. Moreover that viewpoint can normally be shown to correspond more or less closely to the outlooks of different groups within or concerned with organizations. It is fair to say that in general these viewpoints have normally been associated with managerial perspectives. But the social action perspective of Gouldner's *Wildcat Strike* (1965), or the rationalistic approach in Crozier's *The Bureaucratic Phenomenon* (1964) give more weight to contributions other sections make to organizational dynamics. Whether managerial or not, all these perspectives have at one time or another been adopted by sociologists, with the explicit desire to detach themselves from partial viewpoints.

Rosemary Stewart begins her book *The Reality of Organizations* (1972), with a chapter, 'Ways of looking at organizations'. But the question of 'reality' takes us further than 'ways of looking'. Clearly, if we are going to talk about organizations, it is of considerable importance to have criteria for establishing when it is and when it is not legitimate to regard an organization or any element of it as being in existence. I was concerned with this in 'The study of organizations — objectivity or bias?' (1968) to the extent that I accused sociologists of illicitly assuming that the models of the organization theorist were always actualized in organizations, with clear cut goals generating formal rules and authority, instead of treating them as idealized constructions, with their empirical reference always being open to investigation.

Joseph Albini (1971) has demonstrated that it matters whether the American Mafia exists and what its features are. For one thing the response of the police will vary according to whether they are dealing with a form of business enterprise or a very extended kinship system.

But these demands for operational criteria for the use of terms like 'organization' assume that the existence of a particular organization or organizational feature is an empirical question. More radical attacks have been mounted which question the reality of organizations, organizational purposes or structure. Max Weber (1947 pp 101—2), in an early statement of what Karl Popper (1957a p 136) was later to call methodological individualism, considered it illegitimate to impute acts to entities such as 'the state' or 'the nation', since only individuals could act and collective terms were developed for legal and certain practical purposes. Gouldner is acknowledging his debt to Weber when he writes in the same vein:

> But an organization as such cannot be said to be oriented toward a goal, except in a merely metaphorical sense, unless it is assumed that its parts possess a much lower degree of functional autonomy than can in fact be observed. The statement that an organization is oriented towards certain goals often means no more than that these are the goals of its top administrators, or that they represent its societal function, which is another matter altogether. (Gouldner 1959 p 420)

Gouldner, like Weber, is pointing to what has been called the fallacy of misplaced concreteness (Whitehead 1925 p 75) or of reification (Cohen 1931 pp 224—8), that is imputing to abstract entities the qualities of concrete units. But there are some strange twists to the course of these arguments. Thus behaviourism, which resists the imputation of mind and purposiveness to individuals on the grounds of their unobservability and, therefore, aims to counter reification, has been the dominant orientation of academic psychology in this century. *A fortiori*, psychologists have vigorously resisted applying the language of purpose to organizations, regarding it as merely metaphorical. Instead they have advocated systems theory.

Thus in their *Social Psychology of Organizations* (1966 pp 14—19) Katz and Kahn reject the use of the language of organizational objectives and state, 'We shall refer to organizational functions or objectives not as the conscious purposes of group leaders or group members but as the outcomes which are the energic source for a maintenance of the same type of output'. Miller and Rice (1967) adopt a similar strategy of attempting to infer the 'primary task' of the organization, which may differ from the leaders' formulations. But systems theory itself has many times been charged with importing metaphor and false concreteness, and Weber himself warned of the danger of reification (1947 p 103). Indeed it reaches the point in structural-functionalism where society alone appears to have purpose and individuals none. The ideological bias towards conservatism in this position has been pointed out too often to need detailing here.

To deny reality to the foci of a scientist's enquiries must arouse strong feelings on his part, and often vehement counter-charges. Programmatic statements to the effect that only individuals are real, organizations are fictions, ideas cannot influence events, purposes are unreal, structures are metaphors and so on are the background assumptions of the different schools of thought into which so much of the academic world divides itself.

But these assumptions are not merely indicative of divisions in the academic world. They parallel the great political divides also and help to create them. Such a comment is not peculiar to sociologists. The most influential account of the way the axioms of major schools of thought may have political repercussions is contained in Karl Popper's *The Open Society and its Enemies* (1957b), where the collectivism and determinism he detects in the philosophies of Hegel and Marx are viewed as major contributions to political conflict in the twentieth century, and certainly, as a philosopher, Popper has been critical of sociologists, in their attempt to develop a sociology of knowledge. In respect of organizations, I have made the analogous point to the one Popper was making for politics and society as a whole. The way we view organizations still appears to be within the realm of our choice, rather than a necessity in the nature of things, and in that choice we may help to make, rather than merely reflect the world, which brings us to the third phase of our argument.

3 Reflexivity — organizations as theoretical constructs

Social scientific theories have a dialectical relationship with their subject matter, reflecting on society, being created by it and in turn helping to create. In his *Work and Authority in Industry* (1956), Bendix shows how the schools of scientific management and human relations contributed to the managerial ideologies of the United States. Those ideologies were themselves expressions of the interests of the owners and managers of capitalist enterprise which depended on and made the alienated human being possessed of no qualities but his labour power, the man who fitted so well with Taylor's perspective.

Social scientific accounts share with everyday accounts of social activity the quality which I would want to call 'reflexivity'. This is the quality of being both descriptions and component parts of a situation, so that the accounts themselves help to give an objectivity to the practices they refer to. If we accept this idea, the problem of objectivity and scientific nature of any theory of organization takes on an added dimension, for the objective character of the phenomena under investigation is dependent on the constructive activity of human beings. Social phenomena are no longer the products of impersonal forces. As we act, and give accounts of our action, we are creating our society and ourselves.

3.1 Ethnomethodological and sociological approaches to reflexivity

The ethnomethodological school has made fruitful use of the idea of reflexivity to emphasize the original character of the accounts of organizational structure which are given by the members of the organization. Thus Bittner (1965) insists that 'the idea of formal structure is basically a common sense notion' (p 243) and suggests that 'the sociologist finds himself in the position of having borrowed a concept from those he seeks to study in order to describe what he observes about them' (p 242). Bittner does not object in principle to this, but stresses that the 'meaning and import of the formal schemes must remain undetermined unless the circumstances and procedures of its actual use by actors is fully investigated' (p 244). Zimmerman makes a similar point in discussing organizational rules: 'the issue of what such rules mean to, and how they are used by, personnel on actual occasions of bureaucratic work is ignored as an empirical issue' (1971 p 223) by sociologists who make their own assumptions about what the rules mean and take their own competence to apply them for granted. Manning (1971) advocates that particular attention should be paid to the natural language of organizational members, the way they designate roles and activities in everyday contexts.

Yet, in spite of the way reflexivity has been interpreted recently to give priority to everyday accounts, the constructive part that images and concepts may have in the formation of society is an old theme in social thought going back to Hegel and beyond. Merton made use of the idea in writing of the self-fulfilling prophecy (1957 pp 128–9), while Berger and Luckmann offer an account of 'society as objective reality' in which everyday pre-theoretical knowledge especially, but also the complex theoretical systems are essential elements in integrating the institutional order (1971 p 83). Topitsch has said of the social sciences:

> A group of theories in a state of change (the word theory is used here in a very wide sense) relates to a society in a state of change, and these theories are themselves a part of the social scene they represent, and react on it in many different ways. (Topitsch 1971 p 24)

He remarks that this interactive relationship of theory and society has received very little systematic analysis. One of the rare examples of such analysis is Paul Halmos' examination of the sources of social work ideology in social and psychological theory and its subsequent influence on society, where he argues that by interpreting the world 'social scientists – have in fact changed it' (Halmos 1965 and 1970 p 77).

Any mention of the activity of professional groups, such as social workers or managers, must draw our attention to the fact that many occupations base their day to day activities on theory of some kind. Douglas McGregor has asserted, 'Every managerial act rests on theory' (1960 p 6). The assumptions, generalizations and hypotheses of the manager are more often than not built up from his daily experience, and he may believe that his knowledge is in some way 'practical' compared with social science, but in their form they are just as theoretical and, therefore, compete with the formulations of social scientists.

The instance of 'professional knowledge' offers a corrective to the ethnomethodological account which tends to assume the common availability of meanings to groups of undifferentiated actors. It also corrects the complementary tendency on the part of sociologists to assume that theory is the preserve of detached scholars. Precisely because of the range of control that the manager has, he must think in conceptual dimensions which at least attempt to take in the organization as a whole. Thus Bittner may consider 'formal structure' to be a 'common sense notion', but one may suspect that it is employed by the manager far more than by men on the shop floor, and the manager today is probably believing it to be part of his own home-spun theory rather than derived from the social research of the 1930s, which is the most likely source. For an expression of this relationship between theory and everyday practice we may cite Schon:

> When a person enters a social system, he encounters a body of theory which more or less explicitly sets out not only the 'way the world is', but 'who we are', 'what we are doing', and 'what we should be doing' . . . It is in a way misleading to distinguish at all between

social system and theory, for the social system is the embodiment of its theory and the theory is the conceptual dimension of the social system. (Schon 1971 pp 34–5)

These reflections help to throw light on the reasons for the frequency with which the charge of adopting the managerial viewpoint has been levelled at theorists of organizations. For they are already in dialogue with the theories of practical men, and it is those who have power who can give new theories widespread social effect. The differentiation of theorists of organizations from organizational members and managers is itself an important feature of organizational development. Reflexivity is itself a developing, not a static element in society.

3.2 The development of reflexivity in organizations

In *The Genesis of Modern Management* (1968), Pollard shows how in the nineteenth century there were only few and isolated attempts to set down a theory of management in writing. He identifies three major reasons for this: the difficulty at this stage of isolating a separate 'managerial function'; the highly individual position of each manager; and a view of the work force as a body of men, deficient in character and in need of reform. An exception was Robert Owen at the New Lanark Mills, but his was, for the time, a unique appreciation of the administrative processes of a factory.

The early theory of bureaucratic administration was written by bureaucrats and into the twentieth century the leaders of large organizations wrote their own theory. Peter Drucker's account of General Motors includes details of the explicit theory of decentralization which was propagated by Alfred P. Sloan, Jr., its head from 1921 to 1955. This was an elaborate philosophy of management and self-government designed to reduce conflicts of interest between sections and enhance communication generally. Drucker likens it to the American Constitution in the way it consists of a series of yardsticks rather than a set of overall directives: 'General Motors owes its strength precisely to that use of principles and concepts as guides for concrete, unplanned, and unforeseen action of which the "planner" knows nothing' (Drucker 1964 p 70).

Drucker found little evidence of conscious use of theories of governmental organization in General Motors, but Sloan himself established a foundation which had the furtherance of management theory as part of its aims. (Douglas McGregor acknowledges its support for the writing of *The Human Side of Enterprise*, 1960). This is a sign of the functional

differentiation that takes place
and the practitioner. One of the
this gives rise can be found in
Tennessee Valley Authority (196

The TVA was established by
with authority to deepen the Riv
and distribute fertilizer and elect
ment, but at the same time its thr
considerable independence. David
took the major role in expounding a
tion, which, he argued, would revita
excessively centralized power. This w
to managerial dominance, although i ....am singled
out the TVA as an example of just t _ _ *The Managerial Revolution*
(1962). Lilienthal explicitly rejected Burnham's accusations, basing
his own doctrine on Alexis de Tocqueville's classic analysis of centralization in *Democracy in America* (1945). The theory was developed
within the organization through training conferences, and administrative seminars, and Selznick comments that, as basic organization
policy, the theory extended far beyond the views of its chairman
(Selznick 1966 p 22).

Selznick interprets the use of this doctrine as an ideology serving to
define the organization and shape the views of its staff. In other words,
it has latent functions beyond those that were intended. He makes use
of this idea in his later book *Leadership in Administration* (1957),
where he argues that the creative leader will propagate 'socially integrating myths' in order to generate unity of purpose. What was latent
in the TVA he makes manifest for the use of future leaders in a book
which, in its foreword, claims to help 'in broadening the intellectual
horizons of businessmen' (1957 p viii).

De Tocqueville's theory, Lilienthal's application of it in the TVA,
Selznick's interpretation of the TVA theory and then the advice he
gives to administrative leaders, make up an ongoing cycle of experience
and interpretation which has no necessary end point. Whether we
consider such a cycle as information feedback keeping organization
on course, or the emergence of new social forms through the agency of
human creativity is a question of some importance, but in this context
what matters most is that it illustrates the importance that theoretical
formulations have in the process of organizational change.

When Joan Woodward undertook her ten year study of the structure
of one hundred South Essex firms she found that 'about half had made
some conscious attempt to plan organization and to apply the precepts

systematic body of knowledge of organizational
ss contained in management theory' (1965 p 17).
nted that the decade 1953–63 saw the evolution of
ology among managers which was a barrier to their under-
reality (Woodward 1965 p 254). Her hope was that social
would transform this situation.

But from all that has gone before, we can hardly be as sanguine that
social science dispels, rather than assists ideology. Peter Clark has
examined the nature of action research in organizations, where
programmes are initiated to solve practical problems and to generate
more widely applicable knowledge. Here manager and researcher are
placed in roles of mutual assistance in thought and action. He characterizes the knowledge the social scientist brings to bear in this situation
as consisting of the concepts and propositions of his discipline and also
data collected in the particular organization, but he will also have a
focus, a set of key variables for manipulation to induce change, and
these 'will almost certainly incorporate his beliefs about the nature
of man's role in society' (Clark 1972 p 68). One can only hope that
these beliefs are examined with the same care as the organization.

But for a full length treatment of the theme of the application of
social science in organizations which gives it full historical significance
we must turn to the fortunately popular *The Organization Man* (1956)
by William H. Whyte. He argues that a new type of man has been
created through the propagation of a new ideology to replace the
Protestant Ethic. This ideology sees the organization as the source of
creativity and 'belongingness' as the ultimate individual need. The Social
Ethic is propagated through scientism, the belief that the same methods
that have been adopted in the natural sciences can be employed in the
study of man and simultaneously solve ethical problems. Whyte identifies the origins of these beliefs in the work of the Human Relations
movement and shows how they are translated into reality through the
training and control of the individual in the organization.

The historical and cultural specifics of Whyte's account have changed
since 1956 when his book first appeard, but the basic theme is as
relevant now as then. It is the creation of a new social reality in the
illusion that it is a given and stable reality which is being analysed.
Organizational science is part of organizational life and its active
demension cannot be ignored if an adequate understanding of its
relevance to organizations is to be gained.

References

ADAMS, S. (1953) 'Status congruency as a variable in small group performance', *Social Forces*, vol. 32, no. 1, pp 16–22.

ADAMS, J.S. and ROSENBAUM, W.B. (1962) 'The relationship of worker productivity to cognitive dissonance about wage inequities', *Journal of Applied Psychology*, vol. 46, pp 161–4.

ADAMS, J.S. and JACOBSON, P.R. (1964) 'Effects of wage inequalities on work quality', *Journal of Abnormal Social Psychology*, vol. 69, pp 19–25.

ADAMS, J.S. (1965) 'Inequality in social exchange', in BERKOWITZ, L. (ed.) *Advances in Experimental Social Psychology*, vol. 2, New York, Academic Press.

ADORNO, T.W., FRENKEL-BRUNSWICK, E., LEVISON, D.J. and S., and SANFORD, R.N. (1950) *The Authoritarian Personality*, New York, Harper and Row.

AIKEN, M. and HAGE, J. (1970) 'Organizational alienation : a comparative analysis' in GRUSKY, O. and MILLER, (eds) *The Sociology of Organizations : Basic Studies*, New York, Free Press, pp 517–26.

ALBINI, J.L. (1971) *The American Mafia : Genesis of a Legend*, New York, Appleton Century Crofts.

ALBROW, M. (1973) 'The study of organizations – objectivity or bias?' in SALAMAN and THOMPSON (eds) pp 396–413.

ALBROW, M. (1970) *Bureaucracy*, London, Pall Mall Press.

ALBROW, M. (1971) 'Public administration and sociological theory' in *The Advancement of Science*, vol. 27, pp 347–56.

ALBROW, M. (1968) 'The study of organizations – objectivity or bias?' in Julius Gould, (ed.) *Penguin Social Sciences Survey*, Harmondsworth, Penguin Books, pp 146–67.

ALUTTO, J.A. and BELASCO, J.A. (1972) 'A typology for participation in organizational decision-making' in *Administrative Science Quarterly*, vol. 17, no. 1, pp 117–25.

ARGYRIS, C. (1973) 'Peter Blau' in SALAMAN and THOMPSON (eds) pp 76–90.

ARGYRIS, C. (1957) *Personality and Organization*, New York, Harper and Row.

ARGYRIS, C. (1962) *Interpersonal Competence and Organizational Effectiveness*, London, Tavistock.

ARON, R. (1967) *Main Currents in Sociological Thought*, vol. 2, Harmondsworth, Penguin.

BACHMAN, J.G., BOWERS, D.G. and MARCUS, P.M. (1968) 'Bases of supervisory power : a comparative study in five organizational settings', in TANNENBAUM, A. (ed.) *Control in Organizations*, New York, McGraw Hill, pp 229–38.

BACHRACH, P., and BARATZ, M.S.A. (1962) 'Two faces of power', in *American Political Science Review*, LVI 4, pp 947–52.

BAKKE, E.W. (1934) *The Unemployed Man*, New York, E.P. Dutton and Co.

BALES, R.F. (1950) *Interaction Process Analysis : A method for the study of small groups*, Cambridge, Mass., Addison-Wesley.

BALES, R.F. (1953) 'The equilibrium problem in small groups', in PARSONS, T., BALES, R.F. and SHILS, E.A. *Working Papers in the Theory of Action*, Glencoe Ill., Free Press.

BARITZ, L. (1960) *The Servants of Power*, Middletown, Wesleyan University Press.

BARNARD, C.I. (1970) 'Co-operation' in GRUSKY and MILLER (eds) pp 65–73.

BENDIX, R. (1956) *Work and Authority in Industry*, New York, John Wiley.

BENDIX, R. (1970) 'The Impact of Ideas on Organizational Structure', in GRUSKY and MILLER (eds) pp 529–36.

BENNIS, W.G. and THOMAS, J.M. (1972) *Management of Change and Conflict*, Harmondsworth, Penguin.

BENSMAN, J. and ROSENBERG, B. (1960) 'The meaning of work in bureaucratic society', in STEIN, M., VIDICH, A. and MANNING-WHITE, D. (eds) *Identity and Anxiety*, New York, The Free Press, pp 181–97.

BENSON, J.K. (ed.) 1978) *Organizational Analysis : Critique and Innovation*, Beverly Hills, Calif., Sage Publications.

BENSON, J.K. (1975) 'The interorganizational network as a political economy', *Administrative Science Quarterly*, vol. 20, pp 229–249.

BERGER, P.L. (1969) *The Social Reality of Religion*, London, Faber and Faber.

BERGER, P.L. and LUCKMANN, T. (1971) *The Social Construction of Reality*, Harmonsworth, Penguin.

BERLYNE, D.E. (1960) *Conflict, Arousal and Curiosity*, New York, McGraw-Hill.

BETTELHEIM, B. (1961) *The Informed Heart*, London, Thames and Hudson.

BIERSTADT, R. (1950) 'An analysis of social power', in *American Sociological Review*, vol. 15, pp 730–6.

BITTNER, E. (1973a) 'The concept of organizations' in SALAMAN and THOMPSON (eds) pp 264–76.

BITTNER, E. (1973b) 'The police on skid-row : A study of peace-keeping' in SALAMAN and THOMPSON (eds) pp 331–45.

BLAU, P.M. (1956) *Bureaucracy in Modern Society*, New York Random House.

BLAU, P.M. (1964) *Exchange and Power in Social Life*, New York, Wiley.

BLAU, P.M. (1970a) 'The comparative study of organizations' in GRUSKY and MILLER (eds) pp 175–86.

BLAU, P.M. (1970b) 'Decentralization in bureaucracies' in ZALD, MAYER (ed.) *Power in Organizations*, Nashville, Tennessee, Venderbilt University Press, pp 150–74.

BLAU, P.M. (1970c) *The Dynamics of Bureaucracy*, Chicago, University of Chicago Press.

BLAU, P. (1970d) 'Bureaucracy and social change', in GRUSKY and MILLER (eds) pp 249–58.

BLAU, P.M. and SCHOENHERR, R.A. (1971) *The Structure of Organizations*, New York, Basic Books.

BLAU, P.M. and SCHOENHERR, R.A. (1973) 'New forms of power', in SALAMAN and THOMPSON (eds) pp 13–24.

BLAU, P.M. and SCOTT, R.W. (1963) *Formal Organizations : A comparative approach*, London, Routledge and Kegan Paul.

BLAUNER, R. (1960) 'Work satisfaction and industrial trends in modern society' in GALENSON, W. and LIPSET, S.M. (eds) *Labour and Trade Unionism : An interdisciplinary reader*, New York, Wiley, pp 339–60.

BLOOK, C.L. and HULIN, M.R. (1967) 'Alienation, environmental characteristics and worker responses', *Journal of Applied Psychology*, vol. 51, pp 284–90.

BLOOM, R. and BARRY, J.R. (1967) 'Determinants of work attitudes among negroes', *Journal of Applied Psychology*, vol. 57, pp 291–4.

BORGESS, J.L. (1972) *A Personal Anthology*, London, Pan Books.

BRADBURY, M. HEADING, B. and HOLLIS, M. (1972) 'The man and the mask : A discussion of role theory' in JACKSON, J.A. (ed.) *Role*, Cambridge University Press.

BRAVERMAN, H. (1974) *Labour and Monopoly Capital : The degradation of work in the twentieth century*, New York and London, Monthly Review Press.

BRAYFIELD, A.H. and CROCKETT, W.H. (1955) 'Employee attitudes and employee performance', *Psychological Bulletin*, vol. 52, pp 396–424.

BREWER, J. (1970) 'Organizational patterns of supervision : A study of the debureaucratization of authority relations in two business organizations' in GRUSKY and MILLER (eds) pp 341–7.

BRISTOL, L.H. (ed.) (1960) *Developing the Corporate Image*, New York.

BRITTAN, A., (1973) *Meanings and Situations*, London, Routledge and Kegan Paul.

BRONFENBRENNER, U., (1958) 'Socialization and social class through space and time', in MACCOBY, E.E., NEWCOMB, T.M., and HARTLEY, E.L. (eds) *Readings in Social Psychology*, New York, Holt, pp 400–25.

BROWN, H. (1979) 'Fathers and childbirth: changing attitudes and expectations', in *Midwife, Health Visitor and Community Nurse*, vol. 15, 10, pp 398–400.

BROWN, J.A.C., (1954) *The Social Psychology of Industry*, Harmondsworth, Penguin.

BROWN, R. (1973) 'Sources of objectives in work and employment', in CHILD, J. (ed.) *Man and Organization*, London, Allen and Unwin, pp 17–38.

BROWN, R.H. (1978a) 'Bureaucracy as praxis : Toward a political phenomenology of formal organizations', *Administrative Science Quarterly*, vol. 23, no. 3 (September), pp 365–382.

BROWN, R. and BRANNEN, P. (1970) 'Social relations and social perspectives amongst shipbuilding workers – A preliminary statement' in *Sociology*, vol. 4, pp 71–84, 187–211.

BROWN, W. (1965) *Exploration in Management*, Harmondsworth, Penguin.

BUCKLEY, W. (1967) *Sociology and Modern Systems Theory*, Englewood Cliffs, Prentice Hall.

BUCKLEY, W. (1973) 'Society as a complex adaptive system', in SALAMAN and THOMPSON (eds) pp 134–54.

BURNHAM, J. (1962) *The Managerial Revolution*, Harmondsworth, Penguin.

BURNS, T. (1955) 'The reference of conduct in small groups', *Human Relations*, vol. 8, pp 467–86.

BURNS, T. (1964) 'What managers do' in *New Society*, no. 116, (17 December) pp 8–9.

BURNS, T. (1967) 'The comparative study of organizations', in VROOM, V. (ed.) *Methods of Organizational Research*, Pittsburgh, University of Pittsburgh Press, pp 113–70.

BURNS, T. and STALKER, G.M., (1966) *The Management of Innovation*, London, Tavistock (second edition, first printed 1961).

BURRAGE, M. (1973) 'Nationalization and the professional ideal', *Sociology*, vol. 7, no. 2, pp 253–72.

BUTLER, R.J., HICKSON, D.J., WILSON, D.C. and AXELSSON, R. (1978) 'Organizational power, politicking and paralysis', *Organization and Administrative Sciences*, (Winter 1977/78).

CAMPBELL, J.P. and DUNNETTE, M.D. (1968) 'Effectiveness of T-group experiences in managerial training and development', *Psychological Bulletin*, vol. 70, pp 73–104.

CAPLOW, T. (1954) *The Sociology of Work*, University of Minnesota Press.

CAREER CHOICE (1973) 'Market yourself as if you are a new product', London, Morgan-Grampian, pp 26–7.

CARTER, E.C. (1971) 'The behavioural theory of the firm and top-level corporate decisions', in *Administrative Science Quarterly*, vol. 16, no. 4, pp 413–29.

CARTWRIGHT, D. (1965) 'Influence, leadership, control', in MARCH, J.G. (ed.) *Handbook of Organizations*, Chicago, Rand McNally, pp 1–47.

CASTLES, F.S., MURRAY, D.J. and POTTER, D.C. (eds) (1971) *Decisions, Organizations and Society*, Harmondsworth, Penguin.

CENTERS, R.J., and BUGENTAL, D.E. (1966) 'Intrinsic and extrinsic job motivations among different segments of the working population', *Journal of Applied Psychology*, vol. 50, pp 193–7.

CHADWICK, G. (1971) *A Systems View of Planning*, Oxford, Pergamon Press.

CHAMBERLAIN, N.W. (1948) *Union Challenge to Management Control*, New York, Harper and Brothers.

CHILD, J. (1964) 'Quaker employers and industrial relations', *Sociological Review*, vol. 12, no. 3 (November) pp 293–315.

CHILD, J. (1967) 'Industrial management' in PARKER, S.R., BROWN, R.K., CHILD, J. and SMITH, M.A. *The Sociology of Industry*, London, Allen and Unwin, pp 85–98.

CHILD, J. (1972) 'Organizational structure, environment and performance : The role of strategic choice', *Sociology*, vol. 6, pp 1–22. Also in SALAMAN and THOMPSON (eds) (1973) pp 91–107.

CHILD, J. (1973) 'Organization : A choice for man', in CHILD, J. (ed.) *Man and Organization*, London, Allen and Unwin, pp 234—57.

CHOMSKY, N. (1971) *At War With Asia*, London, Fontana.

CICOUREL, A. (1958) 'The front and back of organizational leadership : A case study', *Pacific Sociological Review*, vol. 1, pp 54—8.

CLARK, J.V. (1958) 'A preliminary investigation of some unconscious assumptions affecting labour efficiency in eight supermarkets', unpublished doctoral dissertation (Grad. Sch. Bus. Admin.), Harvard University. Referred to in ADAMS (1965) and HOMANS (1961).

CLARK, B.R. (1956) 'Organizational adaptation and precarious values : a case study', *American Sociological Review*, vol. 21, pp 327—36.

CLARK, P.A. (1972) *Action Research and Organizational Change*, London, Harper and Row.

CLAWSON, D. (forthcoming) *Class Struggle and the Rise of Bureaucracy*, New York and London, Monthly Review Press.

CLELAND, D.I. and KING, W.R. (1972) *Management : A systems approach*, New York, McGraw Hill.

COCH, L. and FRENCH, J.P.R. Jr. (1948) 'Overcoming resistance to change', *Human Relations*, vol. 1, pp 512—32.

COHEN, M.D., MARCH, J.G. and OLSEN, J.P. (1972) 'A garbage can model of organizational choice', *Administrative Science Quarterly*, vol. 17, no. 1, pp 1—25.

COHEN, M.R. (1931) *Reason and Nature*, New York, Harcourt Brace.

COOPER, C.L. and MAUGHAM, I.L. (1971) *T-groups : A survey of research*, London, Wiley.

COSER, L.A. (1956) *The Functions of Social Conflict*, London, Routledge and Kegan Paul.

COTGROVE, S., DUNHAM, J. and VAMPLEW, C. (1971) *The Nylon Spinners*, London, Allen and Unwin.

COTGROVE, S. and BOX, S. (1970) *Science, Industry and Society*, London, Allen and Unwin.

CROZIER, M. (1964) *The Bureaucratic Phenomenon*, London, Tavistock.

CROZIER, M. (1969) 'The vicious circle of bureaucracy', in BURNS, T. (ed.) *Industrial Man*, Harmondsworth, Penguin, pp 250—62.

CYERT, R.M. and MARCH, J.G. (1963) *A Behavioural Theory of the Firm*, Englewood Cliffs, Prentice Hall.

CYERT, R.M., SIMON, H.A. and TROW, D.B. (1956) 'Observation of a business decision', *Journal of Business*, vol. 29, pp 237—48, 67—85.

DAHL, R.A. (1968) 'Power' in SILLS, D.L. (ed.) *International Encyclopaedia of Social Sciences*, vol. 12, London, Macmillan, pp 405—15.

DAHRENDORF, R. (1968) *Essay in the Theory of Society*, London, Routledge and Kegan Paul.

DANIEL, W.W. (1973) 'Understanding employee behaviour in its context : Illustrations from productivity bargaining' in CHILD, J. (ed.) *Man and Organization*, London, Allen and Unwin, pp 39–62.

DANIEL, W.C. and McINTOSH, N. (1972) *The Rights to Manage?* London, Macdonald.

DENZIN, N.K. (1972) 'Symbolic interactionism and ethnomethodology' in DOUGLAS, J.P. (ed.) *Understanding Everyday Life*, London, Routledge and Kegan Paul.

DEUTSCH, K.W. and MADOW, W.G. (1961) 'A note on the appearance of wisdom in large bureaucratic organizations', *Behavioural Science*, vol. 6, no. 1, pp 72–8.

DORNBUSH, S.M. (1955) 'Military academy as an assimilating institution', *Social Forces*, vol. 33, pp 316–21.

DOSTOYEVSKY, F.M. (1972) *Notes from Underground*, translated by COULSON, J., Harmondsworth, Penguin.

DOUGLAS, J. (1971) 'Understanding everyday life' in DOUGLAS, J. (ed.) *Understanding Everyday Life*, London, Routledge and Kegan Paul, pp 3–44.

DOUGLAS, J. (1971) *American Social Order*, New York, The Free Press.

DOWNS, A. (1971) 'Decision-making in bureaucracy', in CASTLES, MURRAY and POTTER (eds) (1971) *Decisions, Organizations and Society*, Harmondsworth, Penguin, pp 66–85.

DRUCKER, P. (1955) *The Practice of Management*, London, Heinemann.

DRUCKER, P.F. (1964) *The Concept of the Corporation*, New York, Mentor.

DRUCKER, P. (1968) *The Practice of Management*, London, Pan Books.

DUFTY, N.F. and TAYLOR, P.M. (1970) 'The implementation of a decision', in WELSCH AND CYERT (eds) pp 111–21.

DUNKERLEY, D. (1972) *The Study of Organizations*, London, Routledge and Kegan Paul.

DUNNETTE, M., CAMPBELL, J and HAKEL, M. (1967) 'Factors contributing to job satisfaction and job dissatisfaction in six occupational groups', *Journal of Organizational Behaviour and Human Performance*, vol. 21, pp 143–74.

DURKHEIM, E., (1938) *The Rules of Sociological Method*, New York, The Free Press.

EHRENREICH, B. and EHRENREICH, J. (1971) *The American Health Empire : Power, profits and politics*, New York, Vintage Books.

ELDRIDGE, J.E.T. (1971) 'Systems analysis and industrial behaviour' in ELDRIDGE, J.E.T. *Sociology and Industrial Life*, London, Michael Joseph, pp 25–39.

ELGER, A.J. (1975) 'Industrial organizations – a processual perspective' in McKINLAY, J. (ed.) *Processing People : Case studies in organizational behaviour*, Holt, Reinhart and Winston.

ELLIOT, P. (1972) *The Sociology of the Professions*, London, Macmillan.

ELLUL, J. (1964) *The Technological Society*, New York, Vintage Books, Random House.

EMERSON, J. (1973) 'Behaviour in private places : Sustaining definitions of reality in gynaecological examinations', in SALAMAN and THOMPSON (eds) pp 358–71.

EMERY, F.E. and TRIST, E.L. (1960) 'Socio-technical systems' in CHURCHMAN, C.W. and VERHULST, M. (eds) *Management Science, Models and Techniques*, vol. 2, Oxford, Pergamon Press, pp 83–97.

EMERY, F.E. and TRIST, E.L. (1969) 'The causal texture of organisational environment', in EMERY, F. (ed.) *Systems Thinking*, Harmondsworth, Penguin, pp 241–57.

ESTES, H. (1962) 'Some considerations in designing an organization structure', in HAIRE, M. (ed.) *Organization Theory in Industrial Practice*, New York, John Wiley, pp 13–27.

ETZIONI, A. (1970) 'Two approaches to organizational analysis : A critique and a suggestion', in GRUSKY and MILLER (eds) pp 215–25.

ETZIONI, A. (1970) 'Compliance theory', in GRUSKY, O. and MILLER, G.A. (eds) pp 103–26.

ETZIONI, A. (1961) *A Comparative Analysis of Complex Organizations*, New York, The Free Press.

FESTINGER, L. (1957) *A Theory of Cognitive Dissonance*, Evanston, Ill., Row, Peterson.

FIEDLER, F.E. (1965) 'Engineer the job to fit the manager', *Harvard Business Review*, pp 115–22.

FIEDLER, F.E. (1967) *A Theory of Leadership Effectiveness*, New York, McGraw-Hill.

FIEDLER, F.E. (1968) 'Personality and situational determinants of leadership effectiveness', in CARTWRIGHT, D. and ZANDER, A. (eds) *Group Dynamics*, New York, Harper and Row (third edition).

FIEDLER, F.E. (1971) 'Validation and extension of the contingency model of leadership effectiveness : a review of empirical findings', *Psychological Bulletin*, vol. 76, pp 128–48.

FIEDLER, F.E. (1972) 'Personality, motivational systems and the behaviour of high and low LPC persons', *Human Relations*, vol. 25, pp 391–412.

FILMER, P. (1972) 'On Harold Garfinkel's Ethnomethodology', in FILMER, P., PHILLIPSON, M., SILVERMAN, D. and WALSH, D. *New Directions in Sociological Theory*, London, Collier-Macmillan, pp 203–34.

✝ FOX, A. (1971) *A Sociology of Work in Industry*, London, Collier-Macmillan.

— FOX, A. (1973a) 'Participation in decision-making', paper presented to one day conference on participation and democracy organized by the Industrial Sociology Section of the British Sociological Association at the Imperial College of Science and Technology, London, 10 March.

— FOX, A. (1973) 'The social organization of industrial work', in SALAMAN and THOMPSON (eds) pp 321–30.

FRENCH, J.R.P. and RAVEN, B. (1959) 'The bases of social power', in CARTWRIGHT (ed.) *Studies in Social Power*, Ann Arbor, University of Michigan, Institute for Social Research, pp 150–67.

FRIEDMAN, E.A. and HAVIGHURST, R.J. (1954) *The Meaning of Work and Retirement*, Chicago, Chicago University Press.

FRIEDSON, E. (1971) 'Dilemmas in the doctor patient relationship', in ROSE, A. (ed.) *Human Behaviour and Social Processes*, London, Routledge and Kegan Paul, pp 207–24.

GALBRAITH, J.K. (1967) *The New Industrial State*, Harmondsworth, Penguin.

GARDNER, B.B. (1965) 'The consultant to business – his role and his problems', in GOULDNER, A.W. and MILLER, S.M. (eds) *Applied Sociology*, New York, The Free Press, pp 79–85.

GALVIN WRIGHT, B.W. (1960) 'Projecting the corporate image', in GALVIN WRIGHT, B.W. *An Advertising Appraisal*, London.

GARFINKEL, H. (1956) 'Conditions of successful degradation ceremonies', *American Journal of Sociology*, vol. 61, pp 420–4.

GARFINKEL, H. (1967) *Studies in Ethnomethodology*, New Jersey, Prentice-Hall.

GARFINKEL, H. (1972) 'Studies of the routine grounds of everyday activities' in SUDNOW, D. (ed.) *Studies in Social Interaction*, New York, The Free Press, pp 1–30.

GARFINKEL, H. and SACKS, H. (1970) 'On formal structures of practical action', in McKINNEY, J.C. and TIRYAKIAN, E.A. (eds) *Theoretical Sociology : Perspectives and developments*, New York, Appleton Century Crofts, pp 337–66.

GEERTZ, C. (1964) 'Ideology as a cultural system', in APTER, D. (ed.) *Ideology and Discontent*, The Free Press, pp 47–76.

GERTH, H.H. and MILLS, C.W. (1948) *From Max Weber : Essay in sociology*, London, Routledge and Kegan Paul.

GIALLOMBARDO, R. (1970) 'Social roles in a prison for women' in GRISKY, O. and MILLER, G.A. (eds) *The Sociology of Organizations*, New York, Free Press, pp 394–408.

GLASER, B.G. (1968) 'Towards a theory of organizational careers', in GLASER, B.G. (ed.) *Organizational Careers : A sourcebook for theory*, Chicago, Aldine, pp 13–16.

GLASER,B. and STRAUSS, A. (1964) 'Awareness contexts and social interaction', *American Sociological Review*, vol. 29, pp 669–79.

GLASER, B. and STRAUSS, A. (1965) *Awareness of Dying*, Chicago, Aldine.

GLASER, B. and STRAUSS, A. (1967) *The Discovery of Grounded Theory*, London, Weidenfeld and Nicolson.

GOFFMAN, E. (1968) 'The underlife of a public institution : A study of ways of making out in a mental hospital', in GOFFMAN, E. *Asylums*, pp 157–280, 439–454.

GOFFMAN, E. (1968) *Asylums*, Harmondsworth, Penguin.

GOLDTHORPE, J.H. LOCKWOOD, D., BECHHOFER, F. and PLATT, J. (1968) *The Affluent Worker*, Cambridge, Cambridge University Press.

GORE, W.J. and DYSON, J.W. (eds) (1964) *The Making of Decisions*, London, Collier, Macmillan.

GOULDNER, A.W. (1954) *Wildcat Strike*, Yellow Springs, Ohio, Antioch Press.

GOULDNER, A.W. (1954a) *Patterns of Industrial Bureaucracy*, Kent, Ohio, Antioch Press.

GOULDNER, A.W. (1955) 'Metaphysical pathos and the theory of bureaucracy', *American Political Science Review*, vol. 49, pp 496–507.

GOULDNER, A.W. (1959) 'Organizational analysis', in MERTON, R.K., BROOM, L. and COTTRELL, L.S. (eds) *Sociology Today : Problems and prospects*, New York, Harper pp 400–428.

GOULDNER, A.W. (1964) 'About the functions of bureaucratic rules', in GOULDNER, A.W. *Patterns of Industrial Bureaucracy*, New York, The Free Press, pp 157–80 (first published 1955).

GOULDNER, A.W. (1970) *The Coming Crisis in Western Sociology*, London, Heinemann.

GROSS, E. (1969) 'The definition of organizational goals', *British Journal of Sociology*, vol. XX, no. 3, pp 277–294.

GROSS, N., MASON, W.S. and MCEACHERN, A.W. (1958) *Explorations in Role Analysis*, New York, John Wiley.

GRUSKY, O. and MILLER, G.A. (eds) (1970) *The Sociology of Organizations : Basic studies*, New York, The Free Press.

GUEST, R.H. (1962) *Organizational Change : The effect of successful leadership*, Illinois, Homewood.

HABERMAS, J. (1970) 'Toward a theory of communicative competence', in DREITZEL, H.P. (ed.) *Recent Sociology*, no. 2, London, Collier-Macmillan, pp 114–48.

HAGE, J. and AIKEN, M. (1967) 'Relationship of centralization to other structural properties' *Administrative Science Quarterly*, vol. 12, no. 1, pp 72–92.

HAGE, J. and AIKEN, M. (1972) 'Routine technology, social structure and organizational goals', in HALL, R.H. (ed.) *The Formal Organization*, New York, Basic Books, pp 55–72.

HAIRE, M. (1962) 'What is organized in an organization?' in HAIRE, M. (ed.) *Organization Theory in Industrial Practice*, New York, John Wiley, pp 1–12.

HALL, R.H. (1963) 'The concept of bureaucracy', *American Journal of Sociology*, vol. 69, pp 32–40.

HALL, R.H. (ed.) (1972) *The Formal Organization*, New York, Basic Books.

HALL, R.H. (1973) 'Professionalization and bureaucratization', in SALAMAN and THOMPSON (eds) pp 120–33.

HALL, R. (1978) *Organizations : Structure and process* (Revised edition) New Jersey, Prentice-Hall (first published 1972).

HALL, R.H., HAAS, E. and JOHNSON, N. (1967) 'An examination of the Blau-Scott and Etzioni typologies', *Administrative Science Quarterly*, vol. 12, pp 118–39.

HALL, T.D. and NOUGAIM, K.E. (1968) 'An examination of Maslow's need hierarchy in an organizational setting', *Organizational Behaviour and Human Performance*, vol. 3, pp 12–35.

HALMOS, P. (1965) *The Faith of the Counsellors*, London, Constable.

HALMOS, P. (1970) *The Personal Service Society*, London, Constable.

HANIKS, F. deP. (1965) *New Thinking in Management*, London, Hutchinson.

HERBERT, H. (1973) 'Narrow corridors of power', *The Guardian*, 30 October.

HEILBRONER, R. (1970) 'How the Pentagon rules us', *New York Review of Books*, July 23, pp 5–8. This article is a review of MELMAN, S. (1970) *Pentagon Capitalism : The political economy of war*, New York, McGraw-Hill.

HERZBERG, F. (1968) 'One more time : How do you motivate employees?', *Harvard Business Review*, Jan/Feb 1978, pp 53–62.

HERZBERG, F. (1968a) *Work and the Nature of Man*, London, Staples Press.

HERZBERG, F., MAUSNER, B., PETERSON, R.O. and CAPWELL, D.F. (1957) *Job Attitudes : Review of research and opinion*, Pittsburgh, Psychological Service.

HICKSON, D.J. (1973) 'A convergence of organization theory', in SALAMAN and THOMPSON (eds) pp 108–19.

HICKSON, D.J., PUGH, D.S. and PHEYSEY, D.C. (1972) 'Operations technology and organizations structure : An empirical reappraisal' in AZUMI, K. and HAGE, J. (eds) *Organizational Systems*, Lexington, Mass., Heath, pp 137–50.

HICKSON, D.J. HININGS, C.R., LEE, C.A., SCHNECK, R.C. and PENNINGS, J.M. (1973) 'A strategic contingencies theory of intra-organizational power' in SALAMAN and THOMPSON (eds) pp 174–89.

HILL, J.M.M. and TRIST, E.L. (1953) 'A consideration of industrial accidents as a means of withdrawal from the work situation', *Human Relations*, vol. 6, pp 357–80.

HININGS, C.R. and FOSTER, B.D. (1973) 'Organization structure of churches : A primary model', *Sociology*, vol. 7, no. 1, pp 93–106.

HININGS, C.R., HICKSON, D.J., PENNINGS, J.M. and SCHNECK, R.E. (1974) 'Structural conditions of intraorganizational power', *Administrative Science Quarterly*, vol. 19, pp 21–44.

HOLLANDER, E.P. and JULIAN, J.W. (1970) 'Studies in leader legitimacy, influence and innovation', in BERKOWITZ, L. (ed.) *Advances in Experimental Social Psychology*, vol. 5, New York, Academic Press.

HOMANS, G.C. (1958) 'Social behaviour as exchange', *American Journal of Sociology*, vol. 63, pp 597–606.

HOMANS, G.C. (1961) *Social Behaviour : Its elementary forms*, New York, Harcourt Brace.

HOUSE, R.J. and WIGDOR, L.A. (1967) 'Herzberg's dual-factor theory of job satisfaction and motivation : A review of the evidence and a criticism', *Personnel Psychology*, vol. 20, pp 369–89.

HOUSE, R.J. (1967) 'T-group education and leadership effectiveness : A review of the empirical literature and a critical evaluation', *Personnel Psychology*, vol. 20, no. 1, pp 1–32.

HULIN, C.L. and BLOOD, M.R. (1968) 'Job enlargement, individual differences and worker responses', *Psychological Bulletin*, vol. 69, pp 41–55.

JACOBS, D. (1974) 'Dependency and vulnerability : An exchange approach to the control of organizations', *Administrative Science Quarterly*, vol. 19, no. 1, pp 45–49.

JACQUES, E. (1951) *The Changing Culture of a Factory*, London, Tavistock.

JACQUES, E. (1961) *Equitable Payment*, London, Heinemann.

JAHODA, M., LAZARSFIELD, P.F. and ZEISEL, H. (1966) 'Attitudes under condition of unemployment', in JAHODA, M. and WARREN, N. (eds) *Attitudes*, Harmondsworth, Penguin Modern Psychology.

JANOWITZ, M. (1959) 'Changing patterns of organizational authority : The military establishment', *Administrative Science Quarterly*, vol. 3, pp 473–93.

KAHN, R.L., WOLFE, D.M., QUINN, R.P. and SNOEF, J.D. (1964) *Organizational Stress : Role conflict and ambiguity*, New York, Wiley.

KAPLAN, A. (1964) 'Power in perspective', in KAHN, R.L. and BOULDING, E. (eds) *Power and Conflict in Organizations*, London, Tavistock, pp 1–32.

KASSOUF, S. (1970) *Normative Decision-Making*, Englewood Cliffs, New Jersey, Prentice-Hall.

KATZ, D. and KAHN, R.L. (1966) *The Social Psychology of Organizations*, New York, John Wiley.

KATZ, D. and KAHN, R.L. (1970) 'Open systems theory' in GRUSKY and MILLER (eds) pp 149–58.

KATZ, F.E. (1968) *Autonomy and Organizations : The limits of social control*, New York, Random House.

KATZ, F.E. (1968) 'Integrative and adaptive uses of autonomy : Worker autonomy in factories', and 'The limits of social control' in *Autonomy and Organizations*, New York, Random House.

KITSUSE, J.I. and CICOUREL, A. (1963) 'A note on the use of official statistics', *Social Problems*, vol. 11, pp 131–9.

KUHN, T.S. (1970) *Structure of Scientific Revolutions*, Chicago, University of Chicago Press.

KYNASTON REEVES, T. and WOODWARD, J. (1970) 'The study of managerial control' in WOODWARD, J. (ed.) *Industrial Organization : Behaviour and control*.

LAMMERS, S.J. (1967) 'Power and participation in decision-making in formal organizations' in *American Journal of Sociology*, vol. 73, no. 2, pp 201–16.

LANDSBERGER, H.A. (1961) 'The horizontal dimension in bureaucracy', *Administrative Science Quarterly*, vol. 6, pp 299–332.

LANT, T. and ROBERTS, K. (1971) *Strike at Pilkingtons*, London, Fontana.

LANGER, E. (1970) 'Inside the New York Telephone Company' and 'The Women of the Telephone Company', in *New York Review of Books*, March 12, pp 16—24 and March 26, pp 21—2.

LAWLER, E.C. III and PORTER, L.W. (1967) 'The effect of performance on job satisfaction', *Industrial Relations : A journal of economy and society*, vol. 7, no. 1, pp 20—28.

LAWRENCE, P.R. (1958) *The Changing of Organizational Behaviour Patterns*, Boston, Harvard University Press.

LAWRENCE, P.R. and LORSCH, J.W. (1967) *Organization and Environment*, Harvard, Harvard University.

LENIN, V.I. (n.d.) *Selected Works*, vol. VII, New York, International Publisher.

LENIN, V.I. (1970) *The State and Revolution*, Peking, Foreign Languages Press.

LEWIN, K. (1947) 'Group decision and social change', reprinted in PROSHANSKY, H. and SEIDENBERG, B. (eds) (1969) *Basic Studies in Social Psychology*, New York, Holt, Rinehart and Winston.

LEWIN, K., LIPPIT, R. and WHITE, R.K., (1939) 'Patterns of aggressive behaviour in experimentally created "social climates" ', *Journal of Social Psychology*, vol. 10, pp 271—99.

LIKERT, R. (1961) *New Patterns of Management*, New York, McGraw-Hill.

LIKERT, R. (1967) *The Human Organization : Its management and value*, New York, McGraw-Hill.

LINDBLOM, C.E. (1958) 'Policy analysis', *American Economic Review*, vol. 48, no. 3, pp 298—312.

LINDBLOM, C.E. (1959) 'The science of "muddling through" ', *Public Administration Review*, vol. 19, no. 2, pp 79—88.

LIPSET, S.M., TROW, M.A. and COLEMAN, J.S. (1956) *Union Democracy*, New York, The Free Press.

LLOYD, L.E. (1962) 'Origins and objectives of organizations' in HAIRE, M. (ed.) *Organizational Theory in Industrial Practice*, New York, John Wiley, pp 28—47.

LUKES, S. (1974) *Power : A radical view*, London, Macmillan.

LUPTON, T. and CUNNISON, S. (1964) 'Workshop behaviour' in GLUCKMAN, M. (ed.) *Closed Systems and Open Minds*, Edinburgh, Oliver and Boyd, pp 103—28.

LUPTON, T. (1971) *Management and the Social Sciences*, Harmondsworth, Penguin.

LYMAN, S.M. and SCOTT, M.B. (1970) *A Sociology of the Absurd*, New York, Appleton Century Crofts.

MANNHEIM, K. (1952) 'Orientations of bureaucratic thought' in MERTON, R.K., GRAY, A.P., HOCKEY, R. and SELVIN, H.C. (eds) *Reader in Bureaucracy*, New York, The Free Press, pp 360—1.

MANNING, P.K. (1971) 'Talking and becoming : A view of organizational socialization' in DOUGLAS, J.D. (ed.) *Understanding Everyday Life*, London, Routledge and Kegan Paul, pp 239—56.

MARCH, J.G. (1955) 'An introduction to the theory and measurement of influence', *American Political Science Review*, vol. 49, pp 431—50.

MARCH, J.G. (1957) 'Measurement concepts in the theory of influence', *Journal of Politics*, vol. 19, pp 202—26.

MARCH, J.G. and SIMON, H.A. (1958) *Organizations*, New York, Wiley.

MARCH, J.G. and SIMON, H.A. (1970) 'Decision-making theory' in GRUSKY and MILLER (eds) pp 93—102.

MARGLIN, S.A. (1976) 'What do bosses do?' in GORZ, A. *The Division of Labor*, Atlantic Highlands, New Jersey, Humanities Press.

MARTIN, R. and FRYER, R.H. (1973) *Redundancy and Paternalist Capitalism*, London, Allen and Unwin.

MARX, K. (1930) *Capital*, London, Everyman Edition, Dent.

MASLOW, A.H. (1954) *Motivation and Personality*, New York, Harper and Row.

MAYO, C. (1933) *The Human Problems of Industrial Civilization*, London, Macmillan.

MAYO, C. (1949) *The Social Problems of an Industrial Civilization*, London, Routledge and Kegan Paul.

McCLELLAND, D.C. *et al* (1953) *The Achievement Motive*, New York, Appleton Century Crofts.

McCLELLAND, D.C. (1961) *The Achieving Society*, Princeton, Van Nostrand.

McCLELLAND, D.C. and WINTER, D.G. (1969) *Motivating Economic Achievement*, New York, The Free Press; London, Collier-MacMillan.

McGREGOR, D. (1960) *The Human Side of Enterprise*, New York, McGraw-Hill.

McLELLAND, D. (1971) *Marx's Grundrisse*, London, Macmillan.

McNEIL, K. (1978) 'Understanding organizational power : Building on the Weberian legacy', *Administrative Science Quarterly*, vol. 23, no. 1 (March), pp 65—90.

MECHANIC, D. (1962) 'Sources of power of lower participants in complex organizations', *Administrative Science Quarterly*, vol. 7, no. 3, December, pp 349—364.

MECHANIC, D. (1963) 'Some considerations in the methodology of organizational studies' in LEAVITT, H.J. (ed.) *The Social Science of Organizations*, Englewood Cliffs, Prentice-Hall, pp 139–82.

MEAD, G.H. (1936) *Movements of Thought in the Nineteenth Century*, Chicago, University of Chicago Press.

MERTON, R.K. (1952) 'Bureaucratic structure and personality' in MERTON, R.K., GRAY, A.P., HOCKEY, B. and SELVIN, H.C. (eds) *Reader in Bureaucracy*, New York, Free Press, pp 361–71.

MERTON, R.K. (1957) *Social Theory and Social Structure*, Glencoe, The Free Press.

MERTON, R.K. (1957) 'Bureaucratic structure and personality', in MERTON, R.K. (1957) *Social Theory and Social Structure*, New York, The Free Press, pp 249–60.

MEZAROVIC, M., SAUNDERS, J.L. and SPRAGUE, C.F. (1973) 'An axiomatic approach to organizations from a general systems viewpoint' in OPTNER, L. (ed.) *Systems Analysis*, Harmondsworth, Penguin.

MEYNAUD, J. (1968) *Technocracy*, London, Faber and Faber.

MICHELS, R. (1949) *Political Parties*, Chicago Free Press.

MICHELS, R. (1970) 'Oligarchy' in GRUSKY and MILLER (eds) pp 25–43.

MILLER, E.J. and RICE, A.K. (1967) *Systems of Organization : The control of task and sentient boundaries*, London, Tavistock.

MILLER, G.A. (1970) 'Professionals in bureaucracy : Alienation among industrial scientists and engineers' in GRUSKY and MILLER (eds) pp 503–15.

MILLS, C.W. (1956) *White Collar*, New York, Oxford University Press.

MILLS, C.W. (1940) 'Situated actions and vocabularies of motive', *American Sociological Review*, pp 904–13.

MINTZBERG, H., RAISINGHANI, D. and THEORET, A. (1976) 'The structure of "unstructured" decision processes', *Administrative Science Quarterly*, vol. 21, no. 2 pp 246–275.

MOUZELIS, N. (1967) *Organization and Bureaucracy*, London, Routledge and Kegan Paul.

MULDER, M. (1971) 'Power equalization through participation?', *Administrative Science Quarterly*, vol. 16, no. 1, pp 31–8.

MÜNSTERBERG, H. (1913) *Psychology and Industrial Efficiency*, London, Constable.

NICHOLS, T. and ARMSTRONG, P. (1976) *Workers Divided: A study in shopfloor politics*, London, Fontana.

NICHOLS, T. and BEYNON, H. (1977) *Living With Capitalism: Class relations and the modern factory*, London, Routledge and Kegan Paul.

NICHOLS, T. (1969) 'Of conflict and organicism, materialism and social responsibility', in NICHOLS, T. *Ownership, Control and Ideology*, London, Allen and Unwin, pp 208–39.

NORMANN, R. (1971) 'Organizational innovativeness : Product variation and reorientation', *Administrative Science Quarterly*, vol. 16, no. 2, pp 203–15.

PAHL, J.M. and PAHL, R.E. (1972) *Managers and Their Wives : A study of career and family relationships in the middle class*, Harmondsworth, Penguin.

PARSONS, T. (1970) 'Social Systems' in GRUSKY and MILLER (eds) pp 75–85.

PARKIN, F. (1971) *Class Inequality and Political Order*, London, MacGibbon and Kee.

PEARLIN, L.I. (1962) 'Alienation from work : A study of nursing personnel', *American Sociological Review*, vol. 27, pp 314–25.

PEREZ-DIAZ, V.M. (1978) *State, Bureaucracy and Civil Society*, London, Macmillan.

PERROW, C. (1961) 'The analysis of goals in complex organizations', *American Sociological Review*, vol. 26, pp 854–66.

PERROW, C. (1970) *Organizational Analysis*, London, Tavistock.

PERROW, C. (1970) 'Departmental power and perspectives in industrial forms', in ZALD, M. (ed.) *Power in Organizations*, Nashville, Vanderbilt University Press, pp 59–89.

PERROW, C. (1972) 'Technology, organizations and environment : A cautionary note', paper presented at the British Sociological Association meeting of the Industrial Sociology Group.

PERROW, C. (1972a) *The Radical Attack on Business*, New York, Harcourt Brace Javanovich.

PERROW, C. (1972b) 'A framework for the comparative analysis of organizations' in BRINKERHOFF, M. and KUNZ, P. (eds) *Complex Organizations and Their Environments*, Dubuque, Wm. C. Brown, pp 48–67.

PERROW, C. (1972c) *Complex Organizations : A critical essay*, Glenview, Illinois, Scott Foresman, revised edition.

PERROW, C. (1973) 'The neo-Weberian model : Decision-making, conflict and technology' in SALAMAN and THOMPSON (eds) pp 281–92.

PERROW, C. (1974) 'Is business really changing?' *Organizational Dynamics*, Spring.

PERROW, C. (1979) 'Demystifying organizations' in SARRI, R.C. and HASENFELD, Y. (eds) *The Management of Human Services*, New York, Columbia University Press.

PETTIGREW, A.M. (1972) 'Information control as a power resource', *Sociology*, vol. 6, no. 2, pp 187–204.

PETTIGREW, A.M. (1973) *The Politics of Organizational Decision-Making*, London, Tavistock.

PITKIN, H. (1972) 'Obligation and consent', in LASLETT, P., RUNCI-MAN, W.G. and SKINNER, Q. (eds) *Philosophy, Politics and Society*, 4th series, Oxford, Blackwell, pp 45–85.

PIVCEVIC, E. (1972) 'Can there be a phenomenological sociology?', *Sociology*, vol. 6, pp 335–49.

POLLARD, S. (1968) *The Genesis of Modern Management*, Harmondsworth, Penguin.

POPPER, K. (1957a) *The Poverty of Historicism*, London, Routledge and Kegan Paul.

POPPER, K. (1957b) *The Open Society and its Enemies* London, Routledge and Kegan Paul.

PRITCHARD, R.B. (1969) 'Equity theory : A review and critique', *Organizational Behaviour and Human Performance*, vol. 4, pp 176–211.

PRITCHARD, R.B., DUNNETTE, M.D. and JORGENSON, D.O. (1972) 'Effects of perceptions of equity and inequity on worker performance and satisfaction', *Journal of Applied Psychology*, vol. 56, pp 75–94.

PUGH, D.S., HICKSON, D.J., HINNINGS, C.R. and TURNER, C. (1969) 'The context of organizational structures', *Administrative Science Quarterly*, vol. 14, pp 91–114.

PUGH, D.S., HICKSON, D.J. and HINNINGS, C.R. (1971) *Writers on Organizations*, Harmondsworth, Penguin.

PUGH, D.S. and HICKSON, D.J. (1973) 'The comparative study of organizations' in SALAMAN and THOMPSON (eds) pp 50–66.

PUGH, D. (1973) 'Role activation conflict : A study of industrial inspection' in SALAMAN and THOMPSON (eds) pp 238–49.

PUGH, D.S. and HICKSON, D.J. (eds) (1976) *Organizational Structure in its Context : The Aston Programme 1*, Westmead, Hampshire, Saxon House.

ROGERS, D. and BERG, I.E. (1961) 'Occupation and ideology : The case of the small businessman', *Human Organization*, vol. 20, no. 3, pp 103–11.

ROETHLISBERGER, F.J. and DICKSON, W.J. (1970) 'Human Relations' in GRUSKY and MILLER (eds) pp 53–63.

ROETHLISBERGER, F. J. and DICKSON, W.J. (1964) *Management and the Worker*, Massachusetts, Harvard University Press.

ROSE, M. (1969) *Computers, Managers and Society*, Harmondsworth, Penguin.

ROSE, M. (1975) *IndustrialBehaviour, Theoretical Development Since Taylor*, London, Allen Lane.

ROSE, M. (1978) *Industrial Behaviour*, Harmondsworth, Penguin Books.

ROWE, K. (1964) 'An appraisal of appraisals', *Journal of Management Studies*, vol. 1, pp 1–25.

ROY, D.F. (1960) 'Banana time : Job satisfaction and information interaction', *Human Organization*, vol. 18, pp 156–168, pp 205–222. Also in SALAMAN and THOMPSON (eds) (1973).

ROY, D. (1969) 'Making-out : A counter-system of workers' control of work situation and relationship' in BURNS, T. (ed.) *Industrial Man*, Harmondsworth, Penguin, pp 359–79.

RUS, V. (1980) 'Positive and negative power', *Organization Studies*, vol. 1, no. 1 (to appear January 1980).

SACKS, H. (1972) 'Notes on police assessment of moral character' in SUDNOW, D. (ed.) *Studies in Social Interaction*, New York, The Free Press, pp 280–93.

SALAMAN, G. and THOMPSON, K. (eds) (1973) *People and Organizations*, London, Longmans.

SALAMAN, G. and THOMPSON, K. (eds) (1973) *People and Organiza*-persistence of an elite : The case of army officer selection', *Sociological Review*, vol. 26, no. 2, May, pp 283–304.

SAMPSON, A. (1973) *The Sovereign State : The secret history of ITT*, London, Hodder and Stoughton.

SAYLES, S.M. (1966) 'Supervisory style and productivity : Review and theory', *Personnel Psychology*, vol. 19, no. 3, pp 275–86.

SCHNEIDER, E.V. (1969) *Industrial Sociology*, New York, McGraw-Hill.

SCHON, D. (1971) *Beyond the Stable State*, London, Temple Smith.

SCHROYER, T. (1970) 'Toward a critical theory for advanced industrial society' in DREITZEL, H.P. (ed.) *Recent Sociology*, no. 2, London, Collier-Macmillan, pp 209–34.

SCHUTZ, A. (1962) *Collected Papers*, The Hague, Nijhoff.

SCOTT, W.G. (1971) 'Decision concepts' in CASTLES, MURRAY and POTTER (eds) pp 19–27.

SCOTT, W.H. *et al* (1963) *Coal and Conflict*, Liverpool, Liverpool University Press.

SELZNICK, P. (1957) *Leadership in Administration*, Evanston, Ill., Row Peterson.

SELZNICK, P. (1966) *TVA and the Grass Roots : A study in the sociology of formal organizations*, New York, Harper and Row.

SHULL, F.A., DELBECQ, A.L. and CUMMINGS, L.L. (1970) *Organizational Decision-Making*, London, McGraw-Hill.

SILLS, D.L. (1970) 'Preserving organizational goals', in GRUSKY and MILLER (eds) pp 227–36.

SILVERMAN, D. (1970) *The Theory of Organizations*, London, Heinemann.

SIMON, H.A. (1960) *The New Science of Management Decisions*, New York, Harper and Row.

SIMON, H.A. (1965) *Administrative Behavior*, New York, The Free Press, (first published 1945, London).

SIMON, H. (1969) 'On the concept of organizational goal' in ETZIONI, A. (ed.) *A Sociological Reader on Complex Organizations*, London, Holt Rinehart and Winston, pp 158–74.

SIMON, H.A., (1971) 'Theories of Decision-making in economics and behavioural science' in CASTLES, MURRAY and POTTER (eds) pp 37–55.

SKINNER, B.F. (1978) *Beyond Freedom and Dignity*, Harmondsworth, Penguin Books.

SOFER, C. (1970) *Men in Mid-Career*, Cambridge, Cambridge University Press.

SOFER, C. and TUCHMAN, M. (1970) 'Appraisal interviews and the structure of colleague relations', *The Sociological Review*, vol. 18, pp 365–91.

SPENCER, H. (1897) *Principles of Sociology*, London, Appleton-Century Crofts, (third edition).

STEWART, R. (1972) *The Reality of Organizations*, London, Pan Books.

STINCHCOMBE, A.L. (1970) 'Bureaucratic and Craft Administration of Production' in GRUSKY and MILLER (eds) pp 261–71.

STOUFFER, S.A., SUCHMAN, E.A., DEVINNEY, L.C., STARR, S.A. and WILLIAMS, R.M., Jr. (1949) *The American Soldier : Adjustment during army life*, vol. 1, Princeton, N.J., Princeton University Press.

STRAUSS, G. (1962) 'Tactics of Lateral Relationship : The purchasing agent', *Administrative Science Quarterly*, vol. 7, pp 161–86.

STRAUSS, G. (1963) 'Some notes on power equalization', in LEAVITT, H.A. (ed.) *The Social Science of Organizations*, Englewood Cliffs, Prentice Hall, pp 39–84.

STRAUSS, A., SCHATZMAN, L., EHRLICH, D., BUCHER, R.·and SABSHIN, M. (1973) 'The hospital and its negoitated order', in SALAMAN and THOMPSON (eds) pp 303–20.

STUDENTS FOR A DEMOCRATIC SOCIETY (1972) 'The military-industrial complex' from the Port Huron Statement in PERROW, C. (ed.) *The Radical Attack on Business*, New York Harcourt Brace Jovanovich, pp 15–16.

SUDNOW, D. (1973) 'Normal crimes : Sociological features of the penal code in a public defender office' in SALAMAN and THOMPSON (eds) pp 346–57.

SUTTON, F.X., HARRIS, S.E., KAYSEN, C. and TOBIN, J. (1956) *The American Business Creed*, Cambridge, Massachusetts, Harvard University Press.

TANNENBAUM, A.S. (1968) *Control in Organizations*, New York, McGraw-Hill.

TANNENBAUM, A.S. and COOKE, R.A. (1979) 'Organizational control : A review of studies employing the control graph method' in LAMMERS, C.J. and HICKSON, D.J., (eds) *Organizations Alike and Unlike*, London, Routledge and Kegan Paul.

TAYLOR, D.W. (1970) 'Decision-making and problem-solving', in WELSCH and CYERT (eds) pp 30–63.

TAYLOR, F.W. (1947) *Scientific Management*, New York, Harper.

TAYLOR, L. and WALTON, P. (1971) 'Industrial sabotage : Motives and meanings' in COHEN, S. (ed.) *Images of Deviance*, Harmondsworth, Penguin, pp 219–45.

THE QUEEN'S COMMISSION, Prepared for the Ministry of Defence (Army) by the Central Office of Information.

THE UNIVERSITY OF HULL APPOINTMENTS BOARD INFORMATION SHEET A/6 (1968).

THOMPSON, J.D. (1967) *Organizations in Action*, New York, McGraw-Hill.

THOMPSON, J.D. and McEWEN, W.J. (1973) 'Organizational goals and environment : Goal-setting as an interaction process' in SALAMAN and THOMPSON (eds) pp 155–67.

THOMPSON, K. (1973) 'Religious Organizations : The cultural perspective' in SALAMAN and THOMPSON (eds) pp 293–302.

TOCQUEVILLE, A. de (1945) *Democracy in America*, New York, Knopf.

TOPITSCH, E. (1971) 'Max Weber and sociology today' in STAMMER, O. (ed.) *Max Weber and Sociology Today*, Oxford Blackwell, pp 8–25.

TRIANDIS, H.C. (1959) 'A critique and experimental design for the study of the relationship between productivity and job satisfaction', *Psychological Bulletin*, vol. 55, pp 309—12.

TRIST, E.L., and BAMFORTH, K.W. (1951) 'Some social and psychological consequences of the longwall method of coal-getting', *Human Relations*, vol. 4, no. 1, pp 3—38.

TRIST, E.L. HIGGINS, G.W., MURRAY, H. and POLLOCK, A.B. (1963) *Organizational Choice*, London, Tavistock.

TURNER, A.N. and LAWRENCE, P.R. (1967) *Industrial Jobs and the Worker : An investigation of response to task attributes*, Boston, Harvard University.

TURNER, B. (1973) 'The industrial subculture' in SALAMAN and THOMPSON (eds) pp 67—75.

UDY, S. (1959) 'Bureaucracy and rationality in Weber's organizational theory : An empirical study', *American Sociological Review*, vol. 24, pp 791—5.

VAUGHN BLANKENSHIP, L. and MILES, R.E. (1968) 'Organizational structure and managerial decision behaviour', *Administrative Science Quarterly*, vol. 13, pp 106—20.

VROOM, V.H. (1959) 'Some personality determinants of the effects of participation', *The Journal of Abnormal and Social Psychology*, vol. 59, pp 322—7.

VROOM, V.H. (1964) *Work and Motivation*, New York, Wiley.

WALKER, C. (1950) *Steeltown*, New York, Harper and Row.

WALL, T.D., STEPHENSON, G.M. and SKIDMORE, C. (1971) 'Ego-involvement and Herzberg's two-factor theory of job satisfaction : An experimental field study', *British Journal of Social and Clinical Psychology*, vol. 10, pp 123—31.

WALSTER, E., WALSTER, G.W. and BERSCHEID, E. (1978) *Equity : Theory and research*, Boston, Allyn and Bacon.

WAMSLEY, G. and ZALD, M.N. (1973) 'The political economy of public organizations', *Public Administration Review*, vol. 33, pp 62—73.

WARREN, D.I. (1968) 'Power, visibility and conformity in formal organizations', *American Journal of Sociology*, vol. 3, no. 6, pp 951—70.

WEBBER, R.A. (1970) 'Perceptions of interactions between superiors and subordinates', *Human Relations*, vol. 23, no. 3, pp 235—48.

WEBER, M. (1947) *The Theory of Social and Economic Organization*, Glencoe, The Free Press.

WEBER, M. (1948) *From Max Weber : Essays in sociology*, translated and edited by GORTH, H.H. and MILLS, C.W. London, Routledge and Kegan Paul.

WEBER, M. (1949) *The Methodology of the Social Sciences*, Glencoe, The Free Press.

WEBER, M. (1964) *The Theory of Social and Economic Organization*, edited and with an introduction by PARSONS, T., New York, Free Press.

WEBER, M. (1968) *Economy and Society*, New York, Bedminster Press.

WEBER, M. (1970) 'Bureaucracy' in GRUSKY and MILLER (eds) pp 5–23.

WELDON, P.D. (1972) 'An examination of the Blau-Scott and Etzioni typologies : A critique', *Administrative Science Quarterly*, vol. 17, no. 1, pp 76–8.

WEEKS, D.R. (1973) 'Organizational theory : Some themes and distinctions' in SALAMAN and THOMPSON (eds) pp 375–95.

WELSCH, L.A. and CYERT, R.M. (eds) (1970) *Management Decision-Making*, Harmondsworth, Penguin.

WHISLER, T.L., MEYER, H., BAUM, B.H. and SORENSEN, P.F. (1967) 'Centralization of organizational control : An empirical study of its meaning and measurement', *Journal of Business*, vol. 40, no. 1, pp 10–26.

WHITEHEAD, A.N. (1925) *Science and the Modern World*, New York, Macmillan.

WHYTE, W.H., Jr. (1956) *The Organization Man*, New York, Simon and Shuster.

WHYTE, W.F. (1948) *Human Relations in the Restaurant Industry*, New York, McGraw-Hill.

WILENSKY, H. (1967) *Organizational Intelligence*, New York, Basic Books.

WILENSKY, H. (1968) 'Careers, life-styles and social integration' in GLASER, B. (ed.) *Organizational Careers*, Chicago, Aldine, pp 50–3.

WILENSKY, H.L. (1970) 'The professionalization of everyone?' in GRUSKY and MILLER (eds) pp 483–501.

WILLIAMSON, O.E. (1975) *Markets and Hierarchies*, New York, Free Press.

WILSON, T.P. (1971) 'Normative and interpretive paradigms in sociology' in DOUGLAS, J.D. (ed.) *Understanding Everday Life*, London, Routledge and Kegan Paul, pp 57–79.

WOODWARD, J. (1970) 'Technology and organization' in GRUSKY and MILLER (eds) pp 273–90.

WOODWARD, J. (1969) 'Management and technology' in BURNS, T. (ed.) *Industrial Man*, Harmondsworth, Penguin, pp 196–231.

WOODWARD, J. (1959) *Management and Technology*, London, HMSO.

WOODWARD, J. (1965) *Industrial Organization : Theory and practice*, London, Oxford University Press.

WOODWARD, J. (1970) *Industrial Organizations : Behaviour and control*, London, Oxford University Press.

WRONG, D.H. (1968) 'Some problems in defining social power', *American Journal of Sociology*, vol. 73, pp 673–81.

ZALD, M. (1962) 'Organizational control structures in five correctional institutions', *American Journal of Sociology*, vol. 68, pp 335–45.

ZIMMERMAN, D. (1971) 'The practicalities of rule use' in DOUGLAS, JACK (ed.) *Understanding Everyday Life*, Routledge and Kegan Paul, 1971. Also in SALAMAN and THOMPSON (eds) 1973 pp 250–63.

ZIMMERMAN, D. and POLLNER, M. (1971) 'The everyday world as a phenomenon' in DOUGLAS, J. (ed.) *Understanding Everyday Life*, London, Routledge and Kegan Paul, pp 80–104.

ZIMMERMAN, D. and WIEDER, D.L. (1971) 'Ethnomethodology and the problem of order : Comment on Denzin' in DOUGLAS J. (ed.) *Understanding Everyday Life*, London, Routledge and Kegan Paul, pp 285–95.

Index